MALE/
FEMALE
ROLES

OPPOSING VIEWPOINTS®

Other Books of Related Interest in the Opposing
Viewpoints Series:

Abortion
America's Children
Child Abuse
The Family in America
Feminism
Homosexuality
Poverty
Sexual Values
Social Justice
Sports in America
Teenage Sexuality

DISCARDED

MALE/
FEMALE
ROLES
OPPOSING VIEWPOINTS®

David Bender & Bruno Leone, *Series Editors*

Jonathan S. Petrikin, *Book Editor*

OPPOSING
VIEWPOINTS
SERIES®

Greenhaven Press, Inc., San Diego, CA

Greenhaven Press, Inc.
PO Box 289009
San Diego, CA 92198-9009

Cover photo: Rocky Thies

Library of Congress Cataloging-in-Publication Data

Male/female roles : opposing viewpoints / Jonathan S. Petrikin,
    book editor.
        p.   cm. — (Opposing viewpoints series)
    Includes bibliographical references (p.   ) and index.
    ISBN 1-56510-174-X (lib. : acid-free paper) — ISBN 1-56510-
175-8 (pbk. : acid-free paper)
    1. Sex role. 2. Sex role—United States. [1. Sex role.] I. Petrikin,
Jonathan S., 1963–   . II. Series: Opposing viewpoints series
(Unnumbered)
HQ1075.M353   1995
305.3—dc20   94-4975
                                                            CIP
                                                            AC

Every effort has been made to trace the owners of copyrighted material.

"Congress shall make no law . . . abridging the freedom of speech, or of the press."

First Amendment to the U.S. Constitution

The basic foundation of our democracy is the first amendment guarantee of freedom of expression. The Opposing Viewpoints Series is dedicated to the concept of this basic freedom and the idea that it is more important to practice it than to enshrine it.

Contents

Page

Why Consider Opposing Viewpoints?   9

Introduction   12

Chapter 1: How Are Sex Roles Established?

Chapter Preface   16

1. Evolution Explains Traditional Gender Roles   17
   Anthony Layng

2. Evolution Does Not Explain Traditional Gender Roles   24
   Carol Tavris

3. Biology Determines Gender Roles   32
   James C. Dobson

4. Biology Does Not Determine Gender Roles   40
   Ruth Hubbard

5. Brain Structure Explains Male/Female Differences   48
   Yves Christen

6. Brain Structure Does Not Explain Male/Female
   Differences   57
   Le Anne Schreiber

7. Economics Determines Gender Roles   66
   Francine D. Blau & Marianne A. Ferber

8. Culture Determines Gender Roles   74
   Linda L. Lindsey

Periodical Bibliography   82

Chapter 2: Have Women's Roles Changed for the Better?

Chapter Preface   84

1. A Glass Ceiling Limits Women's Roles at Work   85
   Business and Professional Women's Foundation

2. The Glass Ceiling Is Not What Limits Women
   at Work   92
   George Gilder

3. Gender Issues Are Helping Women Win
   in Politics   100
   Mary Beth Rogers

4. Gender Issues Are Not Helping Women Win
   in Politics   108
   Marian Lief Palley

5. Women's Opportunities in the Military Are
   Improving   116
   Amy Pagnozzi & Bruce W. Nelan

6. Women's Opportunities in the Military Are
   Dangerous   122
   Elaine Donnelly & Phyllis Schlafly
7. Women Can Have It All   129
   Rosalind C. Barnett & Caryl Rivers
8. Women Cannot Have It All   136
   Nancy Pearcey
Periodical Bibliography   143

Chapter 3: Have Men's Roles Changed for the Better?

Chapter Preface   145
1. Men's Lives Are Changing for the Better   146
   Sam Julty
2. Men's Lives Are Changing for the Worse   151
   Warren Farrell
3. Men Need to Become More Manly   158
   Robert Bly
4. Men Do Not Need to Become More Manly   167
   Fred Pelka
5. Men Need to Form Close Male Friendships   174
   Terry A. Kupers & Larry Letich
6. Men Are Already Forming Close Male Friendships   180
   Alan Buczynski, Mike Yorkey & Peb Jackson
7. Men Are Becoming Better Fathers   186
   Kathleen Gerson
8 Men Are Not Becoming Better Fathers   195
   Wade C. Mackey & Ursula White
Periodical Bibliography   202

Chapter 4: How Does Work Affect the Family?

Chapter Preface   204
1. Working Parents Help Their Children   205
   Faye J. Crosby
2. Working Parents Harm Their Children   212
   Sylvia Ann Hewlett
3. Day Care Harms Children   220
   J. Craig Peery
4. Day Care Does Not Harm Children   229
   Susan Faludi & Rosalind C. Barnett
5. Families Need Government-Subsidized Child Care   236
   Sheila B. Kamerman
6. Families Do Not Need Government-Subsidized
   Child Care   243
   Allan Carlson

Periodical Bibliography   250

Chapter 5: What Is the Future of Male/Female
                Relationships?
Chapter Preface   252
1. Marriage Is Becoming More Popular   253
    Diane Medved
2. Marriage Is Not Becoming More Popular   261
    Norval D. Glenn
3. Men and Women Should Share Domestic
   Responsibilities   268
    Arlie Hochschild with Anne Machung
4. Men and Women Should Not Share Domestic
   Responsibilities   276
    Steven Goldberg
5. Sexual Attraction in the Workplace Is Often
   Counterproductive   284
    Lisa A. Mainiero
6. A New Sexual Dynamic in the Workplace
   Can Be Beneficial   289
    David R. Eyler & Andrea Baridon
Periodical Bibliography   296

For Further Discussion   297
Organizations to Contact   299
Bibliography of Books   303
Index   305

Why Consider Opposing Viewpoints?

"The only way in which a human being can make some approach to knowing the whole of a subject is by hearing what can be said about it by persons of every variety of opinion and studying all modes in which it can be looked at by every character of mind. No wise man ever acquired his wisdom in any mode but this."

John Stuart Mill

In our media-intensive culture it is not difficult to find differing opinions. Thousands of newspapers and magazines and dozens of radio and television talk shows resound with differing points of view. The difficulty lies in deciding which opinion to agree with and which "experts" seem the most credible. The more inundated we become with differing opinions and claims, the more essential it is to hone critical reading and thinking skills to evaluate these ideas. Opposing Viewpoints books address this problem directly by presenting stimulating debates that can be used to enhance and teach these skills. The varied opinions contained in each book examine many different aspects of a single issue. While examining these conveniently edited opposing views, readers can develop critical thinking skills such as the ability to compare and contrast authors' credibility, facts, argumentation styles, use of persuasive techniques, and other stylistic tools. In short, the Opposing Viewpoints Series is an ideal way to attain the higher-level thinking and reading skills so essential in a culture of diverse and contradictory opinions.

In addition to providing a tool for critical thinking, Opposing Viewpoints books challenge readers to question their own strongly held opinions and assumptions. Most people form their opinions on the basis of upbringing, peer pressure, and personal, cultural, or professional bias. By reading carefully balanced opposing views, readers must directly confront new ideas as well as the opinions of those with whom they disagree. This is not to simplistically argue that everyone who reads opposing views will—or should—change his or her opinion. Instead, the series enhances readers' depth of understanding of their own views by encouraging confrontation with opposing ideas. Careful examination of others' views can lead to the readers' understanding of the logical inconsistencies in their own opinions, perspective on why they hold an opinion, and the consideration of the possibility that their opinion requires further evaluation.

Evaluating Other Opinions

To ensure that this type of examination occurs, Opposing Viewpoints books present all types of opinions. Prominent spokespeople on different sides of each issue as well as well-known professionals from many disciplines challenge the reader. An additional goal of the series is to provide a forum for other, less known, or even unpopular viewpoints. The opinion of an ordinary person who has had to make the decision to cut off life support from a terminally ill relative, for example, may be just as valuable and provide just as much insight as a medical ethicist's professional opinion. The editors have two additional purposes in including these less known views. One, the editors encourage readers to respect others' opinions—even when not enhanced by professional credibility. It is only by reading or listening to and objectively evaluating others' ideas that one can determine whether they are worthy of consideration. Two, the inclusion of such viewpoints encourages the important critical thinking skill of objectively evaluating an author's credentials and bias. This evaluation will illuminate an author's reasons for taking a particular stance on an issue and will aid in readers' evaluation of the author's ideas.

As series editors of the Opposing Viewpoints Series, it is our hope that these books will give readers a deeper understanding of the issues debated and an appreciation of the complexity of even seemingly simple issues when good and honest people disagree. This awareness is particularly important in a democratic society such as ours in which people enter into public debate to determine the common good. Those with whom one disagrees should not be regarded as enemies but rather as people whose views deserve careful examination and may shed light on one's own.

Thomas Jefferson once said that "difference of opinion leads to inquiry, and inquiry to truth." Jefferson, a broadly educated man, argued that "if a nation expects to be ignorant and free . . . it expects what never was and never will be." As individuals and as a nation, it is imperative that we consider the opinions of others and examine them with skill and discernment. The Opposing Viewpoints Series is intended to help readers achieve this goal.

David L. Bender & Bruno Leone,
Series Editors

Introduction

"['Should a woman juggle work and family or not?' is a question that] assumes certain sexual scripts and precludes others. The same question is not asked of men."

Faye J. Crosby, *Juggling, 1991.*

The ways in which society has organized itself and divided the work among men and women has changed over the years. In colonial America, men and women shared responsibility both for the production of most of life's necessities and for raising their children. With the Industrial Revolution, however, most production moved to factories, which came to be dominated by men who worked to support their families while their wives stayed home and cared for their children. Not all families were organized this way—18 percent of women worked for pay at the end of the nineteenth century, usually because they were single or poor—but it was the ideal to which most people aspired.

By the early twentieth century, social reformers and labor unions, struggling with employers to raise the living standards of workers, were casting their arguments in terms of a "family wage"—a wage considered sufficient to provide for the male wage earner and his family. As legal scholar Barbara Armstrong put it in 1932: "It is today assumed that a male worker's wage should be a family wage rather than an individual wage." By the 1970s, however, the one-paycheck-per-family norm was fading as women entered the job market in large numbers. Today women make up nearly half of the workforce; this trend, along with the depressing effect on wages of the increased supply of labor, has made the idea of the family wage something of an anachronism. As society adjusts to this new economic reality, observers vigorously debate its effects on the roles of men and women, on the family, and indeed on the shape of society itself.

Some argue that the decline of the family wage and the ideas behind it represents a positive step toward equality for women. According to economic historian Alice Kessler-Harris, the family wage "reflected a rather severe set of injunctions about how men and women were to live." And those injunctions, Kessler-Harris explains, remained largely in force until the passage of the Equal

12

Pay Act of 1963, a measure that outlawed paying men higher wages than women for doing "equal work on jobs the performance of which requires equal skill, effort and responsibility." First proposed in the 1940s in recognition of women's work in the defense industry, the Equal Pay Act, Kessler-Harris maintains, formed the start of ongoing "efforts to redefine justice for women as a function of their individual rights rather than of family responsibilities." Although the battle for pay equity is far from over, Kessler-Harris says, noting that women currently make 70 cents for every dollar made by men, legislative victories like the Equal Pay Act are important validations of women as individuals instead of extensions of their husbands and families.

Many observers agree that the replacement of the family wage with an "individual wage" has coincided with an increase in the financial and personal independence of women. According to Leanna Wolfe, author of *Women Who May Never Marry*, this autonomy finds expression in the 42 percent of the adult population that were single in 1993—a 32 percent increase over 1960 figures. "We can create meaningful social bonds with men and women without marriage," Wolfe explains. "We build our own extended families with people we choose." Now that women earn their own salaries, Wolfe claims, they "don't need to be married to have their basic needs fulfilled"; in fact, marriage is decreasingly seen as socially obligatory for bearing and raising children. Being single, Wolfe notes, is becoming "another option . . . another *desirable* option."

Others lament the decline of the family wage and subsequent changes in the concept and form of the family in America. For example, Allan Carlson, president of the Rockford Institute, an organization that promotes traditional Judeo-Christian values, contends that government affirmative action programs and other feminist-supported efforts to end job discrimination on the basis of sex killed the family wage—making two incomes necessary for most families and consigning others to poverty. Instead of allowing more feminist-sponsored government involvement in their lives and businesses, Carlson insists, Americans should return to the important job of raising their families. Carlson supports measures such as tax credits for families with children to help recreate the economic base of the family and allow women to remain at home to raise their own children.

A return to traditional family roles would benefit everyone, agrees child care researcher Karl Zinsmeister. "It's often claimed today that the two-parent partnership is kind of a historical freak," Zinsmeister notes. "In truth, the mother-father-child household is humankind's universal childrearing institution." The importance of traditional gender roles, he claims, is illustrated by the growing number of poverty-stricken women trying to raise their children alone, as well as the "enormously higher rates of violence, accidents, and criminality" among men who are separated from their families. Indeed, Zinsmeister says, the demise of the traditional family is more than an individual loss since "the surge of fatherlessness and family decay that began about 25 years ago correlates closely to the surges in crime, drug use, child poverty, and educational droop that currently bedevil American society."

The lives and roles of people form the fabric of society, but perhaps not a seamless fabric. As those lives and roles have been informed and defined by gender specialization, redefining the parts women play necessarily changes the whole. Whether society should reassert its interest in what some believe are traditional gender roles or instead adjust to redefined roles is debated in this revised edition of *Male/Female Roles: Opposing Viewpoints*. Against the backdrop of so profound a transformation, the authors discuss the following topics: How Are Sex Roles Established? Have Women's Roles Changed for the Better? Have Men's Roles Changed for the Better? How Does Work Affect the Family? and What Is the Future of Male/Female Relationships? There is much debate over the benefits of current changes in male/female roles because, as history has shown, the quality of each person's life in the future will depend on the kind of society men and women are creating today.

How Are Sex Roles Established?

MALE/
FEMALE
ROLES

Chapter Preface

"Few areas of science are as littered with intellectual rubbish as the study of innate . . . differences between the sexes," asserts feminist writer Barbara Ehrenreich. There are proven differences, Ehrenreich concedes, but, she says, "The question [is], as ever: What do these differences augur for our social roles, in particular the division of power and opportunity between the sexes?"

Ehrenreich's question cuts to the heart of an ongoing, and emotional, debate over the nature and sources of differences between the sexes: Do men and women have different inborn—and therefore unchangeable—strengths and weaknesses? And if they do, should they fulfill different social roles or the same ones?

"Males and females differ anatomically, sexually, emotionally, psychologically, and biochemically," contends James C. Dobson, president of Focus on the Family, a Christian organization advocating conservative family values. Citing research in brain anatomy and hormonal activity, Dobson argues that males, being more aggressive and competitive, are better suited to bringing home a paycheck to their families, while women's maternal instincts and emotionality make them better at raising the children and taking care of the home. For Dobson, traditional male and female roles are natural, and naturally different from each other, because, he says, "we differ in every cell of our bodies."

Nothing could be further from the truth for biologist Ruth Hubbard, who sums up her position with philosopher Simone de Beauvoir's observation that "one isn't born a woman, one becomes a woman." The same holds true for men, Hubbard explains, because "there are enormous overlaps between women and men for all traits that are not directly involved with procreation." Even the most seemingly natural sex differences in physical height and strength are related to socio-cultural factors such as diet and exercise, she argues. Therefore, she concludes, there are no important differences in the sexes' inborn abilities to perform any kind of work or activity. "If society . . . stratifies the work force into women's and men's jobs," Hubbard insists, "it does so for economic, social, and political reasons."

Looking for differences in male/female anatomy is therefore much more than a purely scientific discussion; sex-difference research is, among other things, about finding the biological basis for competing ideas of appropriate gender roles. The following chapter is a forum for ideas that go beyond the question of how sex roles are established to the larger debate over how each person should live and how society as a whole should be organized.

"Mating practices are the result of an evolutionary process favoring genes that most successfully replicate themselves. "

Evolution Explains Traditional Gender Roles

Anthony Layng

Gender roles are global, according to Anthony Layng. Regardless of race, class, or culture, Layng argues, men are more promiscuous, more independent, and less nurturing than are women. These differences are not only biological, Layng concludes, but clearly evolutionary in their tendency to propagate our species. Layng is professor of anthropology at Elmira College in New York.

As you read, consider the following questions:

1. What examples does Layng give in support of his contention that behavioral sex differences are universal? What does the author say should be the impact of these natural gender differences on social policy?
2. How does Layng explain the natural selection of behavior? How does he relate this to Charles Darwin's theory of evolution?
3. How does sociobiological theory explain human sexual aggressiveness/coyness, promiscuousness/faithfulness, domesticity/laziness, and other gender-specific behaviors, according to the author?

Social scientists long have been aware of the distinctive sex roles characteristic of tribal societies around the world, but many are reluctant to conclude that this is anything other than learned behavior. Most American cultural anthropologists have assumed that sex roles are largely arbitrary. This is illustrated by citing examples characteristic of males in one population and females in another—as in the American Southwest, where Navajo weavers are women and Hopi weavers are men.

To suggest that female roles are determined to any significant degree by biological factors invites an implication that the lower social status of women found in most societies also might be attributed to innate differences between the sexes, that "anatomy is destiny." American anthropologists have been influenced by social liberalism to such an extent that any scholarly proponent of biological determinism (racism, sexism, etc.) is likely to be challenged immediately. Their arguments against racism have pointed out that there is no reliable correlation between race and social behavior; people of the same race may have sharply contrasting cultures; and a given population can alter its culture dramatically without, presumably, altering its genes. For instance, the Aztecs and Apache were of the same race, but the former evolved a complex state civilization while the latter remained primitive nomads. The post-World War II Japanese have shown us how much a homogeneous racial population can change its culture in a very short time.

When it comes to sexism—the belief that the distinctive behavior of females and males is influenced significantly by their differing physiology—ethnographic challenges are less convincing. One major difficulty is the fact that there are no societies where men and women act alike. Even where conscious attempts have been made to eliminate behavioral differences between the sexes, distinctions remain. A study of American communes in the 1970s found that none have "come anywhere near succeeding in abolishing sex-role distinctions, although a number . . . have made this their highest ideological priority."

Sexist Societies

Another reason why cross-cultural comparisons have been relatively ineffectual in undermining sexist thinking is that, regardless of the great variability of sex roles from one society to another, there are certain behavior patterns and attitudes that appear to be the same in both traditional and modern societies. For example:

• Women generally prefer older men as mates, while most males prefer younger females.

• In courtship and mating behavior, most men are more sexually aggressive and most women are more coy.

- Males are more inclined to delay marriage.
- Men are more likely to seek a variety of mates.
- Women tend to be more tolerant of adulterous mates.
- Females are more likely to be domestic and nurturing.

In some societies, women prefer men who are considerably older than themselves; in others, the age discrepancy is slight. What is constant is that, on average, the male in each couple is older. Unlike bands of apes, where females are the usual initiators of copulation, "presenting" themselves to males, it is far more common for men to initiate sex, while women are more likely to take a relatively passive role beyond flirtation. Nearly everywhere, shyness or coquettishness is associated strongly with female sexual behavior.

Although some males may have to sell the idea of marriage to their mates, it is far more usual for women to be in the position

Victor Bogorad/*New Times*.

of favoring such a binding relationship and men to be reluctant to commit themselves. However, males are less reticent about participating in purely sexual relationships, often doing so with more than one partner concurrently. Females seem far more inclined to restrict themselves to one mate, or at least to one at a time. These behavioral differences often are reflected in the "double standard"—the attitude that female infidelity is a far more serious moral breach than male unfaithfulness. Typically, both men and women are more inclined to condemn the adulteress. This is not to say that wives do not disapprove strongly of spouses who cheat on them. The point is that a woman far more often will put up with such a husband. Men, on the other hand, are more likely to leave, severely beat, or even kill an unfaithful mate.

Finally, men are far less inclined toward "nesting" and nurturing. It is the women in all societies who are the most domestic and more adept at nursing the sick and comforting those who are troubled. Both sexes generally agree that it is a woman's nature that makes her so well suited to these activities.

Global Uniformity

If women and men naturally are inclined to view each other in programmed ways regardless of their class or culture and naturally are predisposed to act toward each other in similarly uniform ways, it might seem reasonable to conclude that female human nature is clearly distinct from that of males and that an Equal Rights Amendment goes against nature. As an active proponent of the ERA and an opponent to all sexism, I am troubled by such a conclusion, but unable simply to dismiss it.

In light of such global uniformity in behavior and attitudes, it is difficult to account for these patterns solely in terms of socialization. Cultures differ dramatically from one to another, and religious beliefs, kinship systems, social structures, political traditions, and subsistence systems vary. So, why do men in such contrasting societies all behave so aggressively in the pursuit of sex? Why do male hunters, farmers, and warriors tend to show such interest in seducing new sex partners? Why do Latin American and Asian women put up with adulterous husbands? Why do females in primitive tribes and industrial societies usually prefer older men? Why do peasant women and debutantes tend to want marriage before their male counterparts do? Why are both American and African men relatively disinterested in domestic chores? If it is all a matter of learning, of cultural conditioning, why are there not some societies where most men and women do not conform to these patterns?

Are these traits determined to some extent by the biological peculiarities of the different sexes? If so, it is distressing to consider the social and political implications of such a finding. If human nature (and not only nurture) leads females to behave in a distinctive way, is it therefore not suitable that they be treated in a discriminating fashion? If chasing women only is doing what comes naturally to men, then promiscuous females should have less excuse for their infidelities. Should husbands, even of working wives, be excused from house cleaning and child care? Clearly, one need not be a militant feminist to be made very uncomfortable by such questions.

It is further disturbing to liberals to learn about the findings of sociobiology, a new discipline which suggests some rather startling explanations for behavior traits such as those cited above. According to many sociobiologists, mating practices are the result of an evolutionary process favoring genes that most successfully replicate themselves. This theory states that those most successful in this regard give rise to behavior and attitudes maximizing reproductive success.

Supposedly, genetically inherited behavior that causes people to have the most offspring eventually results, through natural selection, in such action becoming more and more common. Genes which induce people to behave otherwise, by the same selective process, are weeded out since people who behave this way have fewer children—that is, they do not produce as many carriers of their genes. Over time, as the result of this process, genes which most successfully cause men and women to produce carriers of these genes become more and more prevalent.

The most convincing illustrations of sociobiological explanations have been provided by studies of animal populations. For example, when a male langur monkey takes over a harem from an older male, he proceeds to kill all the infants of nursing mothers in the troop. From the perspective of Darwin's Theory of Evolution (survival of the fittest), this makes no sense at all, for it destroys healthy and fit infants as well as any others. From a sociobiological perspective, however, this wholesale infanticide is a sound reproductive strategy because it ensures that the genes of this newly dominant male soon will be replicated and in maximum numbers. Were he to wait until each female weaned her infant and ceased to lactate—a prerequisite to coming back into heat—it would be that much longer before he could impregnate them. By killing all the infants carrying some other male's genes, he speeds up the process whereby his genes begin to predominate. Also, he does not waste any energy protecting infants not carrying his genes.

The females of any species, goes this theory, are likely to develop very different kinds of reproductive strategies given the fact that they produce fewer offspring than do males. The genes of males, in competition with those of other males, induce behavior that results in the greatest number of offspring. Females, who are not able to produce nearly as many offspring as are males, compete for quality, rather than quantity, behaving so as to ensure that each child produced will be likely to survive and reproduce. In these ways, males and females alike are directed by their genes to see to it that they reproduce them as successfully as possible.

Reproductive Strategies

Among human beings, the fact that men prefer younger wives is fully consistent with their desire to have children since young women are highly fertile and the most likely to bear full-term healthy offspring. A young wife may devote her entire reproductive potential to producing children fathered by her husband. Since the reproductive strategy of women stresses *quality* of offspring, they are inclined to seek established and mature men as providers and protectors of their children. Male sexual aggressiveness serves to spread male genes. Female coyness helps to assure a potential mate that pregnancy has not occurred already. Her fidelity helps to convince him to stay around to protect what he therefore can assume to be his own offspring. (The sexual aggressiveness of female apes would be inappropriate in a human population, but not for them since male apes are not providers. Given the human sexual division of labor, men and women are economically dependent on each other; apes are not.)

By delaying marriage, a man is free to impregnate more women who will bear his children (his genes) without obligating him to care for them. A woman seeks marriage to monopolize not a man's sexuality, but, rather, his political and economic resources, to ensure that her children (her genes) will be well provided for. She may worry about her husband's infidelities, but only because this can siphon off resources she wants for her children. He, on the other hand, is far more concerned about sexually monopolizing her. He wants assurance that he is the father of any child she gives birth to; otherwise, he will be providing for those who do not carry his genes. Moreover, if she becomes pregnant by another man, it will be many months before she can produce a fetus carrying her husband's genes. With or without her husband's faithfulness, she can get pregnant and produce the maximum number of children carrying her genes. Thus, a wife's affair is less tolerable to her husband for, according to the sociobiological perspective, it threatens to diminish the number of offspring he can produce by her.

The domesticity of women and the wanderings of men also are consistent with the differential reproductive strategies each sex has evolved. In stressing the quality of her offspring, since she can have relatively few, a woman provides a comfortable domicile for her children and stays home to nurture them, to better ensure their survivability so they are most likely to mature and further reproduce her genes. Meanwhile, the man is off chasing women, producing as many children as possible and being far less concerned with sticking around to guarantee their welfare. If he were to limit himself sexually to one woman, he greatly would diminish the number of children he potentially could propagate. In short, from a sociobiological perspective, she "succeeds" by being faithful to her husband since this helps to ensure that he will provide for her children; he does so not only by monopolizing her as a producer of his offspring, but by having children with other women as well.

By this point, you probably are thinking of people who exemplify sociobiologically sound traits of lecherous males and the women who put up with them. Certainly, we all are familiar with this behavior. Even though it often runs counter to accepted moral standards, we frequently hear people say, "That's the way men (or women) are." Sociobiologists seem to be offering theoretical confirmation of this folk wisdom.

Is human social behavior influenced by our genes? Whether further research will confirm or refute sociobiological theory as it applies to human behavior, we shall have to wait until far more information is available. No matter what the effect on our behavior, we should keep in mind that learning plays an important role. Consequently, social policy should not be based on any assumption that biological determinants of human behavior and attitudes are more instrumental than learning, for cultural factors can counteract human genetic predispositions. Our early ancestors were subject to natural selection. Since the time of the Neanderthals, though, human populations have adapted to environmental change almost entirely by altering their learned behavior and attitudes—their culture, not their genes. There are individuals whose behavior conforms to sociobiological generalizations, but, especially among the educated, one finds many contrasting examples—men who do not chase young women, females who are sexually aggressive and/or disinterested in marriage, and couples who choose to have no children at all. . . .

So, even if inborn factors influence male and female human sexual behavior, the extent to which they do so clearly is limited and subordinate to learning and conditioning. Consequently, we neither need fear intellectually the findings of sociobiologists nor allow them significantly to influence interpersonal behavior and social attitudes regarding gender-specific behavior. If men and women continue to behave differently (and it seems there is no clear trend away from this pattern), we may yet learn just why we do not act like the opposite sex.

23

"Sociobiologists . . . can no longer justify traditional sex roles . . . by appealing to the universality of such behavior in other species."

Evolution Does Not Explain Traditional Gender Roles

Carol Tavris

In the following viewpoint, Carol Tavris writes that until now the major contributors to the evolutionary science of sociobiology have been men who, because they naturally identified more with the male animals they were studying, tended to interpret animal behavior in ways that validated traditional human gender roles. That their observations were often wrong is now coming to light, Tavris explains, with the research being conducted by a growing number of women scientists. For example, Tavris reports, it has now been discovered that the females of many species, far from being sexually chaste, as earlier believed, are in fact polyandrous (have several mates) for evolutionarily sound reasons. Tavris is a social psychologist, writer, and lecturer.

As you read, consider the following questions:

1. How does Tavris suggest that sociobiology has, until now, been simplistic and self-serving?
2. How do the results of studying langur monkeys in Tavris's account differ from those cited in Layng's article?
3. How might the findings of female sexuality in Tavris's account influence future gender role interpretations?

Excerpted from pp. 212-21 of *The Mismeasure of Woman* by Carol Tavris. Copyright ©1992 by Carol Tavris. Reprinted by permission of Simon & Schuster, Inc.

It's fun to argue about which sex is "naturally" sexier, but ultimately it is a fruitless debate. The reason is that there is no underlying sexual nature . . . and that trying to find one is as impossible as trying to find a "true self" unaffected by the world in which it develops. Our sexuality *is* body, culture, age, learning, habit, fantasies, worries, passions, and the relationships in which all these elements combine. That's why sexuality can change with age, partner, experience, emotions, and sense of perspective. . . .

To know whether and how men and women differ in bed, we need to consider the worlds in which they live, not just the parts with which they make love. We need to reconnect the genitals to the person. And we need to consider the eye, and ideology, of the beholder who is observing those parts in action, as the Parable of the Primates reveals. . . .

A Gendered Science

The basic ideas behind sociobiology [the comparative study of animals' social organization] date back to Charles Darwin, who in 1871 described what he considered to be a basic dichotomy in the sexual natures of males and females of all species. Males actively pursue females; they are promiscuous; and those who are strongest, most fit in evolutionary terms, succeed in their sexual conquest. Females, said Darwin, are "comparatively passive"; they may choose their preferred suitor, but then remain monogamous and faithful. That this dichotomy conveniently fit Victorian dating and mating patterns was, naturally, pure coincidence.

For a century after Darwin, research on sexual selection and sexual behavior was based on the belief that males are passionate and undiscriminating (any female in a storm will do), whereas females are restrained, cautious, and highly discriminating in their choice of partner (only a male who meets her shopping list of qualifications will do). According to primatologist Sarah Blaffer Hrdy, this stereotype of "the coy female" has persisted in the public mind *"despite the accumulation of abundant openly available evidence contradicting it"* (my emphasis).

The stereotype of the coy female got a major boost in an important paper published in 1948 by Angus John Bateman. Bateman was a distinguished plant geneticist who did dozens of experiments with Drosophila, the tiny fruit fly that many people remember from science experiments in junior high school. Bateman found that successful male fruit flies could, with multiple matings, produce nearly three times as many offspring as the most reproductively successful female. As Hrdy explains, "whereas a male could always gain by mating just one more time, and hence benefit from a nature that made him undiscriminatingly eager to mate, a female, already breeding near capacity after just one cop-

25

ulation, could gain little from multiple mating and should be quite uninterested in mating more than once or twice."

What, you may ask, does a human man have in common with a fruit fly? When it comes to sexual strategies, said Bateman, the answer is everything. Generalizing from his sixty-four experiments with Drosophila to all species, Bateman concluded that there is a universally lopsided division in the sexual natures of all creatures, apart from "a few very primitive organisms." Quite simply, males profit, evolutionarily speaking, from frequent mating, and females do not. This is why, said Bateman, "there is nearly always a combination of an undiscriminating eagerness in the males and a discriminating passivity in the females."

Genetic Behavior

The modern field of sociobiology took this idea still further, attempting to account for complex human social arrangements and customs—warfare and corporate raiding, feeding infants and giving children karate lessons—in terms of the individual's basic need to reproduce his or her genes. Women and men, sociobiologists believe, adopt highly different strategies in order to do this. Males compete with other males for access to desirable females, and their goal is to inseminate as many females as possible. Females, in contrast, are motivated to attach themselves to genetically "superior" males because of the female's greater "investment" in terms of time and energy in her offspring; this, according to sociobiologists, is why females are more faithful and nurturant than males. As biologist Ruth Hubbard observes, "Thus, from the seemingly innocent asymmetries between eggs and sperm [say the sociobiologists] flow such major social consequences as female fidelity, male promiscuity, women's disproportional contribution to the care of children, and the unequal distribution of labor by sex."

Sociobiological explanations of competitive, promiscuous men and choosy, inhibited but flirtatious women fit right in with many elements within the popular culture. "And so it was," Hrdy says, "that 'coyness' came to be the single most commonly mentioned attribute of females in the literature on sociobiology."

It all seems a cruel joke of nature. Certainly many people are convinced, as the King of Siam sings in The King and I, that the male is like the honeybee, flitting from flower to flower, "gathering all he can," whereas the female has "honey for just one man." But notice that it is the King who sings that song; until relatively recently, no one was asking Queens for their view of things. Nor were male observers asking why, if human females were so naturally chaste, coy, and monogamous, social taboos from ostracism to death had to be placed on females who indulged in forbidden sexual relationships. For that matter, why

26

did nonmarital affairs need to be forbidden anyway, if females have "honey for just one man"?

Sociobiologists attempt to explain human social customs by drawing on research on nonhuman animals, from the fields of primatology, evolutionary biology, anthropology, and related disciplines. In the last two decades, however, there has been an explosion of new research that casts doubt on many sociobiological assumptions, a change that is largely a result of the growing numbers of women who have entered these fields. Most of these women saw animal behavior in a different light from most of the male observers who had preceded them. Male primatologists, for example, had tended to observe and emphasize male-male competition and the number of times the male animals "got lucky"; the female animals, to the human men observing them, seemed mysterious and unpredictable. This is not unlike the ways in which human females have seemed mysterious and unpredictable to the human males who have observed *them*.

At first, women who went into these research fields saw the world as they had been taught to see it, through the academic perspective of their mentors. But after a while, they began to ask different questions and to bring different expectations to their observations. Hrdy recalls her own first glimpse of a female langur

> . . . moving away from her natal group to approach and solicit males in an all-male band. At the time, I had no context for interpreting behavior that merely seemed strange and incomprehensible to my Harvard-trained eyes. Only in time, did I come to realize that such wandering and such seemingly "wanton" behavior were recurring events in the lives of langurs.

Eventually, Hrdy learned that female langurs often leave their troops to join up with bands of males; and she also found that often a female, for reasons unknown, "simply takes a shine to the resident male of a neighboring troop." In fact, female langurs (and many other primate species) are able to shift from being in heat once a month to being continuously receptive for weeks at a time, a state not unlike the first phase of (human) love. In many primates, female receptivity is often *situation specific*, rather than being dependent exclusively on cyclical periods of being in heat.

Discovering Female Sexuality

As a result of the efforts of many pioneers like Hrdy, we now know that the females of many animal species do not behave like the patient, coy fruit fly. On the contrary, the females are sexually ardent and can even be called polyandrous (having many male partners). Further, their sexual behavior does not depend simply on the goal of being fertilized by the male, because

27

in many cases females actively solicit males when they are not ovulating, and even when they are already pregnant. . . .

• Many species of female birds are promiscuous. In one study, researchers vasectomized the "master" of a blackbird harem . . . but the females nevertheless conceived.

• Many species of female fish are promiscuous. A female shiner perch who is not ovulating will nevertheless mate with many males, collecting sperm and storing them internally until she is ready to ovulate.

• Many species of female cats, notably leopards, lions, and pumas, are promiscuous. A lioness may mate a hundred times a day with many different partners during the week she is in estrus.

• Many species of female primates are promiscuous. Among savanna baboons and Barbary macaques, females initiate many different brief sexual encounters. Among chimpanzees, Hrdy reports, some females form partnerships with one male, but others engage in communal mating with all males in the vicinity. And among wild tamarin monkeys, a species long thought to be monogamous (at least in captivity), supposedly faithful females will mate with several males. . . .

Pop Anthropology

In the 1960s and 1970s, several books became highly popular for "proving" innate male aggressiveness and male dominance. While drawing their examples mainly from certain mammals, male authors did not hesitate to extend their arguments to prove "the inevitability of patriarchy" among humans. A reading public that revered men touted as eminent scientists did not perceive the serious methodological flaws and factitiousness of their arguments. Authors sophisticated in using "objective" fact to mask preconceptions of male dominance, or perhaps blinded by their own overriding need, made unsubstantiated extrapolations from animal to human life. These works of pop anthropology prepared the ground for sociobiology, which arose soon after the "second wave" of the women's movement. Sociobiology is evoked to challenge feminist assertions of human equality. It too tries to justify male dominance among humans by showing that male dominance, rape, and infanticide exist among animals. Again, the material is carefully selected, slanted, and often false.

Marilyn French, *The War Against Women*, 1992.

In spite of rapidly accumulating evidence that females of many different and varied species do mate "promiscuously" (a word that itself has evaluative overtones), it was not until 1980 or so that researchers realized that this fact threw, well, a mon-

28

keywrench into traditional evolutionary theories. Why would females have more copulations than are necessary for conception? Why would they go off with some guy from a neighboring town, whom none of their friends approves of? Why risk losing the genetic father's support by joining the baboon equivalent of Hell's Angels? And the brooding question over all of them, why did female primates develop continuous sexual receptivity?

These questions stimulated a flurry of new theories to explain why female philandering would make as much survival sense as its male counterpart. Most of these new explanations directly resulted from considering the world from the female's point of view. Traditional theories of sexual selection, after all, were based exclusively on the perspective of the male: Males compete for *access* to the female, who apparently is just hanging around waiting to go out and party with the winner. And it's only from a male point of view that multiple female matings can be considered "excessive," or that female sexual interest is even described as her time of "receptivity." Is she passively "receptive" to the active intentions of the male? The word implies that she's just putting up with his annoying lustfulness yet again.

New hypotheses argue that there are genetic benefits for the offspring of sexually adventurous mothers. According to Hrdy's review of these explanations, the "fertility backup" hypothesis assumes that females need sperm from a number of males in order to assure conception by the healthiest sperm. The "inferior cuckold" hypothesis suggests that a female who has a genetically inferior mate will sneak off with a genetically superior male when she is likely to conceive. (I suppose she knows this by the size of his income.) And the "diverse paternity" hypothesis argues that when the environment is unpredictable, females diversify. Over a reproductive lifetime, females who have numerous partners, and thus different fathers for their offspring, improve their offspring's chances for survival.

Other Hypotheses

Other theories look for the social and environmental benefits of female promiscuity to the mother and her infants. The "therapeutic hypothesis" suggests that having lots of partners and multiple orgasms (in some species) makes intercourse and conception more pleasurable, and therefore more likely to occur. The "keep 'em around" hypothesis maintains that females actively solicit lower-status males (with the tacit approval of dominant males), a behavior that prevents weaker males from leaving the group. Hrdy's own favored theory is what she calls the "manipulation" hypothesis, the idea that females mate with numerous males precisely because paternity becomes uncertain. The result is that male partners will be more invested in, and tolerant of, the female's infants. This idea, Hrdy explains,

> grew out of a dawning awareness that, first of all, individual
> females could do a great deal that would affect the survival of
> their offspring, and second, that males, far from mere dis-
> pensers of sperm, were critical features on the landscape
> where infants died or survived. That is, females were more
> political, males more nurturing (or at least not neutral), than
> some earlier versions of sexual selection theory would lead us
> to suppose. . . .

Hrdy's "manipulation hypothesis" assumes that primate males
respond more benevolently to the offspring of females with
whom they have mated, so the females derive obvious benefits
from mating with more than one male. In numerous primate
species, the mother's multiple sexual partners act like godfa-
thers to the infant, as primatologist Jeanne Altmann calls them.
Each of these males will help care for the female's offspring.
Baboon males, many of whom could have served as the model
for *Three Men and a Baby*, develop special relationships with the
infant, carrying it on their backs in times of danger and protecting it from strangers and hazards. These affectionate bonds are
possible because of the mother's closeness to the males, says
Hrdy, and because the infant comes to trust these males and
seek them out.

Avoiding the Pitfalls

The manipulation hypothesis may or may not hold up with further research, as Hrdy acknowledges. It certainly does not apply
to most human societies, where husbands do not look too kindly
on their wives' "special relationships" with other men, let alone
their previous lovers, husbands, and wooers. Hrdy's work,
nonetheless, shows that theories depend, first and foremost, on
what an observer *observes*, and then on how those observations
can be blurred by unconscious expectations. Hrdy initially regarded those "wanton" female langurs as aberrations because
their behavior did not fit the established theory. Not until researchers began to speculate on the potential benefits of female
promiscuity did they come up with different questions and answers about female sexual behavior than had sociobiologists.

In evolutionary biology, if not in the popular press, the myth
of the coy female (and, for that matter, the myth of the absent
father) is dead. Hrdy is encouraged by the speed with which
primatologists, once aware of the male bias that permeated their
discipline, have produced "a small stampede by members of
both sexes to study female reproductive strategies." This she
takes to be a healthy sign, as do I. But Hrdy cautions against
"substituting a new set of biases for the old ones":

> That is, among feminist scholars it is now permissible to say
> that males and females are different, provided one also stipu-

lates that females are more cooperative, more nurturing, more supportive—not to mention equipped with unique moral sensibilities. . . .

Perhaps it is impossible, as biologist Donna Haraway suggests, for any of us to observe the behavior of other species, let alone our own, in a way that does not mirror the assumptions of our own way of life. It is disconcerting, says Hrdy wryly, that primatologists were finding "politically motivated females and nurturing males at roughly the same time that a woman runs for vice president of the United States and [Garry] Trudeau starts to poke fun at 'caring males' in his cartoons." Informally, scientists admit that their prejudices—such as the tendency to identify with the same sex of the species they are studying—affect their research. One woman primatologist told Hrdy, "I sometimes identify with female baboons more than I do with males of my own species."

Toward Scientific Balance

The recognition of a male-centered bias in primatology and biology proved to be an enormous step forward, allowing scientists of both sexes to revise their theories of animal behavior. Sociobiologists . . . can no longer justify traditional sex roles, particularly male dominance and female nurturance and chastity, by appealing to the universality of such behavior in other species. Other species aren't cooperating.

But that is not the only moral of the Parable of the Primates. The female perspective is invaluable, but, as Hrdy warns, a female-centered bias will provide its own set of distortions. Cultural feminists who look to evolutionary biology to explain women's allegedly sweeter, more cooperative ways are on as shaky ground as the antifeminists they would replace.

31

"Males and females differ anatomically, sexually, emotionally, psychologically, and biochemically. We differ in literally every cell of our bodies. "

Biology Determines Gender Roles

James C. Dobson

In the following viewpoint, James C. Dobson contends that men and women have always behaved differently, had different emotions, even cared about entirely different things. These dissimilarities are universal, Dobson says, because they are biological in origin. Male and female roles cannot be changed, nor should they be, Dobson concludes, since they "counterbalance and interface with one another" in ways that make the family, and hence society, possible. Dobson, a former associate professor of clinical pediatrics at the University of Southern California School of Medicine, is president of Focus on the Family, an organization committed to restoring traditional Christian and conservative family values.

As you read, consider the following questions:

1. The author cites several ways in which women and men are biologically different. What examples does he give?
2. In what ways does Dobson tie behavior to biology? Does he rule out culture as a behavioral influence?
3. How should the differences between the sexes be interpreted, according to Dobson?

I would like to offer some evidence to show that men and women are biologically unique. The women's movement, in its assault on traditional sex roles, has repeatedly asserted that males and females are identical except for the ability to bear children. Nothing could be farther from the truth.

The Human Brain

Let's begin by discussing the human brain, where maleness and femaleness are rooted. Careful research is revealing that the basic differences between the sexes are neurological in origin, rather than being purely cultural as ordinarily presumed. As Dr. Richard Restak stated in his book, *The Brain: The Last Frontier:*

> Certainly, anyone who has spent time with children in a playground or school setting is aware of the differences in the way boys and girls respond to similar situations. Think of the last time you supervised a birthday party attended by five-year-olds. It's not usually the girls who pull hair, throw punches, or smear each other with food. Usually such differences are explained on a cultural basis. Boys are expected to be more aggressive and play rough games, while girls are presumably encouraged to be more gentle, nonassertive, and passive. After several years of exposure to such expectations, so the theory goes, men and women wind up with widely varying behavioral and intellectual repertoires. As a corollary to this, many people believe that if the child-rearing practices could be equalized and sexual-role stereotypes eliminated, most of these differences would eventually disappear. As often happens, however, the true state of affairs is not that simple.

> Recent psychological research indicates that many of the differences in brain function between the sexes are innate, biologically determined, and relatively resistant to change through the influences of culture.

Dr. Restak presents numerous studies that document this statement, and then concludes this chapter by quoting Dr. David Wechsler, creator of the most popular intelligence test for use with adults.

> . . . our findings do confirm what poets and novelists have often asserted, and the average layman long believed, namely, that men not only behave but "think" differently from women.

Both Drs. Restak and Wechsler are right. Males and females differ anatomically, sexually, emotionally, psychologically, and biochemically. We differ in literally every cell of our bodies, for each sex carries a unique chromosomal pattern. Much is written today about so-called sex-change operations, whereby males are transformed into females or vice versa. Admittedly, it is possible to alter the external genitalia by surgery, and silicone can be used to pad the breasts or round out a bony frame. Hormones can then be injected to feminize or masculinize the convert. But nothing can be done to change the assignment of sex made by God at the instant of conception. That determination is carried in each cell, and it will read "male" or "female" from the earliest moment of life to the point of death. The Bible says emphatically, "Male *and* female created he them" (Genesis 1:27, King James Version, emphasis added). Not one sex, but *two!*

Furthermore, it is my deep conviction that each sex displays unique emotional characteristics that are genetically endowed. Cultural influences cannot account for these novelties. Few psychologists have had the courage to express this view in recent years, because some people perceived it to be insulting. But to be *different* from men does not make women *inferior* to men. Males and females are original creations of God, each bearing strengths and weaknesses that counterbalance and interface with one another. It is a beautiful design that must not be disassembled.

The Menstrual Cycle

Just how do female emotions differ from those of males? Let's consider first the importance of the menstrual cycle. I'm reminded of the late 1960s when hairy young men and women became almost indistinguishable from each other. Two of these hippies, a male and female, were involved in a minor traffic accident and were taken to a local hospital for treatment. The nurse who was completing the intake forms could not determine from their clothing and appearance which sex they represented. After considering the dilemma for a moment she asked, "Okay, which one of you has a menstrual cycle?"

The hippie with the bass voice looked at her through his bangs and said, "Not me, man. I gots a Honda."

The question was more significant than merely determining the sex of the patients. Included in this matter of menstruation are many implications for the way females feel about life during the course of the month. It has been said, quite accurately, that the four weeks of the menstrual cycle are characteristic of the four seasons of the year. The first week after a period can be termed the springtime of the physiological calendar. New estrogens (female hormones) are released each day and a woman's body begins to rebound from the recent winter.

The second week represents the summertime of the cycle, when the living is easy. A woman during this phase has more self-confidence than during any other phase of the month. It is a time of maximum energy, enthusiasm, amiability, and self-esteem. Estrogen levels account for much of this optimism, reaching a peak during mid-cycle when ovulation occurs. The relationship between husband and wife is typically at its best during these days of summer, when sexual desire (and the potential for pregnancy) are paramount.

34

But alas, the fall must surely follow summer. Estrogen levels steadily dwindle as the woman's body prepares itself for another period of menstruation. A second hormone, called progesterone, is released, which reduces the effect of estrogen and initiates the symptoms of premenstrual tension. It is a bleak phase of the month. Self-esteem deteriorates day by day, bringing depression and pessimism with it. A bloated and sluggish feeling often produces not only discomfort but also the belief that "I am ugly." Irritability and aggression become increasingly evident as the week progresses, reaching a climax immediately prior to menstruation.

Then come the winter and the period of the menstrual flow.

FILL THIS PRAM WITH MONEY OR I'LL EXPLODE WITH PREMENSTRUAL TENSION!

CASHIER

A.K

©Arja Kajermo. Reprinted with permission.

Women differ remarkably in intensity of these symptoms, but most experience some discomfort. Those most vulnerable even find it necessary to spend a day or two in bed during the winter season, suffering from cramping and generalized misery. Gradually, the siege passes and the refreshing newness of springtime returns.

How can anyone who understands this cyclical pattern contend that there are no genetically determined psychological differences between males and females? No such system operates in men. The effect of the menstrual cycle is not only observable clinically, but it can be documented statistically.

The incidences of suicides, homicides, and infanticides perpetrated by women are significantly higher during the period of premenstrual tension than any other phase of the month. Consider also the findings of Alec Coppen and Neil Kessel, who studied 465 women and observed that they were more irritable and depressed during the premenstrual phase than during the midcycle. "This was true for neurotic, psychotic, and normal women alike. Similarly Natalie Sharness found the premenstrual phase associated with feelings of helplessness, anxiety, hostility, and yearning for love. At menstruation, this tension and irritability eased, but depression often accompanied the relief, and lingered until estrogen increased."

I doubt that these facts will come as a great revelation to men or women. Both sexes know that behavior and attitudes are related to the monthly pattern. I receive interesting letters from men who ask, "How can I cope with my wife's irritability during this phase?" Their question reminds me of an incident shared with me by my late friend Dr. David Hernandez, who was an obstetrician and gynecologist in private practice. The true story involves Latin men whose wives were given birth control pills by a pharmaceutical company. The Food and Drug Administration in America would not permit hormonal research to be conducted, so the company selected a small fishing village in South America which agreed to cooperate. All the women in the town were given the pill on the same date, and after three weeks the prescription was terminated to permit menstruation. That meant, of course, that every adult female in the community was experiencing premenstrual tension at the same time. The men couldn't take it. They all headed for their boats each month and remained at sea until the crisis passed at home. They knew, even if some people didn't, that females are different from males . . . especially every twenty-eight days.

Physical Bases

But there are other ways women are unique. Female emotions are also influenced by two other exclusively feminine functions,

36

lactation and pregnancy. Furthermore, the hypothalamus, which is located at the base of the brain and has been called the "seat of the emotions," is apparently wired very differently for males than females. For example, a severe emotional shock or trauma can be interpreted by the hypothalamus, which then sends messages to the pituitary by way of neurons and hormones. The pituitary often responds by changing the body chemistry of the woman, perhaps interrupting the normal menstrual cycle for six months or longer. Female physiology is a finely tuned instrument, being more vulnerable and complex than the masculine counterpart. Why some women find that fact insulting is still a mystery to me.

How do these differences translate into observable behavior? Medical science has not begun to identify all the ramifications of sexual uniqueness. Some of the implications are extremely subtle. For example, when researchers quietly walked on high school and college campuses to study behavior of the sexes, they observed that males and females even transported their books in different ways. The young men tended to carry them at their sides with their arms looped over the top. Women and girls, by contrast, usually cradled their books at their breasts, in much the same way they would a baby. Who can estimate how many other sex-related influences lie below the level of consciousness?

Emotional Patterns

Admittedly, some of the observed differences between the sexes *are* culturally produced. I don't know how to sort out those which are exclusively genetic from those which represent learned responses. Frankly, it doesn't seem to matter a great deal. The differences exist, for whatever reason. At the risk of being called a sexist, or a propagator of sexual stereotypes (or worse), let me delineate a few of the emotional patterns typical of women as compared with men.

1. The reproductive capacity of women results in a greater appreciation for stability, security, and enduring human relationships. In other words, females are more *future*-oriented because of their concern for children.

2. Related to the first item is a woman's emotional investment in her home, which usually exceeds that of her husband. She typically cares more than he about the minor details of the house, family functioning, and such concerns. To cite a personal example, my wife and I decided to install a new gas barbecue unit in our backyard. When the plumber completed the assignment and departed, Shirley and I both recognized that he had placed the appliance approximately six inches too high. I looked at the device and said, "Hmmm, yes sir, he sure made a mistake. That post is a bit too high. By the way, what are we having for

dinner tonight?" Shirley's reaction was dramatically different. She said, "The plumber has that thing sticking up in the air and I don't think I can stand it!" Our contrasting views represented a classic difference of emotional intensity relating to the home.

3. Anyone who doubts that males and females are unique should observe how they approach a game of Ping Pong or Monopoly or dominoes or horseshoes or volleyball or tennis. Women often use the event as an excuse for fellowship and pleasant conversation. For men, the name of the game is *conquest*. Even if the setting is a friendly social gathering in the host's backyard, the beads of sweat on each man's forehead reveal his passion to win. This aggressive competitiveness has been attributed to cultural influences. I don't believe it. As Richard Restak said, "At a birthday party for five-year-olds, it's not usually the girls who pull hair, throw punches, or smear each other with food."

4. Males and females apparently differ in the manner by which they develop self-esteem. Men draw the necessary evidence of their worthiness primarily from their jobs—from being respected in business, profession, or craft. Women, however, *especially those who are homemakers*, depend primarily on the romantic relationship with their husbands for ego support. This explains why the emotional content of a marriage is often of greater significance to women than men and why tokens of affection are appreciated more by wives, who obtain esteem from these expressions of love and generosity.

5. A maternal instinct apparently operates in most women, although its force is stronger in some than others. This desire to procreate is certainly evident in those who are unable to conceive. I receive a steady influx of letters from women who express great frustration from their inability to become mothers. Although culture plays a major role in these longings, I believe they are rooted in female anatomy and physiology.

6. Perhaps the most dramatic differences between males and females are evident in their contrasting sexual preferences. He is more visually oriented, caring less about the romantic component. She is attracted not to a photograph of an unknown model or by a handsome stranger, but to a *particular* man with whom she has entered into an emotional relationship. This differing orientation is merely the tip of the iceberg in delineating the sexual uniqueness of males and females.

A Summary

These items are illustrative and are not intended to represent a scientific delineation of sexual differences. The reader is invited to add his own observations to the list and to make his own interpretations.

By way of summary, let me offer two *opinions* with regard to masculine leadership. They are as follows:

1. Because of the fragile nature of the male ego and a man's enormous need to be respected, combined with female vulnerability and a woman's need to be loved, I feel it is a mistake to tamper with the time-honored relationship of husband as loving protector and wife as recipient of that protection.

2. Because two captains sink the ship and two cooks spoil the broth, I feel that a family must have a leader whose decisions prevail in times of differing opinions. If I understand the Scriptures, that role has been assigned to the man of the house. However, he must not incite his crew to mutiny by heavyhanded disregard for their feelings and needs. He should, in fact, put the best interests of his family above his own, even to the point of death, if necessary. Nowhere in Scripture is he authorized to become a dictator or slave-owner.

Other combinations of husband-wife teamwork have been successful in individual families, but I've seen many complications occurring in marriages where the man was passive, weak, and lacking in qualities of leadership. None of the modern alternatives have improved on the traditional, masculine role as prescribed in the Good Book. It was, after all, inspired by the Creator of mankind.

If this be macho, sexist, chauvinist, and stereotypical, then I'm guilty as charged. (Please address all hate mail to my secretary, who has a special file prepared for it.)

"Women and men are physically not very different. There are enormous overlaps between women and men for all traits that are not directly involved with procreation."

Biology Does Not Determine Gender Roles

Ruth Hubbard

In the following viewpoint, Ruth Hubbard challenges scientific attempts to find innate or physical differences between men and women—differences that, she says, have traditionally been used to "prove" the inferiority of women. First, except for their reproductive organs, there are no significant physical differences between the sexes, Hubbard maintains. Second, she argues, any differences that are found, with the possible exception of height, are often the result of social conditioning, not inborn capacity. And thus, Hubbard concludes, biology cannot provide an explanation of gender roles and of social organizations in general. Hubbard, professor of biology emerita at Harvard University, has written on the politics of health care since the early 1970s.

As you read, consider the following questions:

1. What examples does Hubbard give to prove her contention that "one isn't born a woman (or man), one becomes one"?
2. What is the motivation behind much of the scientific inquiry into sex differences, according to Hubbard?
3. Why is scientific research into biological sex differences inherently flawed, according to the author?

Excerpted from pp. 119-29 of *The Politics of Women's Biology* by Ruth Hubbard, ©1990 by Rutgers—the State University. Reprinted by permission of Rutgers University Press.

Women's biology is a social construct and a political concept, not a scientific one, and I mean that in at least three ways. The first can be summed up in Simone de Beauvoir's dictum "One isn't born a woman, one becomes a woman." This does not mean that the environment shapes us, but that the concept, woman (or man), is a socially constructed one that little girls (or boys) try to fit as we grow up. Some of us are better at it than others, but we all try, and our efforts have biological as well as social consequences (a false dichotomy because our biological and social attributes are related dialectically [that is, they act on one another in producing an outcome]). How active we are, what clothes we wear, what games we play, what we eat and how much, what kinds of schools we go to, what work we do, all affect our biology as well as our social being in ways we cannot sort out. So, one isn't born a woman (or man), one becomes one.

A Social Construct

The concept of women's biology is socially constructed, and political, in a second way because it is not simply women's description of our experience of our biology. Women's biology has been described by physicians and scientists who, for historical reasons, have been mostly economically privileged, university-educated men with strong personal and political interests in describing women in ways that make it appear "natural" for us to fulfill roles that are important for their well-being, personally and as a group. Self-serving descriptions of women's biology date back at least to Aristotle. But if we dismiss the early descriptions as ideological, so are the descriptions scientists have offered that characterize women as weak, overemotional, and at the mercy of our raging hormones, and that construct our entire being around the functions of our reproductive organs. No one has suggested that men are just walking testicles, but again and again women have been looked on as though they were walking ovaries and wombs.

In the nineteenth century, when women tried to get access to higher education, scientists initially claimed we could not be educated because our brains are too small. When that claim became untenable, they granted that we could be educated the same as men but questioned whether we should be, whether it was good for us. They based their concerns on the claim that girls need to devote much energy to establishing the proper functioning of their ovaries and womb and that if they divert this energy to their brains by studying, their reproductive organs will shrivel, they will become sterile, and the race will die out.

This logic was steeped in race and class prejudice. The notion that women's reproductive organs need careful nurturing was used to justify excluding upper-class girls and young women from higher education but not to spare the working-class, poor, or black women who were laboring in the factories and homes of the upper class. If anything, these women were said to breed too much. In fact, their ability to have many children despite the fact that they worked so hard was taken as evidence that they were less highly evolved than upper-class women; for them breeding was "natural," as for animals.

Finally, and perhaps most importantly, our concept of ourselves is socially constructed and political because our society's interpretation of what is and is not normal and natural affects what we do. It therefore affects our biological structure and functioning because what we do and how our bodies and minds function are connected dialectically. Thus norms are self-fulfilling prophecies that do not merely describe how we are but prescribe how we should be.

Let us consider a few examples. We can begin with a few obvious ones, such as height, weight, and strength. Women and men are physically not very different. There are enormous overlaps between women and men for all traits that are not directly involved with procreation.

For example, there is about a two-foot spread in height among people in the United States, but a difference of only three to five inches between the average heights of women and men. When we say men are taller than women, what we really mean is that the abstraction *average (or mean) height* is a few inches greater for men than women. Overall, women and men are about the same height, with many women as tall as, or taller than, lots of men. The impression that women are shorter than men is enhanced by our social convention that when women and men pair off, it is considered preferable for the man to be taller than the woman. In some countries, such as Bali, differences in height and, indeed, overall body build are much smaller than in the United States.

Cultural Factors

Clearly, height is affected by social factors, such as diet. In the early part of this century, English working-class men were significantly shorter, on average, than men from the upper class, and this difference in height was due to differences not just in the adequacy but in the composition of their diets—proportions of carbohydrates, proteins, fats, vitamins. In the United States we are familiar with a similar phenomenon when comparing the heights of immigrants and their U.S.-born children. We have tended to think that the U.S.-born children are taller than their immigrant parents because they get a better diet. But now that we are learning more about the health hazards of the typical U.S. diet, with its excessive fat and protein content, we should

42

probably defer value judgments and just acknowledge that the diets are different.

"Which one of us is the opposite sex?"

Sex differences in height probably also arise from the differences in growth patterns between girls and boys. Until early adolescence, girls, on average, are taller than boys, but girls' growth rates tend to decrease after they begin to menstruate, whereas boys continue to grow throughout their teens. It is generally assumed that this difference is due to the fact that the increase in estrogen levels after the onset of menstruation tends to slow the growth of girls' long bones. But the age of onset of menstruation, hence of increased estrogen secretion, depends on a number of social factors, such as diet, exercise, and stress. For example, female swimming champions, who, because of their intense, early training, tend to begin to menstruate later than most girls, tend also to be taller than average. We might therefore expect factors that delay the onset of menstruation to decrease the difference in average height between women and men, those that hasten the onset of menstruation to increase it. . . .

Weight clearly has considerable social components. Different societies have different standards of beauty for women, and many of these involve differences in desirable weight. Today we call the women in Rubens's paintings fat and consider Twiggy [a very thin model] anorexic. In our society changes in style not just of clothing but of body shape are generated, at least in part, because entire industries depend on our not liking the way we look so that we will buy the products that promise to change it. To some extent this is true also for men: Padded shoulders are not that different from padded bras. But there is more pressure on women to look "right," and what is "right" changes frequently and sometimes quite drastically. At present, U.S. women are obsessed by concerns about their weight to the point where girls and young women deliberately eat less than they need for healthy growth and development.

Although we may inherit a tendency toward a particular body shape, most women's weight can change considerably in response to our diets, levels of physical activity, and other patterns of living. These also affect physical fitness and strength. When women begin to exercise or engage in weight training and body building, we often notice surprisingly great changes in strength in response to even quite moderate training. Here again, what is striking is the variation among women (and among men).

Physical Strength

People ask whether there are "natural" limits to women's strength and therefore "natural" differences in strength between women and men. In Europe and the United States women and men are far more similar in lower body strength than in the strength of our upper bodies. This fact is not surprising when we consider the different ways girls and boys are encouraged to move and play from early childhood on. We tend to use our legs much more similarly than our arms. Both girls and boys tend to run a lot, and hopscotch and skipping rope are considered girls' games. But when it comes to carrying loads, playing baseball, and wrestling and other contact sports, all of which strengthen the arms and upper body, girls are expected to participate much less than boys are. In general, male/female comparisons are made between physically more highly trained men and less trained women so that so-called sex differences at least in part reflect this difference in activity levels. More and less active men also differ in strength, and so do more and less active women.

If we compare the records of male and female marathon runners, we find that in 1963, when women were first permitted to run the Boston marathon, their record was 1 hour 20 minutes slower than the men's record. Twenty years later, Joan Benoit won in 2 hours, 22 minutes, and 43 seconds, a record that was only about 15 minutes slower than the record of that year's male winner. And she ran the course in over an hour less time than the female winner in 1963. The dramatic improvement women runners made in those twenty years clearly came with practice but no doubt also required changes in their expectations of what they could achieve. Men's records have improved by less than 15 minutes during the entire time since modern marathon competitions began in 1908. Again the question: Are there "natural" limits and "natural" differences between women and men? Only time and opportunities to train and to participate in athletic events will tell. Note that in the 1988 Olympics, the woman who won the hundred-meter sprint took less than one second longer than the male winner, and he set a new world record. This feat is especially remarkable because women are said to compare with men much more favorably in long runs than in sprints.

Arbitrary Work Roles

The stratification of the work force is often explained as though it reflected inherent biological differences between women and men. Women have been disqualified from construction and other relatively well-paid heavy labor because they are said to be too weak for it. But the most prestigious men's jobs and those that pay most, in general, do not require physical strength, while much of women's traditional, unpaid, or underpaid work involves strenuous physical labor. Nurses must sometimes lift heavy, immobilized people, and housework frequently involves carrying and pushing heavy, awkward loads. In many cultures women are responsible for providing the firewood and water, which usually means carrying heavy loads for long distances, often with small children tied to their chests or backs. In the United States, where men are expected to carry the heaviest loads, most men have "bad backs," which is why occupational health advocates argue that loads that are considered too heavy for women should be rated too heavy for everyone.

At present, there is an overemphasis on the reproductive hazards of employment for women and an underemphasis on comparable hazards for men, to the detriment of women, men, and children. Women have been barred from some higher-paying jobs unless they could prove they were sterile, while men in those very jobs, and in others, continue to be exposed to preventable chemical and radiation hazards. Women, too, continue to be exposed to reproductive hazards in traditional women's work, such as nursing and housework, and as x-ray technicians, beauticians, and hairdressers.

In other words, biological differences between women and men are used to rationalize the stratification of the labor force by sex; they do not explain it. One can readily find women or men who qualify for every kind of paid work, except that of sperm donor and what has come to be called surrogate mother. If society instead stratifies the work force into women's and men's jobs, it does so for economic, social, and political reasons. Such stratification is not mandated by biology. . . .

I want to stress that we need have no ideological investment in whether women and men exhibit biological differences, aside from the obvious ones involved with procreation. We cannot know whether such biological differences exist because biology and society (or environment) are interdependent and cannot be sorted out. And in any gender-dichotomized society, the fact that we are born biologically female or male means that our environments will be different: We will live different lives. Because our biology and how we live are dialectically related and build on one another, we cannot vary gender and hold the environment constant. Therefore, the scientific methodology of sex-differences research is intrinsically flawed if scientists try to use it to sort effects of biology and society. Scientists can catalog similarities and differences between women and men but cannot establish their causes.

A Problematic Science

There are other problems with research on differences. One is that it is in the nature of scientific research that if we are interested in differences, we will go on looking until we find them. And if we do not find any, we will assume that our instruments were wrong or that we looked in the wrong place or at the wrong things. Another problem is that most characteristics vary continuously in the population rather than placing us into neat groups. To compare groups, however defined, we must use such concepts as the "average," "mean," or "median" in order to characterize each group by a single number. Yet these constructed, or reified, numbers obscure the diversity that exists within the groups (say, among women and among men) as well as the overlaps between them. That is why statisticians have invented the concept of the standard deviation from the mean to reflect the spread of the actual numbers around the reified average. This problem is obvious when we think about research into differences between blacks and whites. Just to do it, we have to agree on social definitions of who will count as black and who as white because after several centuries of mixing, the biological characteristic, skin color, varies continuously. Research comparing blacks and whites must first generate the group differences

46

it pretends to catalog or analyze.

Differences, be they biological or psychological, become scientifically interesting only when they parallel differences in power. We do not frame scientific questions about differences between tall people and short people, although folk wisdom suggests there may be some. Nor do we, in this society, pursue differences between blue-eyed, blond people and dark-haired, dark-eyed ones. Yet the latter were scientifically interesting differences under the Nazis.

Sex differences are interesting in sexist societies that value one group more highly than the other. Because the overlaps are so large for all the characteristics that are not directly involved with procreation, it is easy to find women and men to perform any task we value. The existence of average sex differences is irrelevant to the way we organize society. To achieve an egalitarian division of labor requires political will and action, not changes in our biology. There is enough variability among us to let us construct a society in which people of both sexes contribute to whatever activities are considered socially useful and are rewarded according to their talents and abilities.

"The differences [between male and female brains] are an established fact. All that remains is to explain them and specify their significance."

Brain Structure Explains Male/Female Differences

Yves Christen

In the following viewpoint, Yves Christen writes that several recent studies find measurable differences between male and female brains. These differences, Christen argues, help explain dissimilarities in the sexes' intellectual abilities—dissimilarities that have been proved by standardized tests and, ultimately, by the different occupational roles played by men and women. Christen holds a doctorate in immunogenetics and is one of Europe's most prolific science writers.

As you read, consider the following questions:

1. What evidence does Christen offer to prove an anatomical difference between male and female brains? How large does the author say these physical differences are? Why haven't these features been found before, according to Christen?
2. What does the author say causes the structural differences in the sexes' brains? What behavioral consequences does the author attribute to this?
3. What aptitudes does Christen say are stronger in each sex? What examples, both work and school related, does Christen offer to prove the existence of these different abilities?

Excerpted from pp. 65-74 of *Sex Differences* by Yves Christen, ©1987 by Editions du Rocher; English translation copyright ©1991 by Nicholas Davidson. Reprinted by permission of Transaction Publishers.

There are times when everyone agrees to assert a position while secretly believing the opposite. This strange sort of consensus makes it possible to avoid a potentially disagreeable argument while more or less unconsciously keeping sight of one's bearings. The question of female psychology clearly reflects such a consensus. Everyone secretly believes that men and women think in very different ways, but no one (at least in intellectual circles) dares to take any position other than the absolute sameness of the sexes in this area.

This ideological burden may turn out to have been a blessing in disguise. A veritable challenge, it has forced scholars to probe deeper, to advance to a more fundamental level of analysis. If the question of sex differences involved psychology alone, it might indeed be difficult to understand clearly. Researchers would consider it frivolous and, frankly, would not dare to study it. But in recent years, the debate has shifted to the fields of brain anatomy, neurochemistry, and endocrinology. Here, on the face of it at least, there should be greater scope for objectivity.

Until just a few years ago, the only thing known for certain in this domain was that women's brains are somewhat lighter than men's; but their total body weight is also lower. The generally accepted conclusion was still that formulated by F.P. Mall in 1909: every scientific attempt to discover a sex difference in the brain had failed. Nothing much, then, to add to the file.

Gendered Brains

However, in the last few years an avalanche of findings has demonstrated the existence of such differences. In the first place, there are numerous studies of animals, particularly birds. The canary is an especially good example. Fernando Nottebohm has demonstrated the existence in the male of a mass of cells that are infinitely more developed than in the female. Moreover, this mass is located in the noblest part of the brain, the frontal lobes. This physiological characteristic is directly involved in song—hence its development in the male. In this instance, a difference in form clearly corresponds to a difference in function.

But birds are not mammals and what one observes in their brains cannot be applied directly to our own species.

More interesting, therefore, are studies of monkeys and rats. In these animals, sex differences have been detected in several parts of the brain—for example, in the hypothalamus, the command center for many activities and notably for sexual behavior; and in the amygdala, a part of the brain located above each ear that may be involved in aggressive behaviors. A coherent picture uniting physiological and behavioral data is beginning to emerge. It has even been shown that there are more cells in certain parts of the brain in one sex than in the other, or, moreover,

49

that they are organized differently.

What about man? Dissection cannot be practiced as readily as with rats in this case. Nevertheless, many autopsies have been performed. They confirm the existence of certain anatomical differences. In 1983, Christine de Lacoste-Utamsing of Columbia University demonstrated that the corpus callosum, which links the two halves of the brain, is considerably larger in women than in men.

Since this initial discovery, several neurophysiologists have confirmed the existence of sex differences in the human brain. Two Dutch researchers, D.F. Swaab and E. Fliers, have managed to demonstrate a difference in the number of cells of a small part of the brain (the preoptic area of the hypothalamus). All these findings are of course the subject of further research and, on various points of detail, they do not elicit unanimity. But one thing, in any event, has been firmly established: *sex differences do indeed exist in the human brain*, and even in metabolism, to judge by the variations in blood flow that have recently been observed. To pronounce on the significance of these differences is, of course, another matter.

Large Differences

The discoveries already reported are so fully confirmed that they appear obvious today. "It is ironic," says Bruce McEwen, one of the leading specialists in this field, "that these studies went from the most complicated and laborious technique and then became progressively simpler"—to the point that the sex differences in the corpus callosum and the preoptic area of the hypothalamus are actually visible to the naked eye.

"Maybe," continues McEwen, "people were afraid to look and didn't believe they could see anything."

While the neuroanatomists were finally seeing what they had been afraid to look for, their colleagues specializing in hormones were also making interesting discoveries. To begin with, they were able to confirm that the brain is indeed the regulator of hormonal activity. It was already known that the glands chiefly responsible for hormone production (the sex glands, the adrenal glands, the thyroid, etc.) are largely regulated by a master gland at the base of the brain, the pituitary. Two Nobel Prize winners, Andrew Schally and Roger Guillemin, were able to demonstrate that the pituitary is in turn controlled by another part of the brain, the hypothalamus.

As the regulator of hormonal activity, the brain is also the director of sexual activity. But—and here we touch on a still more recent set of discoveries—if the brain intervenes in sexual activity, it is itself influenced by sex hormones. Sex hormones interact with the brain; they possess special receptors on the nerve cell membranes. From here to the thought that, in the course of our development, the most precious of our organs is permeated with the very substances that define gender, is just a short step, which experience invites us to take.

A coherent picture progressively emerges: physiological differences in the brain exist and *the brain is influenced by sex as much as it influences sexuality*. This confirms an old intuition that was previously more mythic than scientific, the one that unites sexuality and thought. This is good news for the neuroendocrinologist Roger Gorski of the University of California at Los Angeles, who exclaims enthusiastically: "I've always said that the brain was a sex organ!"

The Bigger Picture

From here, is it possible to carry the biological explanation further? That is the whole question, for, as the psychologist Arthur Arnold says, "The question is no longer even whether there are differences in nervous organization between the sexes, but rather to understand the sequence of events that explains the differences observed." In short, the differences are an established fact. All that remains is to explain them and specify their significance. This is particularly the case for the differences in cerebral asymmetry.

It has long been known that the two hemispheres of the brain, despite their apparent similarity, do not fulfill exactly the same functions. Thus, in most people, the left hemisphere plays an essential role in speech. It is said to dominate the right hemisphere. Until recently, this dominance was thought to be comprehensive. In reality, the right hemisphere is more important in certain activities. It now appears that this cerebral asymmetry, which has long fascinated neurophysiologists, is more pronounced in males than in females. Here the meaning of Christine de Lacoste-Utamsing's discovery becomes clear: if the corpus callosum, which connects the two hemispheres, is so highly developed in woman, it is perhaps because the two sides of the female brain are more intensively interconnected.

Different Languages

From the discoveries regarding cerebral asymmetry flow numerous consequences in the area of psychology. The right side of the brain appears to be more involved than the left side in emotional life. Woman, having a less asymmetrical brain than man, may have, as a highly regarded specialist, Sandra Witelson of McMasters University in Hamilton, Ontario, says, "a bi-hemispherical representation of emotion."

"If that is the case," continues this psychologist, "it could have major implications in daily life. Women, as a result of such a neurological organization, would be less able to dissociate their emotional behavior from verbal analysis."

When it was described in the newspaper *Le Monde* by Dr. Escoffier-Lambiotte, this theory unleashed a flood of angry letters from scandalized readers. The theory, to be sure, still lacks concrete confirmation outside of its theoretical justification and—it must be said—the experiences of daily life. Sandra Witelson herself refers to these: "Ordinary observation, in non-experimental conditions, suggests that women are less able to compartmentalize their emotional responses from their rational analytic behavior. This position is supported, for example, by the effect of emotional stress on the work capacity of men and women." At the same time, it is important not to read too much into these hypotheses, for as Witelson notes: "This difference does not make one sex superior to the other. Different advantages may be associated with the integration of emotion in the rational process and with the independence of both processes."

Pett Peeves   **by Joel Pett**

Biology also encounters psychology. In this domain, research has been under way for many years. Numerous studies have compared the intelligence of women and men. Intelligence quotients (IQ), as well as general evaluations of intelligence, show no significant differences (although IQ tests are designed to minimize any sex differences in scores). But can it be said that the forms of intelligence are the same? Assuredly not.

While noting that IQ's are similar between the sexes, as highly reputed a specialist as L.F. Jarvik has not hesitated to write, "with the information now in hand, it is as unrealistic to deny the existence of intellectual differences between the sexes as it would be to negate their physical dissimilarities." The principal difference involves [male superiority in] spatial aptitudes, which make it possible to visualize a three-dimensional object in space, to rotate it mentally, etc. Almost all studies, in all cultural contexts, with the possible exception of the Eskimos, have confirmed this difference. . . .

The male's superior spatial aptitude may be linked to the prehistoric hunter's need to reconnoiter the surrounding area. Natural selection would thus have imposed this ability as a necessity. Here we again encounter the relationship between the data of psychology and those of sociobiology.

Different Roles

Functional in the past, the male spatial aptitude may still have consequences today, particularly in terms of career choice. In this area there are many small facts that are widely neglected but so important in daily life that they have forced at least one sociologist to reconsider her entire analysis of sex differences. As Evelyne Sullerot frankly explains:

> My work in France involves career counselling for adult women. I decided to study the career orientation and training of girls and women in seven European countries, East and West. Ten years ago, when I began this project, I was convinced—and my publications record this—that social conditioning and education were entirely responsible for all the differences observed between men and women in career choice and career success. . . .
>
> I investigated individual sectors of precision engineering, such as watchmaking, where the tasks do not call for physical strength and the environment is neither dirty, noisy nor rank with the smell of burning oil. I also knew that women had been involved in jewelry making since the Middle Ages, and watchmaking can in a sense be seen as a branch of jewelry making. I had to face the facts: everywhere, women make clocks and watches, rapidly and expertly. With extremely rare exceptions, they do not design the mechanisms, do not invent any, and do not even repair them. In the Soviet Union, girls and boys were initially placed in the same watchmaking schools. Today, there is one course of training for assembly and another for repair; there are only girls in the first and only

53

boys in the second. This division was not intentional, and was even resisted. Yet little by little it imposed itself. I could give many other examples, all of them involving professions in which spatial aptitudes are a factor. . . .

Math: The Deciding Factor

Spatial aptitudes are also closely linked to mathematical ability. It is hard to believe the number of studies, articles, and books that have been devoted to female weakness in this area since the mid-1980s. The starting point for these investigations is the fact that very few women pursue careers in mathematics. (This is also the case in computer science.) David Maines published a study of mathematicians in the Chicago area. The result: 168 people contacted in three universities and a proportion of only 10 percent female PhDs in mathematics. This is certainly an eloquent figure, but one that is susceptible to a variety of explanations. And the explanation offered by David Maines is the closest one possible to the dominant ideology: women are subjected to pressures that do not especially encourage them to pursue careers in mathematics.

Most commentators would not have gone beyond this explanation, which caters to the desire for intellectual comfort, if two psychologists at Johns Hopkins University, Camilla Benbow and Julian Stanley, had not conducted more exhaustive research. Their research was conducted first on 10,000 children in the Johns Hopkins area, and subsequently on a sample of 40,000 Americans! As of the publication of the first part of their work, the results were clear: more boys than girls get good grades in math. Better still, or rather worse, as one ascends the hierarchy of mathematical ability, the differences become more and more overwhelming. Faced with increasingly difficult problems, even relatively high-scoring girls fade away. Intelligence tests that examine mathematical aptitude confirm this major gap.

On its publication in 1980, Benbow and Stanley's study created something of a furor. To tell the truth, it outraged intellectual opinion. Yet its appearance in the most prestigious American scientific journal, *Science*, made it difficult not to take it seriously. Three years later, in the same journal, the authors repeated the provocation. But this time, their sample included 40,000 people, and the results were even clearer with regard to differences at the highest levels of ability. Consider SAT (Scholastic Aptitude Test) scores of 420 and higher: the ratio of male to female success is 1.5, meaning there are 15 boys for every 10 girls reaching this level. But at the 700 level, the ratio reaches 13: in other words, in the Johns Hopkins area, 113 boys scored this high in contrast to only 9 girls. Outside the Johns Hopkins area, the respective figures were 147 and 11. After this, is it still possible to speak of chance and cultural influence? Most experts find that difficult to believe.

Girls make up for their inferiority in mathematics with other qualities. There is no doubt that they regularly outperform boys at school in overall achievement, particularly in English, and above all in reading. They are able to articulate sounds like "ba" and "ma" at an earlier age, and form words and sentences sooner. While boys' superiority in spatial aptitudes appears around the age of 10, girls' linguistic superiority appears very early in life, which strongly suggests that this aptitude is largely independent of environmental constraints. With age, the difference tends to diminish.

What does not diminish, very often, is the general superiority of schoolgirls over schoolboys: among girls there are fewer dunces and more advanced students. This could be the result, to a considerable degree, of a greater aptitude for study. In an examination of over 2,000 student records, Schmidberger has confirmed this quality—which, moreover, increases with age. There is a 9.4 percent female advantage in subjects that require study in the first year, which grows to 22.3 percent in the second year. Girls are more attentive, more docile with teachers, attend class more regularly, etc. The girls' advantage appears so clearly that, in kindergarten, differences due to sex are at least as great as those due to social class. At the secondary level, distinctions arising from social milieu become more determinative. In addition, at the highest social level, sex distinctions finally blur. Among students overall, 32 percent of boys are considered unstable, versus 6 percent of girls; 19 percent of boys participate genuinely in class, compared to 37 percent of girls; 49 percent of boys participate passively, compared to 57 percent of girls. After four years of schooling, there is already a far larger number of boys than girls held back for a year or more. While the girls' good study habits continue for a long time, all the way to the college level, it is no less striking that the number of outstanding female individuals remains limited.

Interpreting the Numbers

Here we touch on an essential question. Whatever else may be said, the average differences between the sexes, even in the case of spatial aptitudes, remain relatively weak. For that matter, at what point is it possible to affirm that a difference is significant? The choice is a matter of appreciation, of a priori, even of prejudice.

If the averages differ little, should it be concluded that there is no social impact? There is an overlap: even when one sex is noticeably more able in a given area, the overlap rules out any notion of absolute superiority or inferiority. Some representatives of the group that is on average less able will perform better than some members of the other group. But conversely, differences in averages, even small ones, can result in major differences in extremes. Several biologists and psychologists have noted this in regard to intelligence: even a slight shift in the distribution curve of intelligence quotients would have vast social consequences, for the number of exceptional individuals (those who make society advance) could be multiplied by a major factor.

With regard to the comparative analysis of the sexes, it is conceivable that the differences at the extremes are more important than the differences in averages. In mathematics, it is among the most gifted individuals that the sex factor appears most overwhelmingly: seven to eight times more boys than girls score over 600 on the SAT.

The boys also occupy the opposite end of the curve. More males suffer from reading difficulties and scholastic failure. Noted by the sexologist Havelock Ellis, contested by some investigators and supported by others, this twofold male extremism (at both the high and low ends of the curve) underlies Arianna Stassinopoulos's antifeminist analysis. As she writes in *The Female Woman:*

> Men are less average than women. They are the geniuses and the idiots, the giants and the dwarfs. . . . The greater variability of men cannot possibly be explained on environmental grounds, as a simple difference in averages might be. If women are not found in the top positions in society in the same proportions as men because, as Women's Lib claims, they are treated as mentally inferior to men and become so, why are there so many more male idiots? Why are the remedial classes in schools full of boys? Why are the inmates of hospitals for the mentally subnormal predominantly male?. . . The reason why Women's Lib does not mention this conspicuous difference between the sexes is that it can only be explained on purely biological grounds.

"The unproven theory that men and women have innately different mental abilities . . . rests upon a string of unproven theories. "

Brain Structure Does Not Explain Male/Female Differences

Le Anne Schreiber

Le Anne Schreiber explains in the following viewpoint that scientific research on the brain tends to focus on anatomical differences between male and female, since these findings are popular and easily published. The problem, Schreiber says, is that these structural "differences," in addition to being scientifically false, are used to prove an equally incorrect assumption: that men and women have different aptitudes that "naturally" result in their different social roles—and, presumably, their different salaries. Schreiber is a former senior editor for the *New York Times* and a journalist who specializes in contemporary social issues.

As you read, consider the following questions:

1. What two important scientific discoveries on the brain does Schreiber find lacking in supporting evidence?
2. What is the problem of "negative evidence" in scientific publishing, according to the author?
3. How is brain research showing male superiority in mathematics wrong, according to the author?

Le Anne Schreiber, "The Search for His and Her Brains," *Glamour*, April 1993. Reprinted by permission of the author.

The 1990s are the decade of the brain, and don't think that's just another media slogan. A congressional resolution in 1989 and a presidential proclamation in 1990 made the designation official, and roughly $2 billion a year in federally funded brain research makes it far more than a catchy phrase. What discoveries can we expect from a ten-year, multibillion-dollar government-sponsored exploration of inner space? What will it mean for women? That depends on which questions the scientists—and the federal agencies that fund them—decide to ask.

Many researchers are trying to answer such basic questions as how the brain develops, acquires language, stores memories, retrieves information and repairs itself after damage. To date, however, the line of research that has been most widely publicized is the one devoted to that most debatable of questions: What makes men and women different? . . .

This emphasis on gender in current brain research makes some people nervous, and with good reason. In every other period of the history of science, the search for sex differences in the brain has been a search for female deficiencies. Today's researchers are quick to assert that they take it as given that male and female brains are *different but equal*, not better and worse. But the fact that the female brain has been referred to as a "default brain" in current sex-difference literature does not inspire confidence. Neither does the fact that current research is frequently cited as evidence for allegedly innate male talents in such areas as science, mathematics, architecture and engineering. Since math achievement is the filter that determines access to many higher-paying occupations, such biological handicapping is a high-stakes issue for women. . . .

Biological Determinism

Blindness to the implications of brain-gender theories can be costly, according to Dr. Anne Fausto-Sterling, a developmental geneticist at Brown University, whose recently updated book, *Myths of Gender*, offers an extremely thorough and cogent critique of recent biological theories of sex difference. "Jobs and education—that's what it's really all about," she says. "About whether boys and girls should attend separate schools, about job and career choices and, as always, about money—how much employers will have to pay to whom. These issues form an unbroken bridge spanning the length of the century."

The gist of current brain-gender theory is this: Although both males and females produce the class of hormones called androgens, males produce higher levels of them early in fetal life, when the developing testes start secreting testosterone—the major androgen. This hormonal surge supposedly washes over the developing male brain, producing structural differences that determine the degree to which an individual exhibits masculine characteristics later in life. The corollary of this theory is that men and women who do not conform to gender stereotypes in their behavior, interests, abilities or temperament were exposed to abnormally low or high levels of androgens in the womb. Although supported only by scant and inconclusive evidence, this theory is often presented as proven fact in the popular press. . . .

So what gives? Is the brain really a sex organ, as structurally different in men and women as more visible parts of our anatomy? Are men and women really born with differing abilities to read maps and find socks? Are men innately better mathematicians and architects? Are women innately better at . . . well, let's see . . . spelling, smelling and reading emotions? Since proponents of brain-gender theories claim to be uncovering the biological bases of our possibilities and limits, it is crucial that we pay close attention to what they are asserting—and on what grounds they base these assertions.

The Initial Interest

The current interest in brain-gender research was sparked in 1982, when Nobel Prize-winning neurobiologist Roger Sperry, Ph.D., demonstrated what others had suspected: that the left and right hemispheres of the human brain house different mental abilities. The left side, for instance, seems to be the locus of certain verbal abilities, and the right side, of certain visual-spatial abilities, which are in turn thought to be related to certain mathematical skills. Dr. Sperry himself did not associate the separate functions of the two halves of the brain with gender; in fact, he emphasized that each person's brain network was vastly more individualized than fingerprints. But other scientists found the possibility of neat differences too tempting to ignore. The hunt for the gendered brain was on.

Since there were no apparent sex differences in the size or shape of the two hemispheres, scientists began to look for differences in the corpus callosum, a thick bundle of nerve fibers that connects the two hemispheres. There were two main working hypotheses. One was that the two hemispheres of the female brain are *less* strongly linked than those of the male's, making the female brain less integrated and less endowed with, for example, mathematical ability. The other was that the female brain's hemispheres are *more* strongly linked than the male's, making it, therefore, less specialized and less endowed with, for example, mathematical ability. When it comes to female brains, the less-equals-less or more-equals-less formulation is a staple of sex-difference research.

The first widely reported finding of a sex difference in the corpus callosum was published in 1982 in *Science*, the prestigious weekly journal that plays an inordinately large role in setting the agenda for science coverage in the popular press. After performing autopsies on nine male and five female brains, physical anthropologist Ralph Holloway and cell biologist Christine de Lacoste-Utamsing claimed to have found a dramatic difference in the shape of the tail end of the corpus callosum. They reported that this section of the corpus callosum, called the splenium, was so much wider in females than in males that it deserved to be regarded as an anatomical sex difference second only to the reproductive organs.

©G. Hallgren 1993. Reprinted with permission.

Although there was no clinical evidence that a wider splenium creates stronger communication between the two brain hemispheres, proponents of brain gender nonetheless used this finding to support the notion that male brains are more specialized, and this theory of "brain specialization" was then offered as an explanation for a host of supposed male mental superiorities, particularly in mathematically related areas. The female's wider splenium, however, was thought to cause more "cross talk" between the two hemispheres—a kind of over-the-fence brain chat that just might be the source of female intuition. It was suggested, for instance, that if the emotions are primarily registered in the right hemisphere and verbal ability resides in the left, then it is innately easier for women to express emotion than it is for men, whose brains store words and emotions more separately.

In the past ten years [to 1993] there have been 16 attempts by various scientists, using both autopsies and magnetic resonance imaging (MRI) technology on much larger samples of both children and adults, to confirm the initial finding of a dramatic sex difference in the corpus callosum. Ten of the 16 studies revealed no sex differences in the shape or size of any part of the corpus callosum. Five studies resulted in mixed or statistically insignificant findings. The most recent study claimed to find a sex-linked difference in the shape of the adult splenium, but also found out that if you tried to guess the sex of a subject by looking at his or her splenium, you would be wrong more than half of the time. Several researchers emphasized that variations in the size and shape of the corpus callosum were greater *among* members of the same sex than *between* the sexes.

Questionable Claims

At present, any claims about sex differences in the corpus callosum are highly questionable at best. Furthermore, scientists don't claim to know very much about how the corpus callosum works. Jonathan Beckwith, Ph.D., professor of microbiology and molecular genetics at Harvard Medical School, puts it this way: "Even if they found differences, there is absolutely no way at this point that they can make a connection between any differences in brain structure and any particular behavior pattern or any particular aptitude."

Equally hypothetical is the notion that these alleged structural brain differences are caused by fetal testosterone. This theory, like the early findings on the corpus callosum, was first reported in *Science* in 1982 and from there was widely disseminated in the popular press. What got lost in translation was the fact that there is no clinical support for this thesis.

The basis of the theory is this: In 1982, Harvard neurologist Norman Geschwind, M.D., suggested that there was a statistical correlation between left-handedness—which is more common in boys—and a whole host of afflictions, including immune-system disorders, autism, dyslexia, myopia and stuttering. He speculated that all these conditions might have a single cause—fetal exposure to excess testosterone. And since left-handedness is associated with right-brain dominance, he further hypothesized in a 1983 *Science* interview that testosterone might cause the fetal male brain to produce "superior right-hemisphere talents, such as artistic, musical or mathematical talent."

To bolster his speculations, Dr. Geschwind cited two studies conducted by other scientists. One was on rat brains, in which parts of the right cortex of male rats were found to be 3 percent thicker than the corresponding parts of the left cortex. This difference was not found in female rats. The other, which involved human fetal brains, found that two convolutions of the right hemisphere develop slightly earlier than those on the left. Dr.

Geschwind chose not to mention that the right brain convolutions developed earlier in *both* male and female fetuses, and therefore could not be caused by hormones from fetal testes.

A House of Cards

And yet the unproven theory that men and women have innately different mental abilities, which rests upon the unproven theory of different brain structures, which rests upon a string of unproven theories about how those structures function, is making its way into the mass media and therefore into the public consciousness as fact. "In science, it's not unreasonable to make hypotheses based on slim data," says Dr. Beckwith, "but one runs into problems when those hypotheses, re-presented as fact or near fact, affect people's attitudes and even social policy. I think scientists should be much more careful than they are in communicating their ideas to the press.". . .

If research on sex differences in the brain is so shaky, how has it been able to establish such a firm footing in the media? . . .

In part, the problem is one intrinsic to the nature of scientific investigation. Almost by definition, scientists look for differences, and if they find one, however slight, they have an easier time getting their research published. Or, as Dr. Ruth Bleier succinctly put it, "There is no field of sex similarities."

"It's called 'the problem of negative evidence,'" explains Dr. Fausto-Sterling. "If you hypothesize no difference and find no difference, you never know if you've just not looked hard enough or not looked in the right place. The only time a finding of no difference is considered significant is when you are trying to replicate experiments that have found a difference, but even then it is difficult to get negative evidence published." As a result, an original finding of difference, however faulty or flimsy, is likely to receive much more widespread publicity than subsequent failures to confirm that finding.

When it comes to sex-difference research, this problem is often compounded by an eagerness on the part of the press and the public to embrace findings that confirm commonly held beliefs. "I think many people have a major investment in believing there are very basic differences between men and women that are responsible for the differences in our status in society," says Ruth Hubbard, Ph.D., Harvard professor of biology emerita and author of *The Politics of Women's Biology*. "It is well to be suspicious when 'objective science' confirms long-standing prejudices."

After all, the starting point of all sex-difference research is the observation that men and women differ—in their behavior, roles, status and achievements as well as their anatomy. Much of the brain research discussed above is devoted to finding biological explanations for alleged sex differences in mathematical ability.

This alleged math gap is in turn used to help account for very observable sex differences in occupational and financial status.

Ironically, research into the biological basis of alleged male mathematical superiority began in the early 1980s, when a decade of social changes had already narrowed the gender gap. In 1990, psychologist Janet Hyde, Ph.D., and colleagues at the University of Wisconsin in Madison used a statistical technique called meta-analysis to assess the results of 100 studies that looked for gender differences in the mathematical performance of more than three million American students.

Their conclusion: Averaged over 30 years, standardized tests show a slight female superiority in math performance at the elementary and middle-school level. There was no gender difference at any age in tests that measured understanding of mathematical concepts, but a moderate male superiority in problem solving did emerge in high school and continued through college and adulthood. Most important, in studies published after 1973, the gender difference was half what it had been in previous years. Differences in course selection beginning in high school account for some but not all of the male advantage in performance on standardized tests in high school and college. Less measurable influences—like parent, teacher and peer encouragement of math achievement—are also a factor.

What does Dr. Hyde think of biological arguments for a math gap? "The bottom line is that they are constructing biological models to explain a nondifference. The math gap is basically zero."

Preserving the Myth

Although Hyde's findings are well-known among sex-difference researchers, they have received less prominent exposure in the popular press than those of psychologist Camilla Benbow, Ed.D., whose research is frequently cited as evidence of innate male mathematical superiority. For 20 years, first at Johns Hopkins University with colleague Julian Stanley and now at Iowa State University in Ames, Dr. Benbow has conducted nationwide searches for gifted children to participate in a program called Study of Mathematically Precocious Youth. Seventh and eighth graders who scored in the top few percentiles on junior high standardized achievement tests are invited to take high-school-level SATs; if they score high enough, they can enroll in accelerated college math courses.

Year after year, Dr. Benbow finds that the best boys outperform the best girls by a significant margin on the math portion of the SAT. Fewer girls than boys choose to enter the talent search and of those who qualify for the accelerated courses, even fewer enroll in them. When Dr. Benbow's results were first published in *Science* in 1980, she was quoted there and elsewhere as favoring a biological explanation for her findings. In a 1983 *Science* article, she was portrayed as an enthusiastic supporter of Dr. Geschwind's testosterone theory of male mathematical superiority.

"What astounds me about Benbow's interpretation of her results," says Dr. Beckwith, "is that there really isn't much research to support the possible biological basis of the differences in math ability between men and women. But if you look at the research on possible environmental factors, it probably outweighs the biological research tenfold."

Dozens of studies that document the importance of parental attitude and other factors upon a child's math performance have not swayed Dr. Benbow from her conviction that males are innately superior in math. She also dismisses as unimportant studies showing that, despite their lower scores on standardized tests, female students get better math grades than males at all levels, including graduate school.

There is evidence that grades are often the only recognition female students receive in the math classroom. Several studies document that in high school and college, boys get significantly more attention from both male and female math teachers. Boys are spoken to more, called on more and receive more corrective feedback, social interaction, individual instruction, praise and encouragement. There is one form of attention bestowed more frequently on girls: In one study of ten high school geometry classes, girls received 84 percent of the discouraging comments.

Psychologist Jacquelynne Eccles, Ph.D., director of the Achievement Research Lab at the University of Michigan in Ann Arbor, studies the impact of parents' attitudes on children's school performance. Several studies document how parents tend to overestimate their sons' math ability and underestimate their daughters'. In 1980, she and colleague Janis Jacobs, Ph.D., found this tendency grew stronger in mothers, particularly in mothers of daughters, who had seen media coverage of Dr. Benbow's findings of male math superiority.

The impact of such distortions is heightened by Dr. Eccles's surprising finding that how parents perceive their children's abilities has an even greater influence on children's self-assessment than the children's previous performance. Given these interlocking factors, it is not surprising that in a 1991 study of sixth through eleventh graders, Dr. Jacobs found that boys had more confidence in their math abilities than girls did, despite the girls' having consistently higher grades. . . .

Interpreting the Question

What, finally, are we to make of the current direction of sex-difference research? It was between 1980 and 1983—that distinct period of time when the pendulum of research interest and funding began to swing from an emphasis on social explanations of difference to an emphasis on biological explanations—that three hypotheses were put forward by three independent sets of researchers working in separate areas: that there was a dramatic sex difference in the corpus callosum, that testosterone organizes male and female brains differently, and that males have an innate mathematical superiority.

All three hypotheses were given prominent coverage in one publication, *Science*, whose partiality for biological explanations is uncritically accepted by the popular press. The evidence supporting each of the three theories was slight, but when combined, as they frequently were in the pages of that journal, they seemed to prop one another up in a way that made the whole look much more solid than its wobbly parts. In the years since, an enormous castle of research and speculation has been built upon that shaky foundation.

Now, already well into the Decade of the Brain, with increased funding and publicity for all types of brain research, we are repeatedly induced to accept this many-turreted castle of speculation as a fortress of established fact. The Discovery Channel runs footage of little boys playing with toy trucks and girls with dolls—while an invisible voice of authority explains that their brains were "wired" in the womb to enjoy these activities. "The more we know about the male brain and the more we know about the female brain," a consulting anthropologist explains, "the more we can apply these things in our daily lives with our friends and our lovers, in our educational system, in our political system, in our business contacts around the world."

Another voice, not to be heard on the Discovery Channel, is that of Harvard's Dr. Ruth Hubbard, who warns: "To try to find the biological basis of our social roles or to sort people by sex when it comes to strength, ability to do math, or other intellectual or social attributes is a political exercise, not a scientific one."

"As the economic role of women changed within
the family, so too did the image of the ideal wife."

Economics Determines Gender Roles

Francine D. Blau and Marianne A. Ferber

Have traditional male and female roles stood the test of time, or
should they change because they are outmoded? The question is
important because it seeks, on the most basic level, to impose
some order on our rapidly changing society. With the decline of
the man-as-sole-earner family, there has evolved a kaleidoscope
of different household types and gender roles, and responsibilities within those households. Such transformations might be un-
settling to many, argue Francine Blau and Marianne Ferber in
the following viewpoint, but they are certainly not unprecedented. Gender roles have changed many times in the past, Blau
and Ferber maintain, pointing out that the male-as-breadwinner/
female-as-homemaker model is a fairly recent development that
resulted from the industrial revolution. Before then, during
America's colonial period, both sexes were indispensable to the
home-based economy, the authors explain, and hence enjoyed
roles that were on a more equal footing. Blau and Ferber are
professors at the University of Illinois at Urbana-Champaign.

As you read, consider the following questions:

1. What four early societal forms do Blau and Ferber discuss?
   What were women's and men's roles in each of these?
2. What kinds of work did men and women do in colonial
   America, according to the authors? How do the authors explain
   the effect of industrialization on the evolution of the family?

Francine D. Blau/Marianne A. Ferber, *The Economics of Women, Men and Work*, 2e, ©1992,
pp. 13-14, 19, 20, 22, 23, 24, 25, 26, 27, 28. Reprinted by permission of Prentice-Hall,
Englewood Cliffs, New Jersey.

We are constantly told today that we live in an era of rapid change—change in economic conditions, in economic and social institutions, in mores and beliefs. And so we do. Changes in the roles of women and men, their relations to each other, and the nature of the families in which most of them continue to live have been taking place at a speed that is quite possibly unprecedented. This situation has inevitably created stresses and strains. Not surprisingly, people who feel insecure in a world of shifting boundaries and values are prone to look back with nostalgia to the "good old days" when women were women, and men were men, and both knew their proper place.

How realistic is this picture some hold of traditional gender roles, unchanging for all time, and pervasive for all places, which is supposed to have existed before the recent era of turmoil and upheaval? The answer to this question has substantial practical implications. If the same roles of women and men have existed always and everywhere, some may conclude that these roles . . . cannot, and perhaps should not, be changed. If, on the other hand, there has been a good deal of variation in the roles of men and women over time, it is likely that there is also room for flexibility now and in the future.

For this reason, it is particularly important to gain some insight into the nature of gender roles through the course of human [societal] development. . . .

Early Economies

In technologically primitive *hunting and gathering societies*, men and women shared in providing food, clothing, and shelter for their families. At the same time, men hunted large animals and defended the tribe, whereas women gathered a variety of vegetable foods, occasionally hunted small animals, and had the main responsibility for food preparation and care of children. Such a division of labor was undoubtedly expedient when women were pregnant or nursing most of their adult lives, and thus could not participate in activities that would have taken them far from home. The greater strength of men also gave them a considerable advantage for such activities as hunting large animals and fighting.

The extent to which men and women contributed to the necessities of life was determined by the availability of various resources, and women's status appeared to vary accordingly. In general, the fact that men provided for the safety of the tribe and furnished most of the meat, always regarded as the prestige food, gave them the advantage. Nonetheless, the common payment of the bride price suggests that women were also valued for their contributions.

In the somewhat more advanced *horticultural societies*, plants were cultivated in small plots located near the home. Men continued to conduct warfare and also prepared the ground by slashing and burning; women prepared the food and cared for infants. But virtually all other activities were shared. Accordingly, men and women tended to be considerably more equal during this stage.

Dianne Reum

Reprinted with permission.

In *pastoral societies*, on the other hand, men tended to monopolize the herding of large animals; this activity often took them far from home. Herding provided the bulk of what was needed for subsistence. Women's contributions were largely confined to tending the primitive equivalent of hearth and home, and females never reached more than a subservient status.

The situation changed radically when horticultural societies were superseded by *agricultural societies*, which arrived with the introduction of the plow. Although women "helped" in the fields, looked after small animals and gardens, and worked in the now-permanent homes taking care of large families, only men owned and worked the land, and the disparity in power and influence became great indeed. The *dowry*, paid by the father of the bride to the groom, who henceforth undertakes her support, and *purdah*, the practice of hiding women from the sight of men, came into use during that period in some of these societies. Both may be viewed as ways of subordinating women as well as symptoms of their subjugation. . . .

The U.S. Experience

In Colonial America, as in other preindustrial economies, the family enterprise was the dominant economic unit, and production was the major function of the family. Most of the necessities for survival were produced in the household, though some goods were generally produced for sale, the proceeds of which were used to purchase some market goods and to accumulate wealth. Cooking; cleaning; care of the young, the old, and the infirm; spinning; weaving; sewing; knitting; soap and candle making; and simple carpentry were carried on in the home. Much of the food and other raw materials were grown on the farm. All members of the family capable of making any contribution participated in production, but there was always some specialization and division of labor.

Among the nonslave population, men were primarily responsible for agriculture and occasionally trade, whereas women did much of the rest of the work, including what would today be characterized as "light manufacturing" activity. But gender-role specialization was by no means complete. Slave women were used to work in the fields. Widows tended to take over the family enterprise when the need arose, and in very early days, single women were on occasion given "maidplots." Even though men and women often had different tasks, and the former were more often involved in production for the market and generally owned all property, everyone participated in productive activity. Even aged grandparents would help with tasks that required responsibility and judgment, and would perhaps also supervise children in carrying out small chores they could adequately perform from a very early age.

Economic Households

All family members, except for infants, had essentially the same economic role. They either contributed goods and services directly or earned money by selling some of these in the market. The important economic role of children, as well as the plentiful availability of land, encouraged large families. High infant mortality rates provided a further incentive to bear many

69

children. In the eighteenth century, completed fertility may have averaged as many as eight to ten births per woman.

Wealthy women were primarily managers, not workers, within the household. This was, no doubt, a less arduous and possibly a more rewarding level of task but one no less absorbing. For most women, regardless of their affluence, there was little role conflict. The ideal of the frugal, industrious housewife working alongside her family corresponded closely to reality. The only women for whom this was not true were very poor women, who often became indentured servants, and, of course, black women, who were generally slaves. The former were, as a rule, not permitted to marry during their years of servitude; the latter might potentially have their family entirely disrupted by their owners' choice. Both had to work very hard, and slaves did not even have the modest legal protection of rights that indentured servants enjoyed.

The one thing all these diverse groups had in common was that they were productive members of nearly self-sufficient households. Government played a very small role, and although there was some exchange of goods and services, chiefly barter, it was not until well into the nineteenth century that production outside the home, for sale rather than for direct use, came to dominate the economy.

Early Industrialization

During the early period of industrialization in the late eighteenth and early nineteenth centuries, women in the United States, as elsewhere, worked in the textile mills and other industries that sprang up in the East. Initially, primarily young farm girls were employed in the factories, often contributing part of their pay to supplement family income and using some to accumulate a "dowry" that would make them more desirable marriage partners. The employment of these young women in factories may have appeared quite natural to observers at the time. They were doing much the same type of work they had done in the home, only in a new location and under the supervision of a foreman rather than the head of the household. Once married, women generally left their jobs to look after their own households, which would soon include children. . . .

As an increasingly larger segment of the population began living in urban centers rather than on farms, and family shops were replaced by factories, women found that their household work increasingly came to be confined to the care of children, the nurturing of the husband, and the maintenance of the home. There were no longer a garden or farm animals to take care of, no need for seasonal help with the crops, and no opportunity to participate in a family business. As husbands left the

70

home to earn the income needed to support their families, a more rigid division developed between the female domestic sphere and the male public sphere.

Separation of Spheres

Thus along with industrialization arose the concept of the *traditional family*, which lingered to a greater or lesser degree well into the twentieth century. The family shifted from a production unit to a consumption unit, and the responsibility for earning a living came to rest squarely on the shoulders of the husband. Wives (and children) grew to be dependent on his income. Redistribution became an important function of the family, as it provided a mechanism for the transfer of income from the market-productive husband to his market-dependent wife and children. Not only did specific *tasks* differ between men and women, as was always the case, but men and women now had different *economic roles* as well. Many workers and social reformers explicitly advocated that a man should be paid a "family wage," adequate to support not only him but also his wife and children.

As before, among the poor, particularly blacks and immigrants, it was often necessary for wives to enter the labor market. But for the middle-class white wife, and even for the working-class wife whose husband had a steady income, holding a job was frowned upon as inconsistent with her social status. If the wife entered the labor market, it was assumed that she was either compensating for her husband's inadequacy as a breadwinner or that she was selfishly pursuing a career at the expense of her household responsibilities.

The status of children also changed. Only in very poor families would they be expected to help to raise the family's standard of living, though some might work to earn spending money or because their parents thought it would be good for their moral fiber. Furthermore, the age when children came to be considered young adults and were supposed to become productive members of the family increased considerably. By the end of the nineteenth century, child labor laws were passed that prohibited employment of "minors."

As a consequence of industrialization and urbanization, more and more goods and services used by households came to be produced outside the home. Nonetheless, much time and effort was still expended to purchase and maintain these commodities, and to use them to attain the desired standard of living. With soap and bleach purchased at the store, and the washing machine doing the scrubbing, laundry became far less of a chore, but it was done far more frequently, and housewives came to take pride in making it "whiter than white." Groceries bought at the super-

71

market and a gas or electric range made cooking much easier, but homemakers would now serve elaborate meals rather than a pot of stew. To do otherwise would not be consistent with the role of dedicated mother and wife, whose every thought was for the well-being of her family. The husband might help her, but this was never to interfere with his "work." The children, too, particularly girls, might be expected to assist their mothers, but the basic responsibility for the household rested with the wife.

The net result of these developments was that the number of hours full-time homemakers devoted to housework, over 50 a week, did not change from the beginning of the century to the 1960s. . . .

The man's authority as "head of the household" was supposed to be absolute in all important matters, for he basically determined the family's lifestyle by providing the money income on which it so crucially depended. Further, the husband's decisions defined the parameters within which the other family members had to operate. Thus, he was dominant within the household as well as in the outside world. It was, however, generally assumed that, within the family, he would see to it that benefits were distributed equally, or according to need, as deemed appropriate.

As the economic role of women changed within the family, so too did the image of the ideal wife. Whereas the colonial wife was valued for her industriousness, the growing *cult of true womanhood* that developed with industrialization in the nineteenth century equated piety, purity, domesticity, and submissiveness with the femininity to which all women were expected to aspire. Their role was in the now consumption-oriented home—as daughter, sister, but most of all as wife and mother. This ideal particularly extolled the lifestyle of affluent middle- and upper-class women, who were to a great extent freed even from their domestic chores by the servants their husbands' ample incomes could provide. . . .

The "Living Wage"

This image of the family was fostered not only by the example of the middle and upper-middle classes, which was the envy of the poor woman bearing the double burden of paid and unpaid work or toiling at home to make ends meet on a limited budget, but also by male workers and their trade unions. Initially, the availability of women and children for work in industry was welcomed by national leaders, because they provided cheap, competitive labor, while agricultural production could be maintained by men. However, attitudes changed as workers became more plentiful with the growing influx of immigrants. Working men were particularly eager to get wives out of the labor force and women out of all but the lowest-paid jobs. Their goals were to reserve the better positions for themselves, make sure they would not be underbid, and give greater force to the argument that a "living wage" for a man had to be sufficient to support a dependent wife and children. Thus, women received little, if any, support from organized labor in trying to improve their own working conditions and rewards.

This was the genesis of the traditional family, once accepted as the backbone of American society. As we have seen, it is in fact comparatively recent in origin, dating back only to the mid-nineteenth and early twentieth centuries. Even in its heyday, it was never entirely universal. Many poor, black, and immigrant married women worked outside their homes; in addition, many others earned income at home, taking in boarders or doing piece work. Throughout this period, market work was quite common among single women, and a relatively small number of women chose careers over marriage as a lifelong vocation. Nonetheless, exclusive dedication to the role of mother and wife was widely accepted as the only proper and fulfilling life for a woman. It was not long, however, before this orthodoxy was challenged. Progressive modernization brought about dramatic changes in conditions of production and in the economic roles of men and women, followed by changes in ideas and aspirations that made rigid differentiation, let alone ranking of the roles of the sexes, increasingly less appropriate. . . .

Conclusions

The overview provided here, though very general, permits us to draw some conclusions. The roles of men and women and the social rules that prescribe appropriate behavior for each are . . . determined by the interaction of technology, the role of women in production, and a variety of social and political factors. There is some reason to believe that women are less likely to be seen as dependents, defined solely in terms of their maternal and family role, when they participate in "productive" work.

It is also likely that the roles of men and women that may have initially developed as a rational response to conditions that existed at one time in the course of economic development continue their hold long after they have ceased to be functional. Thus the view that women should devote themselves to home-making, once a full-time occupation when life was short, families were large, and housekeeping was laborious, lingered long after these conditions had changed substantially. Jobs originally allocated to men, because they required great physical strength, often continued as male preserves when mechanization did away with the need for musclepower. The possibility that such lags in adjustment are not uncommon should be kept in mind when we come to analyze the current situation.

73

"The stereotype is that in filling breadwinning roles, boys will need to be taught . . . competitiveness. In filling domestic roles, girls will need to be taught . . . nurturance."

Culture Determines Gender Roles

Linda L. Lindsey

A culture perpetuates itself by shaping each person to live in society. This process is called socialization, and its lessons are taught to children through a variety of channels—family, friends, school, and even the media. In the following viewpoint, Linda L. Lindsey examines the effects of these cultural influences on the development of one of the most basic levels of identity—gender. It is unfortunate, Lindsey finds, that while sex role socialization is not a uniform or consistent process, its effects are so strong that they prevent most people from developing and drawing on more than a part of their inborn strengths. Lindsey is a sociologist at Maryville College in St. Louis, Missouri.

As you read, consider the following questions:

1. How does Lindsey prove that parents treat their children in gender stereotyped ways?
2. In Lindsey's analysis, how does language define appropriate occupational roles for men and women?
3. In what ways do television and school socialize the sexes, according to the author? What alternative to traditional sex roles does the author say exists?

Linda L. Lindsey, *Gender Roles: A Sociological Perspective*, ©1990, pp. 44, 47, 52, 53, 54. Reprinted by permission of Prentice-Hall, Englewood Cliffs, New Jersey.

I'm Glad I'm a Boy

I don't like girls, I do not, I do not,
I know I didn't like them when I was a tot,
Girls hate lizards and rats, and snakes, bugs and mice,
And all the other things that I think are nice.
I sing a gay song and jump up for joy,
For I'm very happy that I'm a boy.

Poem appearing with an ad for boy's clothing

From the moment a girl infant is wrapped in a pink blanket and a boy infant in a blue one, gender role development begins. The colors of pink and blue are among the first indicators used by a society to distinguish female from male. As these infants grow, other cultural artifacts will assure that this distinction remains intact. Girls will be given dolls to diaper and tiny stoves on which to cook pretend meals. Boys will construct buildings with miniature tools and wage war with toy guns and tanks. In the teen and young adult years, although both may spend their money on records, girls buy more cosmetics and clothes while boys buy sports equipment and stereo components. The incredible power of gender role socialization is largely responsible for such behavior. Pink and blue begin this lifelong process. . . .

The Family Influence

The family is by far the most significant agent of socialization. Even when social change adds other agents, the family maintains the major responsibility for socializing the child during those critical first years of life. Here the child gains a sense of self, learns language, and begins to understand norms of interaction with parents, siblings, and significant others in her or his life. Gender role socialization is pervasive in each of these.

The strength of gender role expectations is suggested in an important study by Jeffrey Rubin and colleagues, which finds that sex typing of infants by parents begins on the day of the child's birth. Though both parents are likely to describe sons as strong, firm, and alert, and daughters as delicate, soft, and awkward, fathers are more stereotyped in their assessments. These findings are especially revealing in light of the fact that the infants did not differ in any health related aspects, such as weight or length. With gender role stereotyping evident on day one of life, it is easier to explain why parents hold such different expectations for their sons and daughters. E.D. Collard finds that mothers of four-year-olds believe boys can perform certain tasks without supervision earlier than girls. While Dick is allowed to cross the street, use scissors, or go to a friend's house by himself, Jane must wait until she is older. . . .

Socialization, perhaps initiated before birth, continues once the proud parents leave the hospital with their daughter or son. The first [objects] acquired by the infant are toys and clothes. In anticipating the arrival of the newborn, friends and relatives choose gifts which are neutral to avoid embarrassing themselves or the expectant parents by colors or toys which suggest the "wrong" sex. Teddy bears and clothing in colors other than pink or blue are safe selections in this regard. Parents may have originally decorated the child's room to accommodate either sex. But within weeks after the arrival of the infant, such rooms are transformed and easily recognizable as belonging to a boy or a girl.

Cathy. Copyright ©Universal Press Syndicate. Reprinted with permission. All rights reserved.

Along with this recognition factor, toys carry with them a formidable force for socialization. Toys for girls encourage domesticity while boys receive not only more categories of toys but ones which are more complex, more expensive, and suggest activities that are not homebound. Little Jane uses her tea set to have a party for her dolls, most likely in her room, while same-age Dick is experimenting with baseball or racing trucks outside in the mud. Certainly these kinds of toys encourage higher levels of physical activity in boys. Parental expectations are tied to the kinds of toys they provide to their children. Although very active play emphasizing motor functions may produce anxiety in parents who fear for the child's safety, research indicates that they discourage girls from engaging in such play more than they discourage boys.

Yet it might be argued that while boys are more vibrant physically, girls are more imaginative in their play. Both Jane and Dick are given prototypical toys at an early age. These are toys which "look like what they are supposed to represent," so that as the child gets older they can pretend *more* with toys which are *less* prototypical. By age two, there is a decrease in pretense of boys while girls' pretense increases. Pretend play is developed early in girls so that by the age of eighteen months, they are actually staging their manner of play, while boys are not, according to researcher Brian Sutton-Smith.

In examining these findings, Sutton-Smith is not as optimistic about the implications. Though girls are more imaginative than boys in the play of early childhood, after age seven the reverse holds true. Girls stage one type of activity, having to do with dolls and playing house, thereby assuming a caretaking, domestic role. Toys given girls bolster this pattern. If boys are restricted in any way, it is in the lack of encouragement in staging activities suggestive of later domestic roles.

Toy selection represents one of many instances of gender role socialization in early childhood. Suggestive of social learning theory, even infants receive reinforcement for behavior which is gender appropriate. In a study of firstborn infants and their mothers, Howard Moss demonstrates that [infant] irritability is a signal for mothers to attend to their babies, and since boys are likely to be more irritable than girls, boys get more overall stimulation. . . . The expectation is for girl babies to be "nicer" than boy babies and, therefore, more passive and controlled. When expectations are translated into rewards, girls soon learn the virtues of passivity. . . .

Speaking of Gender

Language reflects culture and is shaped by it, therefore, it is fundamental to our understanding of gender roles. Once we learn language, we have a great deal of knowledge about how the culture defines the two sexes. The problem is that this knowledge must be discovered because language itself is taken for granted. As we shall see, it is for this reason that language is so powerful an element in determining our gender roles.

We begin with the idea that the English language constantly focuses attention on gender. Nowhere is this clearer than when the word man is used to exclude woman and then used generically to include her. This is the intended meaning when anthropologists speak of culture as man-made or the evolution of mankind. But more often the word is used to distinguish man from woman, such as in the phrases "it's a man's world" or "this is man's work." The word is definitely ambiguous and may be subject to interpretation even within one context. In both instances of usage, it is unclear where women belong, but it implies that they are somehow "part" of man. Sometimes no interpretation is necessary. At a wedding ceremony when a couple is pronounced "man and wife" she becomes defined as his. In learning language, children are also taught that the sexes are valued differently. Not only is language use ambiguous, it is discriminatory as well.

It is awkward to change language to make it more precise. If man is supposed to refer to woman, then he is also supposed to mean she. Because English does not have a neutral singular pronoun, he is seen as the generic norm, with she as the exception. A doctor is he and a nurse is she. More neutral designations are also he words. A consumer, writer, patient or parent is seen as he. In reality, many, if not most, of these people are women. But women are linguistically excluded. Now we see that language is ambiguous, discriminatory *and* inaccurate. . . .

Who Does What

Titles and occupational terms are gender related. We write Dear Sir or Dear Mr. Jones even if we are unsure of the sex of the addressee, especially if it is a business letter. After all business-*men* are seen as the likely occupants of these positions. The same can be said for chairmen, foremen, congressmen, newsmen and garbagemen. Physicians, attorneys, and astronauts are men. Nurses, schoolteachers, and secretaries are women. If either sex deviates occupationally and chooses to enter a nontraditional field, we add linguistic markers to designate this remarkable fact. Children use these markers frequently in referring to females in traditionally male roles or males in traditionally female roles. What emerges is the idea of a female doctor, lady space man, or male stewardess.

Another linguistic marker involves adding appendages or suffixes to words to show where women "belong" occupationally. A poet becomes a poet*ess* and an usher an usher*ette*. . . . Such additions point out that women occupying these roles are exceptions to the rule. They are frivolous or mere imitators, and as exceptions, they are not taken seriously. This is what the acclaimed Broadway and movie performer Whoopi Goldberg means when she states: "I am an actor . . . and I do *not* mean actress. Actresses are sort of cute, you know? What I do is not cute.". . .

The research is conclusive that children's television is generally sexist and gender stereotyped. . . . Television themes can also be differentiated according to how the sexes are portrayed. Females pursue goals related to altruism, home, and family. Self-preservation is an important female goal, too, because female characters are likely to be the targets of threats and violence. Male goals are headed by self-indulgence, wealth, revenge and expressions of hatred. Interestingly, women are more likely to achieve their goals when compared to men. This is not an inconsistent finding if we realize that the goals of women are traditional and socially acceptable. For those television women who step into a "man's world," the outcome is not as optimistic.

Toward the Center

In the nineteenth century, writers such as Oscar Wilde and Marcel Proust exemplified the androgynous male as an artistic ideal necessary to the highest creations; rooted in the vision of a perfect man, androgyny made a man whole by recognizing his female aspects. Bourgeois conventionality, however, deemed it a code name for homosexuality. After being reintroduced in the Seventies, androgyny immediately became politically incorrect. . . .

But at a time when one can be gay or lesbian, transsexual, a cross dresser, a caring man, or a dominant woman and still be accepted in some part of our social landscape, androgyny seems to be moving to the center. . . . A new way of looking at androgyny "would not entail some merging of the sexes into an androgynous mutant, nor would it produce a hermaphroditic creature with male and female genitalia or beards and breasts," says Marilyn Yalom of Stanford. "I have in my mind's eye the image of a piano with its eighty-eight keys. Everyone would have access to a full keyboard. Women would not be limited to the higher-pitched notes, nor the men to the lower scales."

Don Monkerud, *Omni*, October 1990.

Children's television is supported by commercials aimed at products for children, mainly toys and sugared cereal. Younger children, heavy viewers, and boys from low income homes are most susceptible to commercials. Advertisers orient children to the idea that products are waiting to be bought at local stores and that to do without them is an unfortunate hardship. This can be referred to as the be-the-first-kid-on-the-block syndrome. Commercials are blatant in creating desires for toys encouraging domesticity in girls and high activity in boys.

Parents who resist pressure from their children to buy these products or find that the products the children want are unavailable are made to feel guilty, by advertisers and children alike. Remember the frantic search several years in a row for Cabbage Patch® dolls by parents who feared a disappointed child at Christmas or on his or her birthday? Picture, too, the angry exchanges we have all witnessed or taken part in between parent and child in front of the toy, candy, or cereal displays. Parents searching for nonstereotyped toy alternatives may feel demoralized when the offer of a tea set to their son or a truck to their daughter is met with resistance. Tantalized by television, what the child desires is within reach. For toys, the desire is likely to be gender role oriented. The parent stands in between. Who is likely to give up the fight first?

School's Outdated Message

Family life paves the way for the major agent of secondary and continuing socialization, the educational institution. The intimacy and spontaneity of the family is replaced by an environment valuing impersonal evaluation and rewards based on competition and scholastic success. For the next twelve to twenty years school will play a significant role in the lives of most people. . . . It should be noted, however, that regardless of intent, schools are not immune to gender role stereotyping.

Teachers who honestly believe they are treating boys and girls similarly are unaware that they are perpetuating sexist notions. When Jane is ignored or not reprimanded for disruptive behavior, is encouraged in her verbal but not mathematical abilities or is given textbooks which show her that women are housewives at best, or literally invisible at worst, gender role socialization continues. Dick discovers his rowdiness will gain attention from his female elementary school teacher, he can aspire to any occupation except nurse or secretary, and he is rewarded for his athletic skills during competitive games at recess.

Educational institutions are given the responsibility for ensuring that children are trained in the ways of society so that they can eventually assume the positions necessary for the maintenance of society. Schools provide experiences which offer technical competence as well as the learning of values and norms appropriate to the culture. American culture believes that competition, initiative, independence, and individualism are values to be sought, and schools are expected to advance these values. From a functionalist viewpoint, schools are critical ways of bringing a diverse society together through the acceptance of a common value system.

Unfortunately, many schools unwittingly socialize children into acquiring one set of values, to the virtual exclusion of the other. The stereotype is that in filling breadwinning roles, boys will need to be taught the value of competitiveness. In filling domestic roles, girls will need to be taught the value of nurturance. Though both may be positive traits, they are limited to, or truly accepted by, only one gender. As schools begin the task of first discovering, and then working to eliminate, sexist practices, differential gender role socialization can be effectively altered.

We have seen that socialization is neither consistent nor uniform. Though its agents are diverse, patterns of gender roles still emerge. Children are taught that girls and boys should exhibit behavior that is either feminine or masculine. But major contradictions arise in this process. Girls climb trees, excel in mathematics, and aspire to become professors. These same girls are concerned about physical attractiveness, finding the right husband, and raising a family. Boys enjoy cooking, like to play with children, and are not ashamed to demonstrate their emotions. These same boys are concerned about finding the right wife, raising a family, and gaining a rewarding job. Yet they have all been socialized by similar routes.

It is apparent that our views of masculinity and femininity need to shift in the direction of reality. First of all, these terms need not be the opposite of one another. Sandra Bem argues that many people exhibit androgyny, which combines or reconciles traits considered to be feminine or masculine. She has designed an attitude scale, the Bem Sex Role Inventory, which demonstrates that both men and women can score high or low on either set of traits or have a combination of them. Work with the inventory is revealing that large numbers of androgynous people do indeed exist. Biological sex is not an issue here. People know and accept their maleness or femaleness, but gender role rigidity is not as evident. Secondly, androgyny is by definition more flexible. As the situation demands, behavior can be adapted to it. By not being confined to rigid gender roles based on presumptuous assumptions of masculinity and femininity, people can respond according to their desires and abilities. Androgyny would certainly encourage this. Jeanne Block contends that parents who manifest androgynous identification tend to be less stereotyped in notions of masculinity and femininity and offer a wider range of behavioral and attitudinal possibilities to their children.

Androgyny recognizes that socialization into two nonoverlapping gender roles is not a productive way of encouraging behavior that can be adapted readily to a changing society. Society as well as the individual is beginning to demand more.

Periodical Bibliography

The following articles have been selected to supplement the diverse views presented in this chapter.

Jared Diamond — "Turning a Man," *Discover*, June 1992.

Christine Gorman — "Sizing Up the Sexes," *Time*, January 20, 1992.

Barbara Kantrowitz — "Sexism in the Schoolhouse," *Newsweek*, February 24, 1992.

Michael S. Kimmel — "Invisible Masculinity," *Society*, September/October 1993.

Doreen Kimura — "Sex Differences in the Brain," *Scientific American*, September 1992.

Elizabeth Larsen — "Walk a Mile in My Clothes," *Utne Reader*, July/August 1992.

Herbert I. London — "Social Experimentation," *Society*, September/October 1993.

Don Monkerud — "Blurring the Lines: Androgyny on Trial," *Omni*, October 1990.

National Review — "Girls, Girls, Girls," May 25, 1992.

Kathryn Phillips — "Why Can't a Man Be More Like a Woman?" *Omni*, October 1990.

Petra Schnitt — "Boys and Girls Apart," *World Press Review*, September 1992.

Joannie M. Schrof — "The Gender Machine," *U.S. News & World Report*, August 2, 1993.

Meredith F. Small — "Sperm Wars," *Discover*, July 1991.

Thomas Sowell — "Gender Benders," *Forbes*, June 7, 1993.

Douglas Stein — "Interview: Roger Gorski," *Omni*, October 1990.

Tim Unsworth — "Pink or Blue: Gender Roles Have Colored Our View," *Salt*, January 1993.

Daniel Evan Weiss — "Are Men and Women Really Different?" *Glamour*, February 1991.

James Q. Wilson — "On Gender," *The Public Interest*, Summer 1993.

Have Women's Roles Changed for the Better?

MALE/ FEMALE ROLES

Chapter Preface

In the fall of 1991 the United States Senate began hearings to confirm Justice Clarence Thomas to the Supreme Court. The calm of these proceedings was shattered, however, when a woman named Anita Hill accused Thomas of having sexually harassed her when they worked together years before. Reluctantly, the Senate agreed to investigate Hill's allegations. But in the resulting hearings it seemed to many observers that the fourteen male senators looked only into the character of the accuser—not at the truthfulness of her charges. Their line of questioning, which several critics denounced as belittling the seriousness of sexual harassment, made many people angry.

According to feminist writer Naomi Wolf, these proceedings angered a lot of women, in particular. In her book *Fire with Fire: The New Female Power and How It Will Change the 21st Century*, Wolf writes that the Senate's treatment of Hill demonstrated that issues affecting women (such as harassment) were not receiving adequate political representation. This realization resulted, she argues, in a "genderquake" as the numerically superior sex went to the polls in 1992 to elect 7 women senators (a 250 percent increase), 48 congresswomen, 7,424 women state legislators, and even an avowedly feminist president.

The surge in women's political activity and power was accompanied by new legislation and administrative measures affecting women. In 1993, for example, the new administration repealed the military's combat exclusion law, allowing women to fly combat aircraft and engage in a number of combat-related duties. This action meant the possibility of promotion for many military women, and, some felt, the advancement of all women since they were finally recognized as men's equals. "If the boys can go in [to combat], so can my daughter," said Martha Cummins of Lt. Sharon Cummins, a navy pilot who was promoted to a combat squadron.

Not everyone agrees that these administrative innovations are beneficial. For example, in addressing the changes in the military, Eagle Forum president Phyllis Schlafly speaks on behalf of her traditional family-values organization and for many other people when she says that "assigning women to military combat positions goes against human nature, our culture, and centuries of experience."

The battle over women's careers in the military is but one front in the war over women's expanding roles. Other areas disputed in the following chapter include women's place in the workforce, in the family, and in the federal government.

"Women are excluded from management positions not because of their capabilities but because of their gender."

A Glass Ceiling Limits Women's Roles at Work

Business and Professional Women's Foundation

In the following viewpoint, the Business and Professional Women's Foundation reports on the status of women working in corporations, academia, and the government. In all three areas, the foundation determined that, despite "unprecedented strides into the work force" over the last two decades, women are prevented from reaching the top of their professions by a variety of unofficial discriminatory practices, collectively known as the "glass ceiling." The Business and Professional Women's Foundation provides information, education, and research programs designed to help improve the economic status of working women.

As you read, consider the following questions:

1. Where on the corporate ladder does the foundation report that women are grouped? How long does the foundation estimate it will take for women to reach parity with men in top management?
2. This study identifies several barriers to women's advancement. What are they? How do gender role perceptions explain the operation of the glass ceiling in these examples?
3. Why, statistically, is discrimination bad business, according to the authors?

From pages 1-10 of *You Can't Get There from Here: Working Women and the Glass Ceiling*, a report by the Business and Professional Women's Foundation, Washington, D.C., April 1992. Reprinted by permission of the foundation.

Over the past two decades, women and minorities have made unprecedented strides into the work force. Yet, discrimination due to gender and race is still a problem. According to the Department of Labor, "minorities and women have not made significant gains into middle and senior levels of management, notwithstanding their increased experience, credentials, overall qualifications and greater attachment to the work force." More than twenty-five years after Title VII was passed prohibiting sex discrimination in the workplace, women are still conspicuously absent in the ranks of top management. Although women compose 40 percent of all executive, management, and administrative positions, they remain employed in the middle and lower ranks of corporate America. And, the few women who are middle or senior managers are more likely to be concentrated in occupations which are predominantly female. At the current rate of increase, it will be 475 years, or until the year 2466, before women are as equally represented at the top of the career ladder as they are at the bottom.

The Glass Ceiling

This dearth of women in middle and senior level management positions is due to the "glass ceiling" phenomenon, i.e., the *organizational, attitudinal* and *societal* barriers that effectively keep women and minorities from advancing up the career ladder. Unlike sexual harassment, job segregation and pay inequities—obvious examples of sex discrimination—the glass ceiling is a more subtle form of workplace discrimination. Women are no longer prohibited or usually even publicly discouraged from entering certain occupations; however, in most cases, they are kept out of the pipeline for middle and top level management positions. In fact, according to a Department of Labor report, the glass ceiling exists at much lower levels of management than previously thought. Additionally, the glass ceiling is not confined only to the corporate world. The glass ceiling also exists in academia, government and politics. . . .

By the year 2000, two out of three new entrants to the labor force will be women. By the year 2000, almost a third of all new entrants into the labor force will be minorities, who will double their current share of the labor market. Black women will compose the largest share of the increase in the non-white labor force. Between 1985 and 2000, white males, who only a generation ago made up the dominant segment of the labor market, will compose only 15 percent of the net additions to the work force. These changes in the composition of the work force will profoundly alter the available pool of workers. American businesses will face a dramatically different labor force than the one they have long been accustomed to and, in order to remain competitive, the standard operating procedures of businesses may have to alter just as dramatically. More and more, the competitive edge will go to businesses that are able to attract and, perhaps more importantly, retain good employees.

During the last 10 years, there has been only a slight increase in the representation of minorities and women in the top executive positions of the nation's largest 1,000 companies. Minorities and women hold less than 5 percent of these managerial positions, up from less than 3 percent in 1979. Of the top Fortune 500 companies [the nation's largest industrial corporations], women compose a mere 2.6 percent of corporate officers.

The Corporate Glass Ceiling

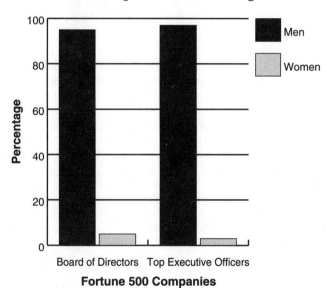

Source: Business and Professional Women's Foundation.

The glass ceiling exists at different levels in different companies or industries. The promotional plateau for women in large companies, however, is often found just short of the "general manager" position. Even in smaller or more progressive companies, though, it is rare to find women at the general management level. Statistics also reveal that minorities and women are less likely to obtain positions in line functions—such as sales and production—which most directly affect the corporation's bottom line and are considered the fast track to the executive suite. Instead women and minorities are more likely to be placed in staff functions.

Of the Fortune Service 500 industries [the largest service industries], women compose 61 percent of all employees, but only 4.3 percent are corporate officers. Representation of women is not much better on corporate boards.

Only 4.5 percent of the Fortune 500 directorships are held by women. Of Fortune Service 500 companies, 5.6 percent of corporate directors are women. And, although a 1988 Korn/Ferry survey reported that 52.8 percent of major U.S. corporations had women board members, up from 42.9 percent in 1986, only 25 percent of the Fortune 1000 companies in 1986 had more than one woman on their board. In fact, according to the Feminist Majority Foundation, there is such tremendous overlap among women sitting on corporate boards that just 39 directors account for 33 percent of the 652 Fortune 1000 directorships held by women.

Academia

The glass ceiling also exists in the world of academia. Women and minorities remain clustered in the ranks of the non-tenured, according to the American Association of University Professors. Furthermore, although women are now receiving the majority of degrees awarded, the situation of professional women in academia is not improving. Recent reports examining the status of women on college campuses are drawing the same conclusions reached in similar reports prepared 20 years ago, according to the *Chronicle of Higher Education*. Female professors, staff members and administrators in academia face a hostile work environment. This poor working climate is attributable to persistent and widespread gender discrimination. Female faculty and staff members are paid less than male colleagues at similar levels, they are more likely to hold lower-level positions, and they also receive fewer job promotions. "We haven't seen enough change," says Patricia B. Kilpatrick, vice president and university marshall at Case Western Reserve. "There aren't enough women in the higher professional ranks or the upper administrative levels."

Although the number of female professors in the country has increased since the early 1970s, their proportion of the total faculty has remained relatively constant. The largest increase occurred at the assistant professor level, where women's representation increased from 24 percent in 1972 to just over 38 percent in 1989. Still, in 1989, only 13.6 percent of full professors were women. . . .

The glass ceiling impedes women's career advancement not only in the private sector, but also in the public sector. In both elected and appointed positions, women are not equally represented. The glass ceiling in government and politics limits the participation of women at the highest levels of the policy-making process. The majority of women in government, especially if they are women of color, still face barriers that restrict their opportunities to advance beyond the lowest-level jobs.

Out of 435 possible seats in the House of Representatives, women currently [1992] hold only 29, just 6.4 percent. Women's representation in the Senate is even worse, at 2 percent. There are no women among the elected leadership positions, such as Speaker of the House or Majority and Minority leaders, within the U.S. Congress. Similarly, there are no women chairs of standing Congressional committees. . . .

Barriers to Advancement

Organizational, attitudinal and *societal* barriers impede women's and minorities' career advancement. "Qualified minorities and women are all too often on the outside looking into the executive suite," according to the Department of Labor's Glass Ceiling Initiative. Seventy-nine percent of Fortune 500 chief executive officers conceded that there are identifiable organizational and attitudinal barriers that prohibit women from reaching the top, according to a 1990 survey by Catalyst, a research consortium concerned with working women's issues. Interestingly, the barriers identified by Catalyst are quite similar to those identified by the Department of Labor.

Recruitment practices, developmental practices and credentials-building experiences, and accountability for equal employment opportunity responsibilities have all been identified as organizational barriers contributing to the glass ceiling. According to the Department of Labor, as well as other research on the glass ceiling, recruitment practices for middle and senior level positions often involve reliance on word-of-mouth and employee referral networking and the use of executive search and referral firms in which affirmative action/equal employment opportunity requirements are not made known. This practice usually produces slates of candidates which are overwhelmingly male and white. Developmental practices and credentials-building experiences, including advanced education, as well as career-enhancing assignments such as to corporate committees and task forces and special projects—which are traditional precursors to advancement—are often not as available to minorities and women. Furthermore, accountability for equal employment opportunity responsibilities does not extend to senior level executives and corporate decision makers. . . .

Job segregation also plays a part in the glass ceiling. The majority of female executives are concentrated in female dominated industries, such as health care and education. Additionally, women executives in both female and male dominated industries are guided into certain types of management positions—mostly staff and support—that offer few openings for getting to the top. According to a 1986 *Wall Street Journal* survey, "The highest ranking women in most industries are in non-operating areas such as personnel, public relations, or, occasionally, finance specialties that seldom lead to the most powerful top management posts."

The "old boys" network also contributes to the glass ceiling. The vast majority of corporate officers are white men. Research has revealed that people at the top usually select for promotions those who resemble themselves. Since mentoring and sponsorship by higher level executives are two of the most important avenues to advancement, and since there are so few women and minorities at the top, these opportunities are less available to women and minorities. . . .

Discrimination by Stereotype

Cliches about why women work also contribute to the stalling of women's careers. One predominant myth is that women are more prone to leave their jobs because they can't handle the dual responsibilities of a job and family. However, "Don't Blame the Baby," a study by Wick and Company that researched why women and men managers change jobs, found that the majority of women quit their jobs to pursue a job with greater career satisfaction, not due to family pressures. Additionally, only 3 percent of women surveyed in a 1986 *Wall Street Journal* study cited family responsibilities as hindrances to their careers while over half cited reasons related to their gender, including the simple fact of being a woman. More than 80 percent of the executive women respondents in a Gallup survey said they believe there are disadvantages to being a woman in the business world. . . .

Outright discrimination does play a major role in preventing women's rise to the top. In a study funded in part by the BPW Foundation, Anne Harlan and Carol Weiss of the Wellesley College Center for Research on Women found that as the number of female managers in a workplace rises, resistance to them falls, until the percentage of women nears 15 percent. Then discrimination, including outright harassment, begins to rise again. In other words, as women's status changes from "token" to competitor, resistance to their success increases.

Differing perceptions of acceptable male and female behavior also block women's career advancement. Though researchers have found that men and women do not differ substantially in management style and competence, the old stereotypes persist. As a result, the same behavior is perceived differently in men than in women. For example, behavior considered assertive in a male is usually seen as aggressive in a female. This means that "managerial" behavior, because it is based on a "male" model, is often seen as inappropriate for women. This perception does seem to be at odds with reality, given a Russell Reynolds Associates' study which reports that significantly more women executives display leadership potential than their male counterparts. Regardless, women remain concentrated in staff management positions which stress "people" skills over line management positions and more and more articles have appeared touting "women's" vs. "men's" management styles. Real people are harmed by the glass ceiling. Real women are excluded from management positions not because of their capabilities but because of their gender. . . .

The Civil Rights Act of 1991, which was signed into law in November 1991, and the introduction in Congress of the Equal Remedies Act represent essential steps toward shattering the glass ceiling. By providing compensatory and punitive damages for victims of sex discrimination, the Civil Rights Act and the Equal Remedies Act create more effective economic incentives for companies to eliminate discriminatory practices, including the organizational practices and attitudinal views which have limited women's careers. The Department of Labor's voluntary Glass Ceiling Initiative is also an important first step in eradicating these barriers to women's and minorities' advancement.

Strengthening existing laws against discrimination will be a futile exercise, however, if such laws are not enforced more effectively. . . . The Equal Employment Opportunities Commission (EEOC), the agency responsible for enforcing Title VII, which prohibits workplace discrimination on the basis of gender or race, has also ignored its mandate to provide non-discriminatory workplaces by failing to protect workers from discriminatory behavior and also failing to provide remedies to workers who have been discriminated against. Furthermore, the Department of Justice, which is authorized to enforce Title VII against state and local governments and to bring suit against federal contractors, has neglected to develop a litigation strategy for enforcing civil rights laws. . . .

Conclusion

Discrimination against women in the workplace is bad business. Businesses cannot afford to continue to under-utilize half of their available work force. Seven out of 10 women age 25 to 54 are currently in the labor force. Women currently compose almost half of the entire work force. Discrimination, whether intentional or unintentional, prevents women and minorities from truly benefitting from their training and efforts and from fully contributing their abilities and knowledge to the productivity of our country. As women become more essential to a productive work force, businesses will be able to ignore their concerns only at their own peril.

"Rather than conceding that they are less apt for workplace success, many women prefer to blame discrimination."

The Glass Ceiling Is Not What Limits Women at Work

George Gilder

In the following viewpoint, George Gilder argues that women and men are mentally and physically different and that these dissimilarities find expression in their contrasting social roles. Therefore it is not surprising, Gilder concludes, that women are to be found less in the upper reaches of the professions than in less-demanding jobs or in the home raising their children. George Gilder is a critic of feminism and the author of several books on men and men's roles, including *Men and Marriage, Visible Man, Naked Nomads,* and *Sexual Suicide.*

As you read, consider the following questions:

1. What evidence does Gilder offer to show that women and men are different physically and mentally? What is the significance of this difference, according to Gilder?
2. How does the author support his contention that women would rather "work less"? How is work defined here?
3. How do feminist charges of a glass ceiling translate into a search for a glass slipper, in Gilder's opinion? What does the author say is the effect of this debate on the economy?

From George Gilder, "Still Seeking a Glass Slipper," *National Review*, December 14, 1992. Reprinted with the author's permission.

Lean back in your chair and look up—the ceiling is opaque, isn't it? At least it is for most of us mere men. I would like to play for the Celtics, run the software division at IBM, write eighty best-sellers like Agatha Christie, be elected to the Senate like Barbara Mikulski, summon God and make Him come like Leanne Payne. I would like to be able to debate, write numberless books, and lead national movements to victory, as Phyllis Schlafly does, while raising five children. I ogle upward at these paragons and am baffled. I do not have the slightest idea how they do it. The ceiling is not glass.

Actually, I think the problem is that for the feminists, the ceiling is a mirror. They look up at the pinnacles of the economy and see themselves in power. The fact is that in a competitive economy, nearly all high-level jobs demand singular gifts, special experience, high ambition, bold willingness to take risks. For a particular slot, there is usually not a broad selection of people available. Often, judging from my experience with small high-technology businesses, there is no one available of either sex. Headhunters earn thousands of dollars by delivering one suitable head. And each year, these high-tech firms account for a larger share of total U.S. employment.

Old vs. New

Men too sometimes find themselves beneath a glass ceiling— shut out of a job for which they are sure they're qualified. But they have to smash the ceiling the old-fashioned way: by leaving the company and starting their own business.

These are the facts of life in enterprise. You don't get to be boss because of credentials or good behavior. You don't zoom to the top in a glass slipper. You get to the top by devoting your life to the pursuit. And at the summit the slopes are slippery. Most of the time there is no glass floor to catch you if you fall.

The new way, if you're a woman or an approved minority, is to call a lawyer, as did Barbara Sogg. She wanted to run the American Airlines LaGuardia Office. But she was "stubborn and uncooperative," according to her superiors, and she had had heart surgery. And she lacked a degree in engineering. Just the sort of person you want in control at the airport. Passed over in favor of a male engineer, she sued. An affirmative-action triple threat, she charged discrimination on the basis of sex, age, and disability, and won a total of $7 million.

Wow. There's a woman who can cut it in modern-day America. She told the *New York Times* that she hoped the verdict would "shatter the glass ceiling that has kept women from many of the top jobs in large corporations."

Of course, in some circles frequented by feminists, the ceiling is indeed transparent. On university campuses, in soft subjects, the worst rule. It is similar in government. With the appropriate norming and other skews, credentials often can prevail. But in the dreaded private sector, outside of a few plush monopolies, performance is nearly everything. When you are competing with the Japanese, there is literally no room for bias of any sort—including affirmative action. And though many people do not want to face it, it is the heavily patriarchal societies of Japan and other Asian countries that we will be competing against more and more in most businesses.

Yet the women continue to complain and sue. They want to be allotted positions at the top. They want to ride up in a glass slipper.

What is going on here? Russell Kirk explained the problem in *The Conservative Mind:* "[Our] people have come to look upon society, vaguely, as a homogeneous mass of identical individuals, with indistinguishable abilities and needs, whose happiness may be secured by direction from above, through legislation or some manner of public instruction."

He is right. The problem is the sociological view: the belief in a society of monads that are all to be treated as human beings. But I have never met a human being, and I hope I never do. In this world, there are only men and women; and they are very different from one another. *Vive la différence.*

But if men and women are different, there is no reason on earth to expect them to show up in comparable numbers in high-ranking jobs. There is no reason to believe that the male advantage in executive roles is an effect of discrimination. In fact, the differences between men and women overwhelmingly favor men in the positions beyond the glass ceiling.

Although there are many contrary claims and myths, anthropologists have yet to document a society in which men do not dominate the "top" jobs and do not tend to rule in male-female relations. As Steven Goldberg has demonstrated in *The Inevitability of Patriarchy,* and as even Margaret Mead admitted, there has never existed a documented matriarchy. In other words, the glass ceiling is not a cultural peculiarity of the United States, reversible by legislation. All societies ever studied have a glass ceiling. . . .

Performance Is Everything

Juliet B. Schor, a Harvard economist, put the feminist argument in [straightforward] terms in a recent book, highly acclaimed, which maintains that the problem with the U.S. economy is that Americans work too hard. She protests—how like a feminist!—that one ought to get these top-of-the-line jobs on flextime, with a lot of vacations and leisure. She does not comprehend that for nearly all the men above the glass ceiling, onerous work is their life, indispensable to support their families and crucial to the success of the economy. These disdained workaholics make it possible for Juliet Schor to pursue a leisurely tenured career in Cambridge.

The winners of the jobs beyond the looking glass are precisely the competitors who push on when ordinary men and women flag. They are competitors for whom the so-called rat race is the focus of their lives. For many reasons, men are overwhelmingly more inclined to an obsessive and successful focus on career than women are.

What Women Need

Women's substantial progress during the '80s helped muffle the call for radical legislation to aid them. There is much less support now than a decade ago for the silly system of government wage-setting figured on the basis of "comparable worth," the inevitably arbitrary judgments of statisticians and bureaucrats about what the pay should be in different occupations. Rapid entry of women into prestigious occupations has also quieted the call for quotas. Even supporters concede quotas aren't really what they have in mind. . . .

The law of supply and demand, along with civil rights legislation, is steadily improving the economic position of U.S. women. Extensive intervention in labor markets to help them is unwarranted and will do more harm than good in implementing the principles of equal pay and equal employment opportunities for equal work.

Gary S. Becker, *Business Week*, December 2, 1991.

Some of the reasons are biological. The evidence is overwhelming that men and women are genetically dissimilar in ways well beyond the obvious physical differences. Feminist psychologists Eleanor Maccoby and Carol Jacklin sum it up in *The Psychology of Sex Differences:* "1) Males are more aggressive than females in all human societies for which evidence is available. 2) The sex differences are found early in life, at a time when there is no evidence that differential socialization pressures have been brought to bear by adults to 'shape' aggression differently in the two sexes. 3) Similar sex differences are found in man and subhuman primates. 4) Aggression is related to levels of sex hormones, and can be changed by experimental administrations of these hormones."

Virtually all feminists who have considered the evidence now acknowledge these differences. But they rarely concede the obvious result: The sex that is the more competitive will tend to win more competitions.

Feminists contend that the male edge in aggressiveness is irrelevant in the modern workplace, where soft skills are allegedly becoming more important. The fact is, however, that from finance to economics, from technology to market research, high-level employment is more and more oriented toward mathematical reasoning. This means that men will increasingly hold the top jobs, because they are overwhelmingly more likely to excel in math.

In a study of 9,927 exceptional students by researchers at Johns Hopkins, the mathematical portion of the Scholastic Aptitude Test was administered on six different occasions between 1972 and 1979 to seventh- and eighth-graders with equal preparation. The researchers found 32.5 per cent more boys than girls scoring high in math, though the girls in the sample exceeded the average in their sex by a greater margin than the boys did. Overall, 7.8 per cent of the boys, but only 1.7 per cent of the girls, scored over 600 out of the 800 possible points, and all the scores over 760 were by boys. This difference is not peculiar to America. In international tests of math and science skills, boys decisively outperformed girls in math in all the 13 countries participating.

Better, Best

Feminists say these differences are not important. They may accept the fact that most men are more competitive, aggressive, technically oriented, and physically strong than most women. But they point out correctly that many women excel most men in all these characteristics. Although only 4 out of 350 chess grandmasters are women, the youngest one of all time is Judit Polgar, a Hungarian girl in a family which has produced one of the other female grandmasters as well.

Nonetheless, the fact that many women are more aggressive or technically adept than most men is irrelevant to the glass-ceiling debate, which necessarily focuses not on averages but on exceptions. Competing for top jobs, women will not face average men. Women will have to excel the men whose aptitudes have led them to specialize in the particular task at hand. It does not help women chess players or wrestlers or commodity traders or microchip entrepreneurs that they might be better at these activities than me. Or better than millions of other men, including most of the men reading this article. What matters is whether they are willing and able to compete near the top male level in their field.

Reinforcing the biological differences are equally powerful cultural and psychological differences. Quite simply, men are dependent on earning money for their sexual role in the world.

In general, without earning money, a man cannot win a woman or marry her. Although feminists claim that all this is changing, the fact is that leading feminists show no inclination to marry flower children. Gloria Steinem pursued her self-esteem with real-estate tycoons. Indeed, the more money a woman earns, the bigger the gap between her income and the larger income of her husband. Marriageable women usually demand that their men outearn them.

Different Roles

The sexual and marital prospects of a woman, on the other hand, are little affected by her earning power. Unlike the man, the woman has options. She can drop out of the rat race any time she wants without jeopardizing her prospects for marriage.

This difference alone would be enough to explain the different numbers of men and women beyond the glass ceiling. But marriageability is just the beginning of it. After marriage, the woman has a deep biological instinct to have children and to care for them and has a deeply respectable role as mother. On the other hand, many surveys show that a man who stays home and cares for the children wins the respect neither of his wife nor of other men. According to the sociological data, couples who switch roles for any extended period are "extremely unhappy and prone to divorce."

In competing for glass-ceiling work, even rising female education and credentials do not countervail these overwhelming social forces. A study by the Institute for Research on Poverty at the University of Wisconsin—a liberal group financed largely by the government—demonstrates a drastic difference between the sexes in the use of what they call "earnings capacity." Earnings capacity is defined in terms of age, education, credentials, experience, location, physical health, alleged discrimination, and other determinants of potential earnings. The study shows that married men of working age use 87 per cent of their earnings capacity, while comparable married women use only 33 per cent. Although the differences are much smaller for singles, the same pattern applies. The men devote more of their energies to their careers—though, because women have more credentials and are healthier, single women who work full time on average outearn single men.

Different Goals

For the glass-ceiling debate, however, the key point is that men with the most earnings capacity exploit it most effectively, working longer hours and more resourcefully the more education and credentials they possess. By contrast, the more education and credentials a married woman possesses, the less likely

97

she is to work full time all year at a highly demanding and remunerative job. While the earnings-capacity utilization of married men rises from 84 to 94 per cent from the bottom to the top tenth of earnings capacity, the earnings-capacity utilization of married women drops nearly one-third, from 35 to 24 per cent, or to a level about one-quarter that of their husbands. (These figures were based on data from the 1970s, but later statistics confirm the pattern.) Women, that is, may seek education and credentials in order to work less rather than to work more. Female physicians, for example, see 38 per cent fewer patients on average than male physicians; female lawyers see fewer clients than male lawyers; female professors write fewer books and research papers than male professors.

This is in no way culpable. It springs from an entirely commendable desire on the part of women to gain more time with their families. The result, however, is overwhelming. The very women who would be best prepared to pierce the glass ceiling shy from the effort.

The fact that more men than women succeed, therefore, is not difficult to explain. What needs to be explained is the pervasive bitterness and resentment shown by many women at these obvious manifestations of the facts of life.

Discrimination or Blackmail?

The reason, though, is clear when you think about it. All the established institutions in society today—in education, politics, the media, and the professions—tell women that they should be doing better in the job market. They know that they neither can nor want to make the efforts and sacrifices that men routinely make in order to reach the top echelons. But rather than admitting that feminism overall is a profoundly wrongheaded and unnatural theory of life, many women prefer to denounce the society. Rather than conceding that they are less apt for workplace success, many women prefer to blame discrimination.

In any workplace competition, discrimination is the great alibi for failure. We all tend to use it when we can. Conservatives talk about a huge conspiracy against them in the marketplace. Liberals talk about an establishment conspiracy against them. But only the 70 per cent or so of the U.S. population now covered as victims under civil-rights laws can actually sue.

Conservatives sometimes get this stuff wrong. The problem of glass-ceiling legislation isn't quotas; it's blackmail. No small business can afford to contest a lawsuit and few large ones want to. It's just too much time and distraction for the key personnel, the ones above the ceiling. I have seen it many times. Unless the amounts demanded are huge—in which case you go bankrupt—what you have to do if someone sues is to pay her off, regardless of the facts of the case. You just cannot continue to function as a business while undergoing a discovery process in a discrimination or, even worse, a sexual-harassment suit. The new Civil Rights Act is not a quota bill so much as a protection racket.

For, in addition to feminists, there is one minority that benefits greatly from such laws, one group that has mostly pierced the glass ceiling already. That group is, of course, lawyers.

Unlike the lower-class clientele involved in many discrimination suits, the glass-ceiling concept focuses on deep pockets: the richest and best-positioned Americans, who can afford to pay lawyers and who work in firms which can sustain lucrative settlements. The concern is not with bias; it is with finance. But when the law itself becomes an object of entrepreneurial manipulation, the entire economy suffers. This is the real meaning and portent of the glass-ceiling debate.

"Issues related to gender—particularly reproductive choice—helped [women candidates] win their races."

Gender Issues Are Helping Women Win in Politics

Mary Beth Rogers

Mary Beth Rogers explains in the following viewpoint that in response to a couple of key issues—abortion and governmental ignorance about sexual harassment—women stepped into the political arena in 1992 . . . and won. In the process, Rogers explains, women were seen playing a variety of "new" roles—from gender-loyal voter to financial power broker to skillful politician—that were part and parcel of an ongoing shift in gender roles. Rogers, who holds the Lloyd M. Bentsen Jr. chair in government and business relations at the University of Texas, Austin, was election manager and then chief of staff for Texas governor Ann Richards.

As you read, consider the following questions:

1. How does electing women to political office resolve the issues of abortion availability and protection from sexual harassment, in Rogers's view? What were women's specific political gains in 1992?
2. What does Rogers say was new and significant about women's 1992 political campaigns? What, conversely, is the product of years of experience, according to Rogers?
3. How does the author explain the generational context of the election results?

From Mary Beth Rogers, "Women in Electoral Politics: A Slow, Steady Climb," *Social Policy*, Summer 1993; published by Social Policy Corporation. Copyright ©1993 by Social Policy Corporation. Reprinted by permission.

Will women be able to sustain the political euphoria produced by the spurt of electoral successes in 1992? That is the key question that emerges from the over-hyped "Year of the Woman." It is a question that is rooted in the reality of governing and the current turmoil in political systems. In 1992, a confluence of factors produced momentum strong enough to propel hundreds of women into elective office, but it is far from clear whether this was an aberration or a continuing trend.

Still, something significant *did* occur for women in 1992. After steady, but slow, gains since the early 1970s, the increase in the number of women seeking and winning electoral office rose dramatically in 1992 not only at the federal level, but even more dramatically in state and local government.

In addition, for most of those who ran, gender was central to their mission and message. Issues related to gender—particularly reproductive choice—*helped* them win their races. Not a single anti-abortion female candidate for a major office won election in 1992. The Year of the Woman, in electoral politics at least, was as much about choice on abortion and the prospect of being denied choice, as about any other single issue.

Of the winners, Washington-based Democratic strategist Wendy Sherman said, "These women made no attempt to hide their feminist orientation. The voters who wanted change endorsed it and are eager for results."

The 1992 Results

Factors besides choice, of course, played a role in the great electoral leap forward. But before examining the issues, let's review the results of the pivotal electoral year of 1992. As of summer 1993:

• Seven women now serve in the US Senate—2 from the same state, California. This is up from 2 in 1990.

• Forty-eight women from 27 states and the District of Columbia serve in the House of Representatives—bringing women to 10 percent of the total in the Congress, up from 4 percent in 1975.

• Women now hold more than 22 percent of all statewide elective executive offices across the country—72 women in all. Three women are governors, 11 women are lieutenant governors and 8 women are attorneys general—including the first female African-American attorney general in the nation, Pamela Carter of Indiana.

• More than 20 percent of the nation's 7,424 state legislators are women, a five-fold increase since 1969. Washington State has the highest percentage of women serving in state legislatures with 39.5 percent.

• Women are mayors of 19 of the 100 largest cities in the nation. And women make up 20 percent of *all* mayors and munici-

101

pal council members serving nationwide in cities with populations over 10,000.

• Today, Georgia has the first female African-American sheriff in the nation, 42-year-old Jackie Barrett, who oversees a $28 million budget and 900 deputies and civilian employees as sheriff of Fulton County (which includes Atlanta). And New Yorker Nydia Velazquez, who was one of nine children and who grew up in rural Puerto Rico, becomes the first Puerto Rican woman to serve in Congress.

A woman's place is in the *House* ... and the *Senate**

*Senators Moseley Braun, Murray, Feinstein, Kassebaum, Boxer, and Mikulski.

Szep/*The Boston Globe*. Reprinted with permission.

How did all of this happen, and why was 1992 so important?

The voting constituency for women office holders—other women—was galvanized into action by two important emotions: fear and anger. Fear was generated by the serious prospect that for the first time since the 1973 Roe v. Wade Supreme Court decision, a woman's right to seek and have a safe abortion was in jeopardy. The Reagan-Bush judicial appointments from district and appellant levels all the way to the Supreme Court, as well as an aggressive anti-choice Justice Department, were closing off options, imposing restrictions and limits on abortion and choice.

Few politicians or pollsters recognized the depth of female concern on this issue, particularly among younger women who looked upon choice as a "right" soon to be taken from them. But it was an issue that drove women to the polls and propelled them to look for pro-choice women on the ballot. Even after the election, political consultants and members of the press still have difficulty understanding the intensity of feeling on this issue. It continues to be revealed in ways that are baffling to the pundits, as when attorney Sarah Weddington (who argued Roe v. Wade) was given a standing ovation and the loudest cheers of the afternoon from a crowd of 14,000 who had come to hear Hillary Rodham Clinton speak at the University of Texas.

The Hill-Thomas Hearings

The anger that fueled 1992 politics and provided the impetus for record numbers of women to seek office grew out of the Anita Hill–Clarence Thomas hearings before the all-white, all-male Senate Judiciary Committee [confirmation hearings were held to investigate Hill's sexual harassment charges against Supreme Court nominee Thomas]. When women watched the hearings, their anger grew in direct proportion to their exclusion from any governing body. It was an anger at being left out, at being misunderstood, at having serious complaints dismissed because men just didn't "get it." It was this anger that led Lynn Yeakel to come close to defeating Senator Arlen Specter, one of Hill's most inane questioners.

"I've been asked hundreds of times why I decided to run for the Senate, particularly given the formidable odds of running against a well-financed, two-term incumbent. The answer is simple: I had to do it," Yeakel said after the election.

Although Yeakel lost, victorious women who shared her frustrations and motivations emphasized their exclusion in campaign advertisements and called attention to the imbalance in power and public policy that their exclusion provoked. In Texas, Rose Spector, a candidate for the state's Supreme Court, used a photograph of the all-male Texas Court in a very effective television spot, and pointed out that something was clearly wrong with that picture—as with the Senate Judiciary Committee. Despite being out-spent almost two to one, Spector became the first woman in Texas elected to the Court.

"We owe Anita Hill a great debt of gratitude because we can now spend time getting women elected instead of explaining why we need them," said Jane Danowitz, of the Women's Campaign Fund.

But there were other reasons as well for the 1992 explosion of women into electoral office.

Women were already in the "political pipeline," serving and

learning how to operate in lower offices and gaining the confidence to take on bigger challenges. Few of the women who made it to Congress or to statewide elected posts were neophytes. Diane Feinstein had been mayor of San Francisco and had run a brutal losing race for governor before taking on the challenge of the US Senate race. Barbara Boxer had served in the US House of Representatives. Carol Moseley Braun was an experienced Chicago politician who had served as a state representative and Cook County's recorder of deeds before seeking the Senate seat. Over time, these women and the others who won had learned the ins and outs of the political game. They learned how to make hard decisions, suffer fools, make deals, build coalitions—skills necessary to run and govern.

"Virtually all the women who have come to Congress are not beginners to government and have dealt with male power structures," said Wendy Sherman. But most importantly, the winners in 1992 were women who had learned how to ask for and raise money. For the first time, women had access to political money in sufficient amounts to make them serious contenders for public office. EMILY's List ("Early Money Is Like Yeast") exploded onto the scene with its record $6.2 million in contributions to Democratic women candidates. Under the visionary leadership of Ellen Malcolm, EMILY's List grew from a $1.5 million PAC [political action committee] in 1990, when its 3,000 contributors put almost $800,000 into Ann Richards' winning race for governor of Texas, to more than 24,000 contributors in 1992.

Women Fund Raisers

The development of specialized techniques of fund raising among women had been under way for a number of years, pioneered by the National Women's Political Caucus, but perfected by EMILY's List and the Women's Campaign Fund. These newer, more sophisticated efforts produced a professional cadre of young women fund raisers who were well beyond the bake-sale mentality of raising money that many female candidates have been trapped in over the past decade. Many of these young women are like Jennifer Treat of Texas, a smooth technocrat who trained at the Women's Campaign Fund and who knows strategy, computers, targeting, and mail techniques that bring a steady stream of dollars into a political campaign. Treat headed an operation that eventually raised $9 million for Ann Richards' 1990 governor's race. This kind of professional fund raising for women made a significant difference in 1992. And every Democratic woman running for the US Senate had an experienced female in charge of fund raising.

There was also a sense of financial solidarity among women—again fueled by fear and anger over choice and Anita Hill. Independent fund-raising efforts demonstrated for the first time on a large scale that women were willing to contribute money for women they did not know and who did not even live in their states. Massachusetts women raised $60,000 for Carol Moseley Braun's race in Illinois. Braun also raised about $100,000 in Texas. Feinstein and Boxer also took about $50,000 each out of Texas. The Hollywood Women's Political Caucus put money into the races of every Democratic woman running for the US Senate. "Money is the major measure of credibility to insiders, the media, to people who shape viable candidacies," according to former Massachusetts Lt. Governor Evelyn Murphy. And feminist women had money in 1992. . . .

Aftershocks

There were aftershocks to the Anita Hill case. There was Tailhook, the military sexual assault scandal in which innocent women were brutally harassed and molested by Navy men; there were rape trials involving famous men; there were countless stories of harassment, appearing one after the other, by women emboldened to talk. American women added it all up—the earthquake called Anita Hill plus the aftershocks—and they [made up] their minds about Anita Hill and Clarence Thomas. . . .

America, and in particular, American women, were uncomfortable with the way the whole issue was handled, were uncomfortable with the way the Senate looked—and the Anita Hill incident became a catalyst for change. . . .

Hill led women to political empowerment, as women finally made the ultimate connection between their lack of power and the lack of women in high political office. Change became the political slogan of the 1992 elections, and who would personify change more than the people who *weren't* on the Senate Judiciary Committee, . . . and who *weren't* ever around the corridors of political power in a meaningful way? *Women were the ultimate outsiders* and 1992 would be the "Year of the Woman," with the November elections tripling the number of women in the Senate and almost doubling the number of women in the House of Representatives.

Barbara Boxer, *Strangers in the Senate: Politics and the New Revolution of Women in America*, 1994.

Women in 1992 benefited from a subtle shift in attitude toward women office holders that is perhaps generational in nature. For ten years, we've watched as female baby boomers have become lawyers, doctors, accountants, engineers, newscasters. . . . Why shouldn't they be politicians? In the 1990 governor's race in

Texas, private polls showed that the group most opposed to Ann Richards' candidacy at that time were rural women over 60 years old. It was hard for them to identify with a 55-year-old divorcee who relished the hardball world of politics. But with shifting demographics and a younger population brought up on *Murphy Brown*, *Designing Women* and *Roseanne*, there is a greater tendency to accept, even identify, with women as "doers."

The change has affected men, as well as women. A whole generation of men has attended professional schools with women, worked with them on the factory shop floors, and no longer views the female politician as a two-headed cow. So for the first time since they began running for office in large numbers in the 1970s, women found they had to fight fewer battles simply because they were female.

And what role did the gender gap—the difference between women and men voters— play in the 1992 elections? While generational politics may soon displace the gender gap as an organizing factor in future elections, there is no doubt that in 1992, all things being equal, women were more likely to vote for a female than a male candidate. The 2 to 5 or 6 percentage points generated by a gender gap in well-conceived, highly strategic campaigns, with a specific message targeted to female voters, *can* make a difference—again, especially when choice on abortion is perceived to be one of the defining issues. . . .

Estrogen v. Testosterone

The burst of electoral activity, increasing the percentages of women holding office from low, single-digit levels to double-digit levels over a 20-year period has a spill-over effect on other government appointments as well. The Clinton cabinet is 27 percent female (4 women), as opposed to Bush's 14 percent (2 women). And halfway through her term of office, Ann Richards has selected women for more than 48 percent of the 4,000 appointments she will make. Texas, thanks to Governor Richards, has its first female banking commissioner (who regulates state chartered banks), a female director of the key business development agency, the first female on the powerful state transportation and highway board, and on and on.

These appointments provide women opportunities to learn and to develop leadership skills. Many of them will no doubt seek elective office in the future. And the numbers of women holding elective office *will* increase.

At some point, perhaps shortly after the turn of the century— and the next census count—the "critical mass" of female office holders may at last be reached. When that occurs, feminists will have to address once again the serious question that has dogged every effort since suffrage to expand rights and opportunities in public life for women: does it make any difference in the overall situation for society?

For now, expectations are high—even from unexpected sources.

Thomas P. "Tip" O'Neill Jr., the 80-year-old retired speaker of the House, told new women members of Congress, "You average the women out and the men out, and the women are more intelligent. They're really something, all of superior caliber. Talented. Bright. They work harder than men do. . . . Pat Schroeder and those *girls* [italics added] are able as hell."

Even the Wilderness Society has high hopes, expecting that "the historic number of women elected to Congress will be a boon to environmental protection legislation."

"It was as if estrogen had been prescribed as the perfect antidote for the country's testosterone poisoning," wrote columnist Ellen Goodman after the 1992 election euphoria.

There is no doubt that some changes will occur immediately from the increase in sheer numbers of women in public office. More female judges and prosecutors will make it more difficult for convicted rapists to walk away from their crimes with mere slaps on the wrists. Issues affecting women's health, child care and work-related issues, such as sexual harassment, will be addressed with greater sensitivity.

But will government be better?

That may be too much to ask, and it places too much of a burden on the women who were victorious in 1992. Women have long suffered from a double standard in public life. With full equality, that burden should be expected to drop away. But not yet.

As Ellen Goodman says, "How long will it be before we read the first story asking why six [now seven] women in the Senate haven't yet changed the institution?"

As long as the 1992 euphoria is tempered by a realistic assessment of where women still *are* in electoral politics and what, as a minority in power, they are likely to be able to accomplish, the gains in the "Year of the Woman" can serve as a solid foundation for the slow, but steady, climb to equality that still must be undertaken.

"Gender and support for feminist agenda items were not sufficient to gain women's votes."

Gender Issues Are Not Helping Women Win in Politics

Marian Lief Palley

Some women won political office in the 1992 presidential elections, but, argues Marian Lief Palley, their numbers were still relatively small, they did not necessarily represent women's issues, and they were not universally supported by women voters. Seen in this political context, Palley concludes, the year of the woman looks more like the year of the anti-incumbent—albeit one in which only two incumbents were defeated by women. Palley, professor of political science and international relations at the University of Delaware, has written extensively on the role of women in politics.

As you read, consider the following questions:

1. What does Palley suggest was the perceived role of women candidates in the 1992 elections? Conversely, how does Palley characterize the importance of the "liberal cultural agenda" in general (and the Thomas-Hill conflict in particular)?
2. How successful were women candidates overall, according to the author? How important does Palley say women's votes were to the success of women candidates?
3. On balance, what was the effect of women's issues in the political year of the woman, according to Palley's analysis?

From Marian Lief Palley, "Elections 1992 and the Thomas Appointment," *PS: Political Science & Politics* 26 (1):28-31 (March 1993). Reprinted with permission of the American Political Science Association.

It is tempting to look at the results of the 1992 election season and to observe women candidates' successes and say, yes, it was the "year of the woman." It might also be inviting to attribute women's electoral gains to the attention that the Clarence Thomas [Supreme Court] confirmation hearings received and the anger many women felt towards the all-white male Senate Judiciary Committee with its cavalier treatment of Anita Hill and its insensitivity to sexual harassment. Yet, women's electoral gains must be viewed within the wider lens focus of changing patterns of American politics.

The Thomas-Hill interaction was seen by some as a reflection of institutionalized gender inequality and insensitivity. It underscored the need to press forward with the liberal cultural agenda, which incorporates feminist concerns with gender equity and electoral opportunity. Though the Thomas confirmation hearings made many people aware and angry, other conditions also helped to make 1992 an opportunity year for women and minorities. In particular, there was redistricting, a large number of retirements from Congress, and anti-incumbency feelings running high among American voters. Furthermore, though women were serving in political office, albeit in state and local positions, and thus were in "the pipeline" and ready for the opportunity to contest statewide and congressional positions, they were often seen as the ultimate outsiders. To be perceived as an outsider in an anti-incumbency era enhanced the candidacies of many women. Also, due to redistricting, many seats which women candidates contested were open seats for which their opponents lacked high degrees of political organization and the ability to "call in favors."

Of course, to dismiss completely the impact of the Thomas hearings would be a mistake since the hearings energized some women to run for public office and generated momentum for campaign fund raising to support female candidates. The hearings also made voters aware of the changes that had occurred on the Supreme Court during the Reagan and Bush administrations. However, the effect of the hearings and its broader implications must be seen in a web of other political happenings.

The Political Context

"The economy, . . ." was the rallying cry for the Clinton-Gore 1992 election campaign. All other issues and messages in the Democratic quest for the presidency were subsumed under this overarching concern with economic issues. The national Democratic ticket did not focus its primary attention on cultural agenda items such as reproductive rights, freedom of choice, or the appointment of Clarence Thomas to the United States Supreme Court.

However, the discomfort that Thomas's nomination and confirmation brought to many voters, both male and female, did precipitate events that ultimately led to greater female participation in electoral politics. Women's groups such as EMILY's List [Early Money Is Like Yeast] and the National Women's Political Caucus had their fund raising effectiveness for female candidates enhanced. EMILY's List saw its contributions quadruple to approximately $6 million. In 1992 it was the largest donor to congressional campaigns. And, more women were successful in their electoral bids.

The Elusive Gap

Ethel Klein, a political scientist and strategist who has studied the gender gap [between men's and women's voting practices] extensively, emphasizes that "it is an issue vote and can be triggered only by policy discussions that incorporate women's perspectives.". . . Yet Klein also emphasizes that "different groups of women base their value preferences on different sets of issues" and that all the traditional variables that affect actual votes, such as socioeconomic class, age, or even region of the country, come into play. . . .

If the pitfall in the past was to assume that women's interests were identical to men's, it is equally misleading today to equate the gender gap with an emergent female voting bloc, let alone a monolithic one.

Karen M. Paget, *The American Prospect*, Fall 1993.

Despite the apparent lack of sustained attention by the national Democratic ticket to reproductive rights, abortion rights, and the selection of federal judges, these issues were kept alive by the Republican Party. A culture war has been raging for several decades in the United States between the egalitarians and patriarchists with men and women operating on both sides. The Bush-Quayle campaign as well as many state and local candidates focused sufficient attention on cultural agenda items to keep these issues alive despite the economy-focused Clinton-Gore strategy, which minimized discussion of these divisive concerns.

Avoiding Gender Issues

Before one can understand the election results it is necessary to define the context of the contests. The pre-convention Republican Party debates focused attention on the cultural agenda. The discussions of traditional family values, opposition to abortion rights, and support for such issues as prayer in the schools pushed the Republican Party to the right of the political spectrum. President Bush articulated his support for these views, and when the party platform was drafted these positions were included in the platform. There were Republican women who were very uncomfortable with positions they deemed to be anti-women, but these women did not prevail. In 1988 the debate on cultural issues had been tempered by Lee Atwater who had described the Republican Party as a "big tent" that could accommodate a diversity of views. The 1992 national Republican Party as it came out of its convention was no longer a "big tent."

At the August convention the highlighting of right-wing positions and their spokespeople on prime-time television made the Bush-Quayle stance on cultural agenda items clear. They were anti-choice, symbolically pro-traditional families, and adherents of the broader agenda that had been outlined by the spokespeople of the right such as Pat Robertson, Pat Buchanan, and Phyllis Schlafly. The decision to devote one evening at the convention to "family values" further reinforced the right-wing stance of the Bush-Quayle campaign.

In contrast to the Republicans, the Democrats ran a convention in which restructuring the economy and affordable health care were highlighted. Discussions focusing on the cultural agenda were minimized. During the campaign that ensued, voters knew that Bill Clinton was supportive of gender and race equality. They also knew that if elected he would appoint judges to federal courts who would be defenders of a more liberal cultural agenda than the judges whom Presidents Bush and Reagan had appointed. Moreover, there was no ambiguity regarding his position on abortion rights. He defined himself very clearly as a pro-choice supporter. They also knew that he maintained an egalitarian perspective on other cultural and social agenda items.

Both Clinton and his running mate, Al Gore, could run a campaign without focusing on these issues in part because the president and vice president were discussing these points. Put in somewhat different terms, the Clinton-Gore positions were known to be in opposition to the Bush-Quayle stances. They did not need to be constantly engaged in the cultural agenda debate.

Mixed Messages

In 1992, 6% of the members of Congress (House of Representatives and Senate) were women and 18% of state legislators were women. This represented a substantial gain over 1971 when only 3% of congressional members and just 5% of state legislators were female. In 1992 11 women ran for the Senate, and 106 women ran for seats in the House of Representatives. Ten of the 11 Senate candidates were Democrats; 70 of the 106 House candidates were Democrats. After the ballots were counted it was clear that 47 women were elected to the House of Representatives. Twenty-four new women representatives were in Washington in 1993 (21 are Democrats and 3 are Republicans); and, with the addition of 4 more women in the Senate (all Democrats), 6 of the 100 U.S. senators will be female in the 103rd Congress. In other words, 11% of the representatives in the new Congress are women, and 6% of the new Senate are women.

These numbers represent a substantial gain in female representation in Congress. If, however, one is concerned about proportionality, it is worth noting that the November 1992 electorate was 54% female and 46% male. Of course, gender and support for feminist agenda items were not sufficient to gain women's votes. Some women lost elections in states and districts in which women voters outnumbered men voters. Also, even where women were victorious at the polls, not all women supported their efforts.

Some particular female "wins" and "losses" bear notice. In California, two Democratic women, Barbara Boxer and Dianne Feinstein, were elected to the U.S. Senate. Boxer, an outspoken advocate of feminist agenda items and a strong critic of the Thomas nomination and the committee hearings, entered the campaign in response to the Thomas nomination and confirmation. Whether or not she would have given up her congressional seat to run for the Senate were it not for the Thomas hearings is, of course, not clear.

Feinstein, a former mayor of San Francisco, is also a defender of feminist positions. She is not, however, as strongly identified as a women's issues candidate. Also, Feinstein is a defender of the death penalty and a "friend" of the business community. Put in somewhat different terms, she was seen as being a more centrist candidate than Barbara Boxer. In fact, perhaps as a result of these different views of the two women by voters, Boxer won her election with a 48% plurality of the vote; Feinstein on the other hand won a 55% majority of the votes cast in her race although Boxer received 5% more of the women's vote than Feinstein.

What About Gender?

Women insurgents, not unlike men challengers, were most successful in their candidacies when they were not contesting seats held by incumbents. This is a particularly interesting point given the anti-incumbency attitudes that seemed to have developed in the year prior to the election. However, there were members of both the House of Representatives and the Senate who chose not to stand for reelection (53 representatives did not seek reelection); there was redistricting that altered some districts so much that incumbents chose not to seek reelection; there were new districts drawn in response to demographic changes; and there were incumbents who lost in primary elections. Thus Carol Moseley Braun (D-IL) defeated incumbent Senator Alan Dixon in the primary. However, once in a partisan race for reelection, most incumbents had an incumbency advantage (93% of House incumbents who sought reelection won their contests).

Where women were successful in winning elections they ran good campaigns. Some women may have lost in part due to their political inexperience. Lynn Yeakel, the Democratic candidate for the Senate from Pennsylvania, entered the race in response to the Thomas hearings. She ran against Republican Arlen Specter, the senator who led the prosecuting-style charge against Anita Hill during the Clarence Thomas confirmation hearings. By most accounts Yeakel ran a relatively poor campaign in terms of issue focus and tactics, and she was defeated by Senator Specter.

Year of What Woman?

It's old news that 1992 may be The Year of the Woman in American politics. The political news that deserves the big headlines is being made outside the United States, where the legal and social barriers that kept women from national office are falling faster than the Berlin Wall throughout the world.

In fact, the United States lags well behind many nations in terms of the percentage of women holding national office.

In 1992, women filled only 6.4 percent of the seats in the U.S. House of Representatives. That's well below the international average of 11 percent in the 143 nations with equivalent national assemblies.

In the U.S. Senate, women are even harder to find. Only 2 percent of all senators are women. Around the world, 11 percent of the seats in equivalent assemblies are held by women, according to the Inter-Parliamentary Union, an international organization of countries with elected national assemblies.

Richard Morin, *The Washington Post National Weekly Edition*, April 27-May 3, 1992.

In the Specter-Yeakel race, Lynn Yeakel lost in a close race to a well-financed, articulate incumbent. Despite his support of Clarence Thomas's nomination to the Supreme Court and his attacks on Anita Hill, Senator Specter has a record of supporting women's rights issues and, in particular, freedom of choice. During the Democratic primary campaign Yeakel directed her attention to the role Arlen Specter played during the Thomas-Hill drama. After she won her primary race and became the senator's Democratic opponent, she was dubbed a one-issue candidate by the Specter campaign organization.

Yeakel was not able to overcome Specter's incumbency advantage. Specter was able to raise twice as much money as she was able to raise—$8 million versus $4 million. Also, he had retained his popularity with the voters, and had a background of support for the liberal cultural agenda and, in particular, feminist agenda items. He had targeted labor, Jewish, and African-American voters and was successful in his efforts. Yeakel did not adequately target and appeal to these groups. . . .

Incumbency, Not Gender

Of the 4 nonincumbent women who were successful in their senatorial bids, not one of them was running against an incumbent senator and therefore the incumbency problem that Yeakel experienced in Pennsylvania did not arise. In addition to the 2 female winners in California, Carol Moseley Braun and Patty Murray (D-WA) both scored victories, each winning 55% of the votes cast. Like Yeakel in Pennsylvania and Boxer in California, both Murray and Braun entered the political fray in response to their anger over the Clarence Thomas confirmation proceedings. Senator Barbara Mikulski (D-MD), a forthright opponent of the Thomas nomination, was returned to office with 71% of the votes cast.

Women who were energized by the Thomas appointment to the Supreme Court also contested a number of seats in the House of Representatives. These candidates were often the beneficiaries of open seats and redistricting. Not all of the female hopefuls were elected, but many women did run for congressional office. Twenty-two of the 24 new women elected to Congress won in open districts while only 2 women defeated incumbents. Twenty-three women were incumbents who were returned to office.

Most of the women who contested congressional seats supported the feminist cultural agenda. In fact, each of the first-time elected women to the House of Representatives is an abortion rights advocate. This does not mean that these women ran as "women's candidates" or as "women's advocates." Virginia Democrat Leslie L. Byrne defeated Republican Henry N. Butler in the Washington, D.C., suburban district of Fairfax County. She became the first woman to represent Virginia in the House of Representatives. She did not make a special point of discussing the role of sex as an issue except when she was addressing women's groups. She was a member of the state legislature for seven years and in that capacity she says that "I never was a women's issues–type of legislator because I really felt that all issues were important to women. . . . But it's the way you look at issues and how it affects people's real lives that I think is the real difference."

In California, 7 women, all of whom are Democrats, were elected to the House of Representatives. Also, women won 22 of the 80 seats in the state Assembly and 6 of the 20 state Senate seats. And, women won in local races too. The new mayor of San Diego, Susan Golding, won against her male opponent; in San Francisco, 3 of the 6 newly elected supervisors are women.

However, not all women candidates were defenders of the liberal cultural agenda. Helen Deich Bentley (R-MD), who represents a Baltimore, Maryland, suburban district, was reelected with 65% of the vote. . . . In 1990 the Americans for Democratic Action's *National Journal* gave her 0% liberal/89% conservative rating on social issues.

Economy, Not Gender

Some final observations need to be made regarding presidential voting and the Thomas appointment to the Supreme Court. The economy was clearly the major concern of American voters when they cast their ballots for president on November 3, 1992. Cultural agenda issues such as family values and abortion rights were of secondary concern—with only 15% (family values) and 13% (abortion rights) of voters identifying these issues as ones which helped them decide how to cast their votes. However, it would be a mistake to dismiss these concerns entirely from the voting calculus. To some voters these issues were important. In states where the votes were close, it is possible that the saliency of these issues affected the electoral results.

The selection of Clarence Thomas to serve as an associate justice of the Supreme Court and the confirmation hearings that followed provided some women with the necessary impetus to run for public office. Not all women were successful. Women challengers, like their male counterparts, were most likely to be successful if they were not opposing an incumbent. Also, there was no new substantial political awakening that took place—although the acceptability of women as outsiders who would change "politics as usual" may help explain phenomena such as the dual Boxer/Feinstein victories in California. In the presidential race as William Schneider put it, "Clinton did not win because the country suddenly lurched to the left, but because the voters want him to get the economy moving." And, the newly elected women were selected for a variety of reasons. The successful candidates were usually substantially well focused, tactically deft, and likely to be seen by their constituents as representatives of change.

=====

"Women will never make it into the Star Trek generation . . . until they're given equal opportunity to do the jobs open only to men."

=====

Women's Opportunities in the Military Are Improving

Amy Pagnozzi and Bruce W. Nelan

In Part I of the following viewpoint, Amy Pagnozzi charges that the arguments used to "protect" women by denying them combat roles in the armed services are feeble, irrelevant, and unfair. Pagnozzi, a writer for the *New York Daily News*, supports efforts to increase women's military opportunities. In Part II, Bruce Nelan, a senior writer for *Time* magazine, notes that the Defense Department's May 1993 announcement that women may fill certain military combat positions was largely a recognition of the role women played in the Persian Gulf War. Although older officers still resist the idea, he reports, the change is supported by many younger ones who have worked with female soldiers on difficult assignments.

As you read, consider the following questions:

1. How does Pagnozzi view the "mother as life giver and nurturer" argument for denying women a role in combat?
2. What reasons do female officers give for seeking equal opportunity in combat positions, according to Nelan?
3. What military positions does Nelan report are being opened to women? How physically demanding are these jobs?

Amy Pagnozzi, "The Real Reason Men Want to Keep Women Out of Combat," *Glamour*, December 1992. Reprinted with permission. Bruce W. Nelan, "Annie Get Your Gun," *Time*, May 10, 1993. Copyright 1993 Time Inc. Reprinted by permission.

I

"It does not make much sense, but that is the way I feel."
—*Air Force Chief of Staff Gen. Merrill A. McPeak, telling the Senate Armed Services Committee why he would always assign a male pilot to a combat position over a female one, even if she was more qualified.*

One thing you can say for Gen. McPeak—the guy's direct. It's more than can be said of most of the academics, ideologues and military men and women appointed by President Bush to hold hearings on whether women should be permitted to play military combat roles. . . .

During the months of debate [by the Presidential Commission on the Assignment of Women in the Armed Forces] you didn't need radar to see where many members' thoughts were heading. An agenda seemed to be lurking just beneath the surface, subtle as a Scud:

Shoot those women down!

To accomplish this, anything and anyone was potential ammunition. Two female prisoners of war were sexually assaulted behind enemy lines in Iraq? Have one testify—she can talk about the "special" hazards faced by female POWs. But Maj. Rhonda Cornum, the 37-year-old flight surgeon whose helicopter was downed in Iraq, knew what the commission was after. The sexual attack upon her was unpleasant, she testified, but amounted to merely an "occupational hazard" in the making of war.

She could have added that sexual assault is an occupational hazard for *all* women, everywhere—and that if the commissioners are keeping score on sexual assaults against American women in the Gulf, it's Iraqis, 2; Americans, 22.

The Real Hazards

According to the *New York Times*, American forces investigated 22 cases of servicewomen being attacked by our own boys during Desert Shield and Desert Storm. Remember that the Gulf conflict lasted only a matter of months. Remember Tailhook [an annual Navy and Marine aviators' convention where several women charged they were sexually molested in September 1991], where naval aviators lined up in a hotel hallway to rip the clothes off women passersby—often their fellow fliers. And now they tell us sexual assault happens only to women POWs?

In making an issue of Maj. Cornum's experience, the commission conveniently ignored the fact that male POWs are also vulnerable to sexual assault. The commission chose to see motherhood as another "problem" with assigning women to combat roles, even though there are far more single fathers in the military than single mothers. The commissioners listened to testimony stating that women, overall, aren't equal to men in physical strength, yet strength is irrelevant in many combat positions.

Though often seen only as helpmates—secretaries, drivers, nurses, admirals' aides at best—women in the armed services are better educated than their male peers; women are absent far less frequently, suffer fewer drug and alcohol problems and get promoted faster . . . until they're ruled out of the running due to lack of combat experience. Given this record, one can only guess that lurking behind the stance that women aren't good enough for combat is the fear that we will be *too* good—not just at fighting but at killing.

What Men Want to Believe

Women being shot at, even being killed, isn't the point, admitted retired Marine Corps Gen. Robert H. Barrow in congressional testimony. "It is *killing* . . . and it is . . . uncivilized! And women *cannot do it!* . . . I think the very nature of women disqualifies them. . . . Women give life. Sustain life. Nurture life. They do not *take* it."

Would that this were true, not just of women, but of all human beings. But Gen. Barrow is talking about how men *want* women to be. . . . The commission voted for some gains for servicewomen [in early 1993]. But [combat positions for women was not one of them]. Among the commission's members are a vice president of the far-right Heritage Foundation, an Air Force reservist affiliated with the ultraconservative group Concerned Women for America, an ex-chief of the Coalition for Military Readiness who has spoken out against women in combat, and others who are likely to want to restrict women to their roles as life givers.

The most feeble argument the commission entertained was the one concerning male morale, previously used until the end of World War II to exclude black men from combat units. Will men's innate sense of chivalry cause them to worry unduly about women soldiers' safety, the commissioners wonder? Will women distract the men sexually? If the answer to either is yes, how much self-discipline can these fighters really have?

The deaths of five American servicewomen in hostile action in the Gulf proved that missiles are not gender-specific. If women can and will die for our country, we must insist on our right—however repugnant—to kill for it as well.

II

At the infamous 1991 Tailhook convention in Las Vegas, when male Navy officers and reservists were not assaulting frightened women or drinking from the navels of cooperative ones, they took part in a series of professional seminars. A female naval officer asked a panelist at one such session when women would

118

be permitted to fly combat airplanes. Her question drew hisses and boos and the call "We don't want women!" from the audience. The senior officer on the panel, an admiral, treated it as a joke by ducking under the table.

Female officers insisted those assaults and jeers at Tailhook were two forms of the manhandling that would go on until the second-class status of women in the Navy was ended. To get respect and a fair chance at promotions, they said, they would have to be allowed to serve on warships and fly jet fighters and bombers. "Women will never make it into the Star Trek generation," said Lieut. Paula Coughlin, who exposed the Tailhook scandal, "until they're given equal opportunity to do the jobs open only to men."

Closer to Combat

In January 1994 Defense Secretary Les Aspin unveiled new rules easing the way for female soldiers seeking roles closer to direct ground combat. . . . The new definition would exclude women from most jobs in infantry, . . . but women can now be assigned to units that directly support those ground combat elements and frequently accompany them forward within range of enemy fire. . . . Officials estimated that up to 7,000 jobs in the active U.S. military could open to women as a result. . . .

Around Camp Pendleton Marine Corps base, the comments of men and women alike supported Aspin's stand—and said he should go even further, that women should serve side by side with men in all combat positions.

"If a woman feels strongly enough about the military to put her life at risk, no one should say no," said Stephanie Dielke, a former medic. When she entered the Army in 1972, Dielke said, she served in the first unit to get full field training comparable to that offered the men. Although only 20 percent of the women were expected to finish the course, Dielke said, 46 of 48 did, excepting only one with a broken ankle and another with appendicitis. "I think the females of the species have spent enough time proving themselves," Dielke said.

Otto Kreisher, *San Diego Union-Tribune*, January 14, 1994.

The path to the stars, especially those worn on uniforms, was opened last week. Defense Secretary Les Aspin ordered all the services to remove restrictions on women flying combat aircraft and said he would ask Congress to lift the ban on women serving aboard warships at sea. The change has long been visible on the horizon, but it was hurried along by a Navy eager to do something to smooth the choppy wake left by its official report on Tailhook. As the damaging document was readied for release two weeks ago, Navy brass quietly assured servicewomen at the Pentagon that, as one put it, "something was coming up soon that we would really like."

Aspin called the new role for women "historic." There are only about 800 female pilots in uniform now, so the number of women combat flyers will be relatively low for some time—a few hundred out of more than 41,000 pilots in all the services. It is still a dramatic departure in American society and its armed forces. The new era was symbolized at Aspin's Pentagon press conference by Air Force Captain Sharon Preszler, 28, a soft-spoken strawberry blond. "I can be a killer," she said firmly. "I can and will kill in defense of my country."

That vision, of America's mothers and daughters going into battle and coming back maimed or in body bags, was precisely what traditionalist commanders had fought against for so long. Just last month, the Air Force Chief of Staff, General Merrill McPeak, told a group of female officers, "I think it is a mistake to open up bombers and fighters to women. I have a culturally based hang-up. I can't get over this image of old men ordering young women into combat." Elaine Donnelly, president of the Center for Military Readiness in Livonia, Michigan, blasted the Administration after last week's announcement, accusing Bill Clinton of preparing "to order the nation's daughters into killing zones and rape motels which he himself avoided."

The general and the country were in fact overtaken by events. Whatever the rules may have said, 40,000 American women went to war in Operation Desert Storm as technicians, drivers, tanker and helicopter pilots and dozens of other hazardous occupations. Some were killed, some were captured, some earned Purple Hearts. "That was the defining moment for women in combat," says one of Aspin's senior aides. "All the old bugaboos were met and proved no big deal."

"Women in combat is no longer a question," says Air Force Captain Sandy Kearney, who flew a C-141 cargo plane in the gulf. "We've already been there." Other Desert Storm veterans agree that women have proved that they can operate in combat as well as men. "War is not a hormonal event," says Major Rhonda Cornum, an Army flight surgeon who was shot down, wounded and captured by the Iraqis. "It is a profession with discipline."

Although older officers still resist the idea of serving alongside women in combat, many younger male pilots thought the move was overdue. Women have long been handling difficult assignments in heavy transport planes and refueling tankers with great skill and professionalism. Navy Lieut. Michael Pocker flies helicopters along with women pilots at North Island Naval Air

Station in San Diego. "We've been doing it for eight years," Pocker remarks. "It works. The standards for men and women are the same, period.". . .

If the services still want to bar women from certain jobs, they will have to provide official explanations of why and receive special approval. The Navy is likely to try to keep women off submarines and amphibious assault craft, mainly because of privacy. Its support ships have been reconfigured to provide separate bunk space and toilets for the 8,900 women already on sea duty, but submarines and some other ships are too cramped for this to work well. Even so, the number of women at sea will double or triple.

The issue of women in combat is still not entirely resolved. Before Aspin's order went out, about half the 1.75 million slots in the armed forces were closed to the 201,000 women in uniform because they could not serve in combat units. Under the new rules, they are still ineligible for about 40% of the slots. The reason: those assignments are in "combat arms" of Army and Marine ground forces, mainly infantry, armored units and artillery. While a few slots might open up for women in missile artillery, no one is talking about putting women into tanks or foxholes. A reporter last week asked General Gordon Sullivan, the Army Chief of Staff, if he would favor women "hitting the beach." Sullivan replied, "No."

In fact very few women are calling for the chance to become a grunt. "Nobody is pressuring us on this count," says a Defense official. Women Air Force and Navy pilots are officers, eager to rise through the ranks to senior command. Combat units in the Army and Marines are made up mostly of enlisted personnel without the same opportunities. Some women do argue that any female who meets the physical requirements for combat units should be able to volunteer, but there is no sign of a ground swell. Captain Melea Riley, who commands a training battalion including both men and women at Fort Jackson, South Carolina, says, "I have never come across a woman who said she would like to be in a combat infantry unit." Cornum, the bemedaled flight surgeon now back at Fort Rucker, Alabama, confirms that, "Personally," she says, "I've never met a woman who wanted to be in the infantry."

Last week's decision does open the door to another intriguing debate—about the draft. The Supreme Court ruled in 1981 that women were excluded from registration because any reinstated draft would be intended to increase the pool of people available for combat. Now that combat planes and ships are open to women, might they be considered part of the available personnel pool in a major conflict? The Pentagon says that for now it has no plans to ask for any changes in the Selective Service system.

"The purpose of the military is not to provide jobs, promotions, and a laboratory for social experimentation; it is to deter aggression or win a war."

Women's Opportunities in the Military Are Dangerous

Elaine Donnelly and Phyllis Schlafly

In Part I of the following viewpoint, Elaine Donnelly argues that the congressional repeal of combat exclusions for women aviators in 1991 was a mistake. The decision will lead to assigning women to all combat units, she predicts, which will have negative consequences for women, the armed forces, and national defense. Donnelly is a former member of the Defense Advisory Committee on Women in the Services and an activist in the Michigan Republican Party. In Part II, Phyllis Schlafly charges that the Defense Department's May 1993 decision to go ahead with the repeal (despite a presidential commission's recommendation to the contrary) is not an advance for women but a foolish surrender to political radicals. Schlafly is a conservative writer and activist on behalf of traditional family values.

As you read, consider the following questions:

1. What motives do Donnelly and Schlafly ascribe to feminists who want combat roles for women?
2. What specific evidence do the authors offer to demonstrate that women are not fit for the combat assignments now being offered to them?

Elaine Donnelly, "What Did You Do in the Gulf, Mommy?" *National Review*, November 18, 1991, ©1991 by National Review, Inc., 150 E. 35th St., New York, NY 10016. Reprinted by permission. Phyllis Schlafly, "Public Is Deceived About Women in Combat," *Conservative Chronicle*, May 26, 1993. Reprinted with permission.

I

The Gulf War, universally abhorred by feminist ideologues, served nonetheless as a vehicle to put into practice their most cherished theories. With relentless efficiency, the Pentagon tested the hypothesis that in a unisex world, men and women are interchangeable in all occupations—that it makes no difference who does the soldiering and who does the mothering.

But the experiment was not a success. As it stretched from weeks into months, feminist theories began to crumble in the face of fundamental realities of human nature. The nation was traumatized, for example, by the sight of babies being left behind by helmeted young mothers on their way to the Gulf. Pictures of male soldiers leaving their children behind have always tugged at the heart, but there was an extra dimension of uneasiness because of the number of single mothers and of couples who were both in the service. In a *Newsweek* poll 89 per cent of respondents said they are still troubled by the idea of mothers going to war.

Then there were the sexual tensions that did not respond to bureaucratic mandates for professionalism in the workplace. In spite of Pentagon management of the news, there were many reports of illegal fraternization, genuine sexual harassment, and elevated pregnancy rates—all of which seriously affected readiness and morale.

These problems cannot be blamed on women alone, or on men as a group. Rather, they were due to unrealistic expectations for a unisex world which do not allow for human characteristics, normal emotions, and personal weaknesses.

Double Standards

When the going got rough in Saudi Arabia, feminists who wring their hands about sexual harassment in the workplace were nowhere to be found. While criticizing Middle Eastern society for not allowing women to drive cars, they ignored the plight of enlisted women who had to put up with little or no privacy in co-ed field tents, makeshift showers, unsanitary latrines, and the constant companionship of men equipped with military-issue condoms that were not intended for the women swathed in veils.

But of course feminist leaders rarely denounce conditions that they insist *other* women can endure. In 1989, Canadian Assistant Defense Minister Mary Collins reportedly commented that sexual incidents in the field may be "the price of equality" for military women.

Civilian feminists consistently make inconsistent demands in the name of military women. When it comes to co-ed field tents and mothers going to war, they insist on strict equality. But when it comes to physical requirements that are directly related

123

to the job, they insist on double standards.

During Senate hearings in June [1991] on the issue of women in combat, members of the Armed Services Committee heard a great deal of testimony about "gender-norming"—the practice of routinely scoring women's physical test results differently from men's. When I visited West Point in 1985, I noticed, for example, that a female cadet's "A" performance on the obstacle course was the same as that graded "C" for a man.

Gender-Norming

Gender-norming is designed to fudge the truth that everyone knows: on average, women are not as physically strong as men. Faced with this inconvenient truth, the Pentagon has made "adjustments" for women.

In 1982, for example, the Women in the Army (WITA) project was to match individual physical capabilities to the demands of Army jobs. But the Pentagon-based Defense Advisory Committee on Women in the Services (DACOWITS) complained that sex-neutral standards to qualify recruits were unfair because they tended to disqualify women.

Henry Payne reprinted by permission of UFS, Inc.

The Pentagon promptly gave in on the point, and downgraded the test to nothing more than a "recruiting guidance tool." The result is that a woman who doesn't meet the qualifications can still get a strenuous job. This is not the policy in Canada, where physical training standards in infantry boot camp were not lowered to accommodate women. In 1989, 101 out of 102 women failed to make the grade, so they didn't get the job.

Gender-norming, dual standards, flexible requirements, and "equivalent" training are counterproductive because they destroy the meaning of the word "qualified." In close combat all soldiers are interdependent; their lives depend on the strength, stamina, and speed of all unit members.

"Close combat" is defined as finding, closing with, and killing or capturing the enemy; it is more than the experience of being in danger. In that brutal environment, women don't have an equal opportunity to survive, or to help their fellow soldiers survive. It's not realistic to expect that for men war will be hell, but for women it will just be heck.

Legislating Equality

Congress was pondering issues like this [that] would begin the repeal of women's combat exemptions, starting with female aviators.

The Senate Armed Services Committee defeated [a repeal] amendment on an overwhelming bi-partisan vote. But the full Senate passed it in July 1991, over the objections of the chiefs of the Army, Navy, Air Force, and Marines.

Together with other military witnesses, the service chiefs had testified that repeal of the law could not be limited to female aviators only. They warned that it would be impractical and politically untenable to bar women from Navy carriers on which fighter aircraft land. And because it would be inconsistent to treat enlisted women differently from officers, it would only be a matter of time before women were assigned—on the same *involuntary* basis as men—to all fighting units, including submarines, amphibious forces, tanks, and infantry.

There was strong but generally silent opposition from enlisted women, who will have to endure the worst of this—or give up their careers—if combat exemptions are repealed. Active-duty men and women who opposed the bill could not say so publicly without risking a negative mark in their personnel files. Aggressive female officers, on the other hand, swarmed door to door in the halls of Congress, taking advantage of the reluctance of Pentagon officials to enforce regulations against lobbying by uniformed personnel. The officer-lobbyists argued that combat exemptions are a barrier to career advancement, disregarding Defense Department figures that clearly indicate *all* military women are being consistently promoted at faster rates than men.

A conference committee . . . [decided to] wait until a presidential commission determined what the financial costs and social

125

consequences would be. [The commission voted against the repeal in early 1993.] . . . Accomplished, patriotic servicewomen who serve their country well may want to consider whether it is in their best interests for the Pentagon to continue taking direction from feminist activists with an ideological axe to grind.

The sexual incidents, for example, will never be ended as long as the military pretends that men and women are emotionless, perfectly interchangeable units whose physical differences can be disguised with unisex housing and gender-norming schemes.

Nor will family and child-care problems be resolved as long as the military promises more than it can possibly deliver. Before the next war begins, a balance must be found in the three-way conflict of interest among children, their parents, and the requirements of national defense.

The purpose of the military is not to provide jobs, promotions, and a laboratory for social experimentation; it is to deter aggression or win a war with as few casualties as possible. Nothing should be done that detracts from that responsibility.

II

The Clinton administration's announcement that women will be assigned to military combat was made on the same day, May 12, 1993, that *Ms.* magazine was doing a publicity stunt called "Take your daughter to work.". . .

One of the evening TV newscasts showed a policewoman who took her daughter to work with her. In answer to the newsman's question as to what she learned, the little girl replied, "I learned that women could boss men."

Bossing men (the feminists call it "empowerment") has been a goal of the movement ever since the National Organization for Women whined in a 1973 convention resolution that "military decisions are exclusively made by male supremists."

A totally androgynous society has been a goal of the feminists ever since their top legal whiz, Professor Thomas I. Emerson, wrote in the *Yale Law Journal* in April 1971: "As between brutalizing our young men and brutalizing our young women there is little to choose."

Worlds of Difference

Most civilized Americans think there is a lot of difference between brutalizing men and women. We expect men to protect women from being brutalized by the bad guys of the world.

If feminists want to reject this protection, that's their privilege.

But the rest of American women should not be required to sacrifice this principle in order to facilitate the "career opportunities" (as Defense Secretary Les Aspin called it) of a handful of ambitious feminist officers.

Training for combat and for survival as a POW [prisoner of war] will require women to accept violence from American men as part of their training, and to accept violence from enemy men as an occupational risk.

Men and women will have to be taught to accept violence against women as no different from violence against men, and those who harbor "stereotypes" will be put through sensitivity training to purge their old-fashioned notions.

Preserving Civilization

If you are behind on causes that are politically correct, add: Women should have the right to engage in combat. If the subject has interested you at all, you will know that a presidential commission narrowly voted against women-in-combat. . . .

When actually exposed to the specific arguments [against equal military opportunity], advocates of women in combat are left with a single point. It is that if Lieutenant Jane is as good a flier as Lieutenant John—perhaps better, even—why should she not be permitted to do what John is permitted to do, namely to fly in combat? Opponents offer three arguments, though any one of these—lawyers call this "pleading in the alternative"—is sufficient.

The first argument is utilitarian: Combat duty, especially on the ground, tends to demand the final measure of strength. Women are, on the whole, about 40 per cent weaker than men.

The second argument is sociological: The fraternization that brings on an effective bond in fighting units must not be distracted, as inevitably it will be, by romance or privacy. . . .

Finally, in suggesting that the male predisposition to protect the female should be ignored, aren't we sticking our meddling little fingers into the chemistry of relationships from which much that is concededly civilized issues, for instance, the call to protect the hearth, to honor the mother and care for the child?

William F. Buckley Jr., *National Review*, April 26, 1993.

The polls show that a majority of Americans seem to buy the argument, "If women are as qualified to serve, why not?"

But women are *not* as qualified to serve, and the armed forces have been concealing this fact from the American people by double standards for men and women and by gender norming (which means rigging test scores in favor of women).

For example, male Marines are required to do 40 pull-ups within two minutes, but female Marines only do what is euphemistically called a "flexed-arm hang." A woman may get the same grade for effort that a man gets for actual performance.

Women are not allowed to fail, and men are not allowed to tell the truth about this organized deception. The armed forces practice what is called "zero tolerance" for those who dissent from this fraud.

Instead of competing against men, the women just compete against other women for designated quota slots. According to the *New York Times*, at least 10 female aviators will be "leapfrogged" over 600 male pilots who have been waiting for years for advanced training.

The argument that putting women in combat is the remedy for the Tailhook scandal is the biggest non sequitur of all time. If military women can't defend themselves against some drunks in a Las Vegas hotel, how can they protect themselves against sadistic Iraqis or Serbs?

Aspin said in his news conference that he is even instructing the Navy to "consider" putting women on submarines. It would be instructive to compare the width of the passageways on submarines with the width of the corridors in the Las Vegas hotel that the Tailhook women found they could not walk through safely.

Sidestepping the Facts

President Clinton and Aspin are ignoring the findings and recommendation of the Presidential Commission on the Assignment of Women in the Armed Forces, which concluded after a year's study that the assignment of women to combat units on land, sea and in the air would have a negative effect on combat readiness, unit cohesion and military effectiveness. The American people have the right to know *why* the commission recommended against women in combat.

It surely doesn't help morale to know that assignments are made on the basis of politics, affirmative action quotas and preferential treatment. But what else can we expect from an administration that is dominated by people who don't understand or respect the military? . . .

Assigning women to military combat goes against human nature, our culture, and centuries of experience. It's another Clinton cave-in to the radical feminists.

"Having a baby does not increase psychological distress for working women—unless the birth results in their dropping out of the labor force."

Women Can Have It All

Rosalind C. Barnett and Caryl Rivers

Addressing what they call the myth of the miserable working woman, authors Rosalind C. Barnett and Caryl Rivers argue in the following viewpoint that employed women, and especially working mothers, are happier and more emotionally satisfied than their more domestic peers. The authors maintain that full-time work actually reduces stress and increases self-esteem, allowing mothers to enjoy their families more than if they stayed at home with them all the time. Barnett is a psychologist and senior research associate at the Wellesley College Center for Research on Women. Rivers is a professor of journalism at Boston University and the author of *More Joy than Rage: Crossing Generations with the New Feminism.*

As you read, consider the following questions:

1. What are some of the ailments that working women are said to suffer from, according to Barnett and Rivers? Who is popularizing this disinformation, and what possible motives could they have, according to the authors?
2. What studies do the authors offer to disprove the notion of the unhealthy, unhappy working mother? What are the benefits of working, according to these studies?
3. What do Barnett and Rivers say are the dangers of not working?

"You Can't Do Everything," announced a 1989 *USA Today* headline on a story suggesting that a slower career track for women might be a good idea. "Mommy Career Track Sets Off a Furor," declaimed the *New York Times* on March 8, 1989, reporting that women cost companies more than men. "Pressed for Success, Women Careerists Are Cheating Themselves," sighed a 1989 headline in the *Washington Post*, going on to cite a book about the "unhappy personal lives" of woman graduates of the Harvard Business School. "Women Discovering They're at Risk for Heart Attacks," Gannett News Service reported with alarm in 1991. "Can Your Career Hurt Your Kids? Yes, Say Many Experts," blared a *Fortune* cover in May 1992, adding in a chirpy yet soothing fashion, "But smart parents—and flexible companies—won't let it happen."

Media Hype

If you believe what you read, working women are in big trouble—stressed out, depressed, sick, risking an early death from heart attacks, and so overcome with problems at home that they make inefficient employees at work.

In fact, just the opposite is true. As a research psychologist whose career has focused on women and a journalist-critic who has studied the behavior of the media, we have extensively surveyed the latest data and research and concluded that the public is being engulfed by a tidal wave of disinformation that has serious consequences for the life and health of every American woman. Since large numbers of women began moving into the work force in the 1970s, scores of studies on their emotional and physical health have painted a very clear picture: Paid employment provides substantial health *benefits* for women. These benefits cut across income and class lines; even women who are working because they have to—not because they want to—share in them.

There is a curious gap, however, between what these studies say and what is generally reported on television, radio, and in newspapers and magazines. The more the research shows work is good for women, the bleaker the media reports seem to become. Whether this bizarre state of affairs is the result of a backlash against women, as *Wall Street Journal* reporter Susan Faludi contends in her book, *Backlash: The Undeclared War Against American Women*, or of well-meaning ignorance, the effect is the same: Both the shape of national policy and the lives of women are at risk.

Too often, legislation is written and policies are drafted not on the basis of the facts but on the basis of what those in power believe to be the facts. Even the much discussed *Workforce 2000* report, issued by the Department of Labor under the Reagan administration—hardly a hotbed of feminism—admitted that "most current policies were designed for a society in which men worked and women stayed home." If policies are skewed toward solutions that are aimed at reducing women's commitment to work, they will do more than harm women—they will damage companies, managers and the productivity of the American economy.

Freedom of Choice

Women have greater opportunities than ever before for achieving economic and professional success. The opportunities are greater to define our roles as individuals and women. We have much more freedom of choice in career, mate, offspring, and lifestyle. In 1955, it would have been difficult and in many cases impossible for our mothers to become MBA's; M.D.'s; C.P.A.'s; clergy; electricians; computer technicians; dentists and newscasters.

Rosalyn Wiggins Berne, *Vital Speeches of the Day*, November 1, 1990.

One reason the "bad news" about working women jumps to page one is that we're all too willing to believe it. Many adults today grew up at a time when soldiers were returning home from World War II and a way had to be found to get the women who replaced them in industry back into the kitchen. The result was a barrage of propaganda that turned at-home moms into saints and backyard barbecues and station wagons into cultural icons. Many of us still have that outdated postwar map inside our heads, and it leaves us more willing to believe the horror stories than the good news that paid employment is an emotional and medical plus.

In the 19th century it was accepted medical dogma that women should not be educated because the brain and the ovaries could not develop at the same time. Today it's PMS, the wrong math genes or rampaging hormones. Hardly anyone points out the dire predictions that didn't come true.

You may remember the prediction that career women would start having more heart attacks, just like men. But the Framingham Heart Study—a federally funded cardiac project that has been studying 10,000 men and women since 1948—reveals that working women are not having more heart attacks. They're not dying any earlier, either. Not only are women not losing their health advantages; the lifespan gap is actually widening. Only one group of working women suffers more heart attacks than other women: those in low-paying clerical jobs with many demands on them and little control over their work pace, who also have several children and little or no support at home.

As for the publicity about women having more problems with

heart disease, much of it skims over the important underlying reasons for the increase: namely, that by the time they have a heart attack, women tend to be a good deal older (an average of 67, six years older than the average age for men), and thus frailer, than males who have one. Also, statistics from the National Institutes of Health show that coronary symptoms are treated less aggressively in women—fewer coronary bypasses, for example. In addition, most heart research is done on men, so doctors do not know as much about the causes—and treatment—of heart disease in women. None of these factors have anything to do with work.

Work Equals Health

But doesn't working put women at greater risk for stress-related illnesses? No. Paid work is actually associated with *reduced* anxiety and depression. In the early 1980s we reported in our book, *Lifeprints* (based on a National Science Foundation-funded study of 300 women), that working women were significantly higher in psychological well-being than those not employed. Working gave them a sense of mastery and control that homemaking didn't provide. More recent studies echo our findings. For example:

• A 1989 report by psychologist Ingrid Waldron and sociologist Jerry Jacobs of Temple University on nationwide surveys of 2,392 white and 892 black women, conducted from 1977 to 1982, found that women who held both work and family roles reported better physical and mental health than homemakers.

• According to sociologists Elaine Wethington of Cornell University and Ronald Kessler of the University of Michigan, data from three years (1985 to 1988) of a continuing federally funded study of 745 married women in Detroit "clearly suggests that employment benefits women emotionally." Women who increase their participation in the labor force report lower levels of psychological distress; those who lessen their commitment to work suffer from higher distress.

• A University of California at Berkeley study published in 1990 followed 140 women for 22 years. At age 43, those who were homemakers had more chronic conditions than the working women and seemed more disillusioned and frustrated. The working mothers were in good health and seemed to be juggling their roles with success.

In sum, paid work offers women heightened self-esteem and enhanced mental and physical health. It's unemployment that's a major risk factor for depression in women.

This isn't true only for affluent women in good jobs; working-class women share the benefits of work, according to psychologists Sandra Scarr and Deborah Phillips of the University of Virginia and Kathleen McCartney of the University of New

Hampshire. In reviewing 80 studies on this subject, they reported that working-class women with children say they would not leave work even if they didn't need the money. Work offers not only income but adult companionship, social contact and a connection with the wider world that they cannot get at home. . . .

How Families Benefit

What about the kids? Many working parents feel they want more time with their kids, and they say so. But does maternal employment harm children? In 1989 University of Michigan psychologist Lois Hoffman reviewed 50 years of research and found that the expected negative effects never materialized. Most often, children of employed and unemployed mothers didn't differ on measures of child development. But children of both sexes with working mothers have a less sex-stereotyped view of the world because fathers in two-income families tend to do more child care. . . .

What's more, children in two-job families generally don't lose out on one-to-one time with their parents. New studies, such as S.L. Nock and P.W. Kingston's *Time with Children: The Impact of Couples' Work-Time Commitments*, show that when both parents of preschoolers are working, they spend as much time in direct interaction with their children as families in which only the fathers work. The difference is that working parents spend more time with their kids on weekends. When only the husband works, parents spend more leisure time with each other. There is a cost to two-income families—the couples lose personal time—but the kids don't seem to pay it.

One question we never used to ask is whether having a working mother could be *good* for children. Hoffman, reflecting on the finding that employed women—both blue-collar and professional—register higher life-satisfaction scores than housewives, thinks it can be. She cites studies involving infants and older children, showing that a mother's satisfaction with her employment status relates positively both to "the quality of the mother-child interaction and to various indexes of the child's adjustment and abilities." For example, psychologists J. Guidubaldi and B. K. Nastasi of Kent State University reported in a 1987 paper that a mother's satisfaction with her job was a good predictor of her child's positive adjustment in school.

Again, this isn't true only for women in high-status jobs. In a 1982 study of sources of stress for children in low-income families, psychologists Cynthia Longfellow and Deborah Belle of the Harvard University School of Education found that employed women were generally less depressed than unemployed women. What's more, their children had fewer behavioral problems.

But the real point about working women and children is that

work *isn't* the point at all. There are good mothers and not-so-good mothers, and some work and some don't. When a National Academy of Sciences panel reviewed the previous 50 years of research and dozens of studies in 1982, it found no consistent effects on children from a mother's working. Work is only one of many variables, the panel concluded in *Families That Work*, and not the definitive one.

What is the effect of women's working on their marriages? Having a working wife can increase psychological stress for men, especially older men, who grew up in a world where it was not normal for a wife to work. But men's expectations that they will—and must—be the only provider may be changing. Wethington and Kessler found that a wife's employment could be a significant buffer *against* depression for men born after 1945. Still, the picture of men's psychological well-being is very mixed, and class and expectations clearly play a role. Faludi cites polls showing that young blue-collar men are especially angry at women for invading what they see as their turf as breadwinners, even though a woman with such a job could help protect her husband from economic hardship. But in highly educated, dual-career couples, both partners say the wife's career has enhanced the marriage.

The First Shift

While women's own health and the well-being of their families aren't harmed by their working, what effect does this dual role have on their job performance? It's assumed that men can compartmentalize work and home lives but women will bring their home worries with them to work, making them distracted and inefficient employees.

The only spillover went in the other direction: The women brought their good feelings about their work home with them and left a bad day at home behind when they came to work. In fact, Wethington and Kessler found that it was the *men* who brought the family stresses with them to work. "Women are able to avoid bringing the contagion of home stress into the workplace," the researchers write, "whereas the inability of men to prevent this kind of contagion is pervasive." The researchers speculate that perhaps women get the message early on that they can handle the home front, while men are taking on chores they aren't trained for and didn't expect.

Perhaps the most dangerous myth is that the solution to most problems women suffer is for them to drop back—or drop out. What studies actually show is a significant connection between a reduced commitment to work and increased psychological stress. In their Detroit study, Wethington and Kessler noted that women who went from being full-time employees to full-time housewives reported increased symptoms of distress, such as depression and anxiety attacks; the longer a woman worked and the more committed she was to the job, the greater her risk for psychological distress when she stopped.

What about part-time work, that oft-touted solution for weary women? Women who work fewer than 20 hours per week, it turns out, do not get the mental-health work benefit, probably because they "operate under the fiction that they can retain full responsibility for child care and home maintenance," wrote Wethington and Kessler. The result: Some part-timers wind up more stressed-out than women working full-time. Part-time employment also provides less money, fewer or no benefits and, often, less interesting work and a more arduous road to promotion.

That doesn't mean that a woman shouldn't cut down on her work hours or arrange a more flexible schedule. But it does mean she should be careful about jumping on a poorly designed mommy track that may make her a second-class citizen at work.

Don't Be Fooled

Many women think that when they have a baby, the best thing for their mental health would be to stay home. Wrong once more. According to Wethington and Kessler, having a baby does not increase psychological distress for working women—*unless* the birth results in their dropping out of the labor force. This doesn't mean that any woman who stays home to care for a child is going to be a wreck. But leaving the work force means opting out of the benefits of being in it, and women should be aware of that.

As soon as a woman has any kind of difficulty—emotional, family, medical—the knee-jerk reaction is to get her off the job. . . .

Women don't need help getting out of the work force; they need help staying in it.

"The message was that you have to give up so much to have children . . . [but] what is ignored is how much you have to give up when you have a job."

Women Cannot Have It All

Nancy Pearcey

Much to the surprise of the daughters of modern feminism, stay-at-home motherhood is enjoying a resurgence, declares Nancy Pearcey, author of the following viewpoint. She reports that career women—many of whom delayed childbearing as they pursued professional goals—are finding the experience of raising their children at home to be much more enjoyable and emotionally fulfilling than their old ideal of balancing job and family. Pearcey is a science and social issues writer based in Washington, D.C.

As you read, consider the following questions:

1. According to Pearcey, who gave motherhood a bad reputation? Which segment of the population does the author say is becoming more involved with motherhood? What accounts for this switch?
2. Is the decision to stay home with the children a permanent one, according to the author?
3. What lessons does Pearcey say today's new mothers are learning about themselves?

Nancy Pearcey, "Rediscovering Motherhood." This article appeared in the May 1991 issue and is reprinted with permission from *The World & I*, a publication of The Washington Times Corporation, copyright ©1991.

The number of births in America in 1990 jumped to four million, the first time that annual figure had been reached since the end of the postwar Baby Boom, reports the National Center of Health Statistics. Birth rates had already been rising among women over thirty as this group seeks to make up for postponed childbearing. But the increase in the number of births may indicate that more women in their twenties are having children as well, reports the *Washington Post*. Motherhood is becoming popular again.

Many of today's new mothers were raised in a feminist era, when the implicit assumption, especially among educated women, was that motherhood is a trap and that true fulfillment is possible only through a career. The careerism common among men in the fifties spread to women in the sixties. Having babies was at best something done on the side, during leisure hours.

Women raised in such a social climate often entered energetically into careers and put any idea of having a family on hold. It was only after several years on the fast track that they began to feel a nagging sense that something was missing. Having "made it" at work, which they had been led to regard as the most significant arena of accomplishment, many of these women are puzzled by their desire to have children—and are nothing less than astonished at the actual experience of having them.

Surprised Mothers

Hobnob with new mothers for a time and you are likely to hear musing such as "I had no idea that having a baby would be so much fun" and "I was completely surprised by the intensity of the emotional bond I have with my baby." Surprise at the joy of motherhood is a novel phenomenon. In virtually all cultures and at all times, the birth of a baby has been regarded as an occasion for rejoicing. In her book *Mothering: The Emotional Experience of Motherhood after Freud and Feminism,* Elaine Heffner says there is nothing new about women's feeling the desire to have and raise children. "What is new," she remarks, "is the number of women who are startled by such feelings."

Lonna Wilkinson is a dancer and choreographer who had her first child at age thirty-eight. "For women of my generation," she says, "motherhood really got a bum rap. None of us were going to be *mothers,* for goodness' sake—there were more important things to do."

Eileen Bakke, English teacher and mother of three, takes up the same story: "Women of our age were taught to define ourselves by our accomplishments," she says. "But as we got into our thirties, we began to say, 'This isn't all it was cracked up to be. What I really want to do is invest myself in lasting, loving relationships. What I want is a family.'"

137

Initially many women supposed that family life could simply be tacked onto a vigorous career life. Karla Harris is a fund-raiser who had her first child at age thirty-four. "I thought I could do it all—hold a good job, keep a clean house, go to the health club regularly, and still mother my child adequately," she says. "But when I actually had my baby, I found I couldn't. I wasn't doing any of them well."

The Work/Family Conflict

One of the initial surprises in becoming a mother is the realization that you can't have it all after all. As Bakke puts it, "In college, there was all this emphasis on 'You can be everything a man can be.' But there was no discussion of how to fit job and family together. A lot of women were caught by surprise when they realized that you can't just keep adding things into your life without there being some give somewhere—some giving up."

Stephanie Wood worked with retarded children until she had her first child at age thirty-one. "I feel feminism sold us a bill of goods," she says. "The message was that you have to give up so much to have children and that the only way to be fulfilled is to have a job. What is ignored is how much you have to give up when you have a job. In order to get ahead, you have to put yourself on the back burner and do everything the way the company or the client wants it done. You have to push aside your spouse, your family, your outside interests."

Eventually women like Wood decided they were unwilling to continue relegating their personal lives to the left-over time from work. Having children is a major psychological event in a woman's life, and women want to treat it like one.

Motherhood Wins Out

Carlie Dixon was thirty-five when her first child was born. At the time, she had practiced law for nine years and was a partner in a Washington, D.C., law firm. She fully intended to return to work after the birth of her child. "It was just assumed," Dixon says, "that if you were a career woman, if you had gone to professional school and put in long hours on the job and finally made it to partner, you weren't going to give all that up."

Dixon confesses that she had a "completely unrealistic view of what it means to be a mother." Her conception of having a baby was that it was "like getting a new pet—that they're relatively easy to take care of, they sleep a lot, it's painless to hand them over to others to take care of all day, and you're still free to continue living your life on your own terms."

As a result, Dixon says, "I was completely unprepared for the emotional attachment I would have with this child. I didn't realize how much I would want to spend time with him. Here I was, highly educated, thirty-five years old, highly successful in the business world, and about one of the most basic experiences in human life I knew nothing. I felt there was this big secret that nobody had told me."

"A love affair" is how Cathy Dwiggins, a clinical specialist in child and adolescent psychiatric nursing who adopted a child at age thirty-eight, describes motherhood. "You never love someone in quite the same way because no one is dependent on you in the same way," she says. "It's scary. You sense that you are very vulnerable because you know it would be devastating if anything happened to your child."

A House Divided

There is literally no peace (and I challenge any employed mother to say upon her honor that I'm wrong) in a house where the mother has a full-time outside job. Her anxieties see to that. If Baby is happy, she tortures herself with the conviction that he loves his nanny more than her. If he's fretful and insecure, she is wounded to the heart by the feeling that she is neglecting him. . . .

At this point, she may resort to broad hints and invidious suggestions (I held various jobs as nannies and mother's helpers during college; I was once asked to keep a daily record of the amount of time I spent changing diapers, feeding, and "interacting" with my charge), which infuriates the nanny, and plunges the household still further into tension. . . .

Sooner or later the nanny quits, or is fired, and the family starts the whole process over again with a new one. And all the while, if you asked this harassed and exhausted woman why she insisted on having outside employment, she would tell you with a perfectly straight face that her career was essential to her self-image and fulfillment. Gee, sounds great.

Kathleen Wagner, *Fidelity*, April 1992.

Clinical psychologist Brenda Hunter describes the intensity of the parent-infant bond in these words: "When a woman has a baby, she is emotionally vulnerable. She has a rush of feelings for this tiny, dependent person, feelings that she never expected to have. Many of the women I work with are not prepared for the overwhelming feelings that maternity draws out." For the past twenty-five years, Hunter explains, "our culture has stressed careerism for women and has treated motherhood as an extracurricular activity. When a baby is actually placed in a new mother's arms, the mother is taken completely off guard by the intensity of the experience."

Alongside the euphoria of falling in love comes the unprecedented responsibility of caring for a dependent infant. As a teacher, Bakke knew how children act and think, and she felt well prepared for motherhood. Yet the actual experience of it went well beyond her expectations. "You are still not prepared for the twenty-four-hour responsibility," she says. "That was the biggest surprise for me: the constant, around-the-clock, seven-days-a-week commitment to this new human being. Life does not just go on as before."

Dwiggins describes motherhood as "the hardest, most stressful work I have ever done. It's very demanding. You simply don't live for yourself anymore. Your life is dominated by this tiny person because his needs are so imperative. If a child cries in the middle of the night, you have to get up and see what's wrong. It pulls you out of yourself as nothing else does."

Motherhood has been given bad press in recent years because of the depth of self-giving it requires. Yet, ironically, many women cite precisely that as one of the benefits of mothering. Debby Beisner, portrait painter and mother of four, says having children taught her "how insulated and self-centered I am. It's been good for me to be taken out of myself and learn to care for others." Bakke concurs: "What I love about parenting is that it's made me develop patience and the capacity for selfless giving. I think that's growing up."

Social Pressure

The common stereotype is that motherhood means suppressing one's interests and talents. But contemporary women are rediscovering that being a mother can be a catalyst for developing new interests and new talents. As Karla Harris puts it, "Books like *The Feminine Mystique* made everyone feel you were a martyr to stay home and raise children, that you did it because you were supposed to, not because you enjoyed it—that it was a chore, not a choice. That's not the way it is. I'm home raising my child because I want to."

If the social pressure on mothers a generation ago was to stay home, the social pressure today is to keep working. After having her baby, recalls Harris, "everyone kept saying to me 'When are you going back to work? What about *you* and *your* life?'" Her answer is "This *is* for me. I'm doing this as much for me as for my children."

Much psychological ink has been spent on the growth and development of children. But little has been written on the growth and development of women as mothers. If you ask mothers what changes they see in themselves since having children, they speak eloquently of gains they have made in self-knowledge, confidence, and maturity.

For Wilkinson, "motherhood has been very liberating. When you're in a career, there are certain expectations and requirements that you have to fulfill. You develop a sort of professional persona. Having a child made me more spontaneous. It's brought me in touch with myself in a new way."

Margaret Hilton, who worked for a labor union until she had her first child at age thirty-four, reports a similar experience: "Children's emotions are raw, close to the surface. They don't have the polite exterior we're used to in interacting with adults. You pick children up and hug them, and on the other hand you get so angry with them." As a result, says Hilton, "I'm much more aware of my own emotions now—the good and the bad."

Parenthood can be a time for self-evaluation. As Dixon says, "The challenge of teaching a child good habits and attitudes has inspired a lot of self-examination—looking at how I was raised and deciding what things I want to pass on." Ruth Henderson, mother of four, puts it this way: "Being a mother has made me so much more scrupulous to maintain integrity in my lifestyle because I am aware that I am a model for my children. Your life is an open book, and they're reading it."

Parenthood can also be a time for healing old wounds and broken relationships. It is a maxim in psychoanalytic literature that the birth of a child evokes memories of one's own childhood. *The Joys and Sorrows of Parenthood*, published by the Group for the Advancement of Psychiatry, explains: "In the process of learning to be a mother, a woman reexperiences what happened to her when she was being mothered. . . . In each period of the child's growth, parents rework what happened to them many years ago." Because of this, motherhood can be what Hunter calls "a healing time"—a time for facing both the joyful and the painful feelings hanging on from one's own childhood.

Today's Woman

Mothers of the fifties were the first women to have both smaller families and longer life spans, which means they were the first to have several years of life after their children had grown up. Many were not well prepared to fill those years with productive work; nor was society prepared to reaccept them into the public arena, in terms of offering them educational opportunities and responsible positions in the workplace. Daughters who saw their mothers face decades of the "empty-nest syndrome" without any marketable skills were determined that they would not repeat the same experience. Young women earned their degrees and developed marketable skills *before* they dared to have children.

Now the tide has turned. Today women in their twenties are reading articles about time running out on their elder sisters; twentysomething women are worried that if they wait too long they may not find a husband or be able to have children. They're afraid of the biological clock running out. Many are choosing to have their families first and put off careers until later. They seem less fearful that if they don't get on the career track early they will never have the chance again. Instead, they expect to be able to take courses and work up to a career gradually while their children are growing up.

Biologically, it makes more sense for a woman to have her children while she's young and physically energetic, and then to use the rest of her life for a career. As Harris puts it, "You have the energy to be up all night when you're twenty-five. You don't when you're thirty-five." Moreover, taking time to raise a family no longer eliminates the opportunity for meaningful work later on. Mothers reentering the work force are proving to employers that raising children and running a home are demanding responsibilities that produce skills transferable to the marketplace. As Harris says, "I'm much better prepared to go back into the work force because of raising children. I've gained personal assets that will be very valuable to any future employer—maturity, patience, organizational skills, personal interaction skills, a long-term perspective."

What we are seeing is an adjustment on all sides to the reality that, because of longer life spans, child-rearing is becoming a stage of adult life, not its entirety. It is a time when parents perform a valuable function for society in giving the next generation a secure start on life, and they deserve social esteem for doing it. It is also a time that offers unique satisfactions. A 1989 survey by the Roper Organization found that the percentage of women who described having children as "very satisfying" was 66 percent, compared with 35 percent who described their jobs in the same terms. After decades of getting a "bum rap," to use Lonna Wilkinson's phrase, it appears that motherhood is coming back into its own as a positive, life-changing, and intrinsic part of a woman's life.

Periodical Bibliography

The following articles have been selected to supplement the diverse views presented in this chapter.

John L. Adams — "Juggling Job and Family: Making It Work at Work," *Vital Speeches of the Day*, December 1, 1993.

Barbara Ehrenreich — "Why Women Finally Are Winning," *Time*, June 22, 1992.

Deirdre English — "Through the Glass Ceiling," *Mother Jones*, November/December 1992.

Susan Faludi — "Looking Beyond the Slogans," *Newsweek*, December 28, 1992.

Dawn Gibeau — "Women in Theology: It's No Longer a Man's World," *The National Catholic Reporter*, April 24, 1992.

Glamour — "Women at War: Letters from the Gulf," June 1991.

Michele Ingrassia et al. — "Daughters of Murphy Brown," *Newsweek*, August 2, 1993.

R. Cort Kirkwood — "Life on the Front Lines: The Presidential Commission on Women in the Military," *Chronicles*, March 1994. Available from 434 N. Main St., Rockford, IL 61103.

Richard Miniter — "Women's Successes Smash Business Myths," *Insight*, February 21, 1994. Available from 3600 New York Ave. NE, Washington, DC 20002.

Karen Moderow — "Choosing Home," *Moody*, February 1994.

Elena Neuman — "More Moms Are Homeward Bound," *Insight*, January 10, 1992.

Priscilla Painton — "The Maternal Wall," *Time*, May 10, 1993.

Leon J. Podles — "Men Not Wanted: A Controversial Protest Against the Feminization of the Church," *Crisis*, November 1991. Available from PO Box 1006, Notre Dame, IN 46556.

Dan Quayle — "Murphy Brown Revisited," *The Washington Post National Weekly Edition*, December 20-26, 1993.

Maggie Ross — "The Anglican Ordination of Women: Asking the Wrong Questions," *Creation Spirituality*, November/December 1993. Available from PO Box 19216, Oakland, CA 94619.

Amy Saltzman — "Trouble at the Top," *U.S. News & World Report*, June 17, 1991.

James P. Scanlan — "The Curious Case of Affirmative Action for Women," *Society*, January/February 1992.

Felice N. Schwartz — "Women As a Business Imperative," *Harvard Business Review*, March/April 1992.

Have Men's Roles Changed for the Better?

MALE/ FEMALE ROLES

Chapter Preface

"In the . . . dancing and drumming by firelight, in the third-degree agony of squatting alongside red-glowing rocks in the stifling darkness [of a sweat lodge], he felt himself cleansed and reborn." This excerpt from the *Newsweek* cover story of June 24, 1991, describes a typical experience inside the "men's movement." Since the early 1990s, this movement has grown beyond the men's group retreats *Newsweek* described to include a variety of books, conventions, and other mainstream methods of helping men to bring out and deal with their usually hidden—and often painful—emotions. As *Newsweek* put it, men have become the latest of "American culture's sanctioned grievance carriers." So where did this outpouring of masculine grief come from?

Perhaps no one could better answer that question than Warren Farrell, a feminist writer and leader of the 1970s who later began to focus on those people who he felt were left out by the women's movement: men. In his book *The Myth of Male Power: Why Men Are the Disposable Sex*, Farrell argues that feminism achieved many necessary things but damaged men's lives in the process. "Men condemned . . . 'discriminations against women,'" Farrell says, "even as they accepted the necessity of discrimination against men" in the form of affirmative action for women and various government programs supporting women only. Taxpaying men still fulfill all the duties for women they did in the 1950s, Farrell maintains, but reap none of the rewards since their "liberated" wives have left them to "marry" the government.

Susan Faludi, author of the book *Backlash: The Undeclared War Against Women*, has a different interpretation of the current male focus. Throughout American history, Faludi writes in *Backlash*, men have become obsessed with their own masculinity whenever they perceived "efforts by contemporary women to improve their status." The result, Faludi says, is always a cultural backlash "that stops women long before they reach the finish line [of full equality]." A study by the Business and Professional Women's Foundation similarly finds that resistance to the entry of women in the workplace remains fairly low until their participation rate reaches about 15 percent, at which point outright discrimination begins.

Both interpretations of the new male-oriented discourse share one thing in common, however: They both credit feminism as the starting point for the men's movement. As Farrell explains, men, like women, are in the process of restructuring themselves. What the "new man" might look like is argued in this chapter.

1 VIEWPOINT

"[There is] a new awareness men have for their concerns: one that shares with other men, that does not follow traditional go-it-alone pathways."

Men's Lives Are Changing for the Better

Sam Julty

Feminism may have been primarily a women's movement, but men too are reaping the benefits of the continuing realignment of gender roles. That is the conclusion of many of those who, like Sam Julty, author of the following viewpoint, make up the pro-feminist branch of the men's movement. Julty argues that although the men's movement is something of a misnomer—since it is much smaller and less politically organized than its predecessor, the women's movement—its usefulness in redefining masculinity for and ending the isolation of some men could be harnessed to improve the lives of all men. Already, the author claims, some men are breaking down the barriers that separated them from one another and from the larger society. Julty, who founded and directed the Center for Men's Studies in Berkeley, California, was a prominent men's issues writer and the author of *Men's Bodies, Men's Selves*.

As you read, consider the following questions:

1. How does Julty define a movement? What does he say caused the rise of the feminist movement in the 1960s and 1970s?
2. What does Julty say was the impact of the women's movement on men?
3. What evidence does the author offer to show that men are "on the move"?

From "Men on the Move" by Sam Julty, *Changing Men*, Winter/Spring 1991. Reprinted with permission.

There are times when we are so busy detailing the deliberate ways men must change that we lose sight of the subtle ways they already have changed. Though men have always been a diverse population group, the one segment more visible than others was the rough and tough who often set the standard for what "real" men should be. Today, that standard is no longer the only yardstick by which men can be measured. Different types of men are now clearly visible. In poetic terms, poets now mingle more freely with hunters.

Another area of change not often appreciated concerns the growing number of fathers involved with the *daily* care and nurturing of their children. Of course I realize studies show that many women say more men need to spend even more hours sharing childcare chores. But this fact remains: more men are involved with childcare today than two or three decades before. From a historical perspective, this tells me that the insidious barrier between father and child, erected at the onset of the factory system 150 years ago, is now wearing thin.

All of us know that the changing roles of women have had their effects on men, but we seldom look at the ways those changes have affected men in different age groups. My observations lead me to generalize that most men under age 40 are influenced strongly by the new value systems concerning their manhood, causing many of them to structure their lives accordingly. On the other hand, most men over age 40 are influenced and conflicted by new and old value systems, which allow changes to be demanded of them rather than originating with them. Men in both age groups, however, share a similar affinity: they continue to be used as purveyors of sexist ideology.

Is There a Men's Movement?

As we continue our involvement with different men's issues, it is important to be sure who we really are. In a number of articles in *Changing Men* [a magazine covering antisexism and other issues concerning men today], its writers like to use the term "men's movement." Though it does have a glorious ring to it, saying we are in a movement falls short of accuracy. At best, it's a fantasy wish; at worst, it's a misrepresentation.

Perhaps the term is used carelessly because there is a failure to understand what a political movement really is. Simply put, it's a *temporary alliance* of *diverse* groups making *limited* demands. If you study the abolitionists or the suffragists of the past, and the civil rights, peace and feminist movements of recent times, you will find that each earned its appellation as a movement only after several like-minded groups *united* around one or two major issues and challenged their adversaries.

To those who insist we are in a men's movement I ask: when

has any men's organization allied itself with any other to make a specific demand of any power structure on behalf of men? It hasn't happened—yet. Until it does, we cannot call ourselves a movement. If we must define what we are, it would be more accurate to say that each of today's men's organizations is an advocacy group.

Advocacy groups can mature into a political movement when their collective demands are relevant to a historical need. . . .

The historical needs that prompted the rise of the feminist movement in the 1960s are a contemporary example of how political/social movements harmonize with historical needs. As ev-

---

Redefining Male Power

A large number of men are discovering a new kind of power, the kind that is expressed in having a wonderful circle of intimates and feeling secure because of it, the power that derives from knowing one is living according to one's principles even if that means one does not accumulate all one might, the kind that comes from sharing the burden with others one can respect as equals. In a community of equals a new kind of power can be realized, not the kind where a man stands alone and conquers real and imagined enemies; rather, a man would be able to discuss problems with a network of sympathetic people who might help him devise a collaborative strategy for solving a large array of problems and coping with a variety of threats. When I see men at gatherings celebrating their newfound sense of brotherhood and the relief they feel that they are not as totally alone in the universe as they once felt they were, I know I am part of something that is very powerful and I feel powerful being a part.

Once men begin to expand upon what Kenneth Boulding terms their *integrative power*, a whole set of connections become obvious. Men who are attuned to the plight of others are not able to ignore sexual harassment at work, homelessness, racism, drastic cutbacks in social welfare programs, inattention to the plight of AIDS sufferers, ecological disasters such as the destruction of the rain forests and the ozone layer, and the threat of war and nuclear annihilation.

Men who get in touch with their feminine side, and begin to value their role as father, friend, and team player, need not give away their power in the public arena. In fact, by working collaboratively with others who share a vision of better gender relations, men will discover a whole new level of power. And, by their example, they will begin to redefine masculinity as well as power.

Terry A. Kupers, *Revisioning Men's Lives: Gender, Intimacy, and Power*, 1993.

---

eryone knows, there have been women's advocacy groups in this country since its early days, even a movement that fought for and won the right to vote for women. None, however, succeeded in creating as many legal and social changes witnessed these past 25 years as did the feminist movement. To understand what made this effort different from the others we have to take a wide look at what was happening in the 1960s and 1970s.

Our national economy was in the midst of a series of significant changes. We shifted from being the leading creditor nation to being the leading debtor nation. Add to that the growing presence of computers and automation in a workplace that was steadily shifting its base away from manufacturing toward service, in a marketplace that was now competing internationally. To thrive in this new environment, investors sought to lower operating costs.

Computers and automated machinery eroded the base of the blue-collar job market from a mix of skilled, semiskilled and unskilled workers to a mix of semi-skilled and unskilled. The base of the office job market expanded to include workers with limited or marginal skills. To assure lower labor costs most of the new non-union jobs were offered to women at low pay rates.

As the presence of women in the workplace enlarged, a dichotomy emerged. On the one hand, women were working at jobs, earning money, supporting themselves or contributing to the support of a family. On the other, women were expected to remain subservient to masculine authority on the job and by extension in other areas of their lives. Like all contradictions, this one couldn't endure for long without protest. It did not take long before singular disappointments by women merged with multiple resentments, which propelled alliances to seek social remedies. The rest is history.

Men on the Move

Though there is no men's movement, I believe there is movement among men that indicates some elevated degree of social consciousness. For instance, the concerned way many men reacted to the horrible shooting of 14 women students [by a young man who blamed women for his rejected application to the school] in Montreal, Canada, in the winter of 1989. For an entire week after the event, men in the U.S. and Canada wrote letters to newspapers and called radio talk-programs to express their feelings about this tragedy, what men must learn from it and the ways sexism is linked to violence against women. Another example of movement among men is the continued growth of the number of men's support groups, especially among middle-aged and older men. Recently, I spoke to a group of men at a local Senior Center on ways they can form a support group. I learned that there were such groups in over a dozen Senior Centers in the area. Subsequently I learned that there were men's support groups at union halls and at aid centers for homeless men. It is interesting to note that many of them do not use the term "men's support group." The accepted euphemism is "men's discussion group." That tells me that men who attend these groups welcome a safe forum at which they can air their feelings and share their thoughts, but hesitate to admit the need for support from other men.

Another significant area of movement is the continued growth of different men's advocacy organizations and publications. Though some may focus on issues unimportant to others, and some are not as "politically correct" as others would like them to be, this growth tells us men are gathering to deal with specific issues affecting them as men.

Linking Together

Though some may say the increased number of men's support groups and men's organizations are nothing more than new examples of so-called "male bonding," serving a negative outcome, I believe they represent a new awareness men have for their concerns: one that shares with other men, that does not follow traditional go-it-alone pathways. On another level I can see increased opportunities for different men's groups to link together to make collective demands for men.

In the 1930s the new industrial trade unions thrived by the slogan "An injury to one is an injury to all." That not only provided support for members within a union, but extended the hand of solidarity to members of other unions and to workers who were not in unions. I believe it is time we men begin to embrace that concept concerning groups of men who need a hand.

Are we not aware that 95% of all people with AIDS are men and boys? Are we not moved by the fact that over 80% of all the homeless are men? If we, the pro-active men, can put some energy into finding ways to enable different, and differing, men's groups to work together to extend a helping hand to men who could use one, we would be going a long way toward putting our energies where our mouths now are. . . .

Perhaps some readers may say the developments I cite are trivial, that some of my assessments are off-base or that this may not be the right time for men's organizations to reach out. If so, I welcome their comments. While I do not consider any of the changes I mentioned as harbingers of an earth-shaking social revolution by men, I remain firm in my belief that these and other changes need to be acknowledged, assessed and perhaps understood when we write about, talk about and work with today's men.

"People who succeed monetarily and spiritually *don't think of men as being the sex that has the power as much as being the sex most willing to pay the price of power."*

Men's Lives Are Changing for the Worse

Warren Farrell

In the following viewpoint, excerpted from his book *The Myth of Male Power,* Warren Farrell asserts that men's lives are undergoing a change for the worse—a change that, he says, is a direct result of feminism. In its bid to secure employment for women, feminism influenced government to pass quotas, which took jobs away from men, Farrell maintains; and in its efforts to provide governmental support to women and their children, he argues, feminism not only excluded the now unimportant male from his family but also impoverished him through taxes that were raised to pay for this new subsidy. Farrell, a well-known writer on men's issues, was a feminist leader in the 1970s who later became disenchanted with the movement.

As you read, consider the following questions:

1. What kind of relationship does Farrell say women have with the government? How does he support his belief that this relationship exists?
2. Why does the author believe that a woman's "right to choose" her lifestyle can lead to a man's earlier death?
3. How do men succeed, according to Farrell? How does this compare with the way that Farrell says women succeed?

TRUE OR FALSE? Employers are prohibited from practicing sex discrimination in hiring and promoting employees.

ANSWER: False. The U.S. Supreme Court ruled in 1987 that in job areas dominated by men, *less* qualified women could be hired. It did not allow less qualified men to be hired in areas dominated by women (e.g., elementary school teacher, nurse, secretary, cocktail waiting, restaurant host, office receptionist, flight attendant). The law also *requires* sex discrimination in hiring by requiring quotas, requiring vigorous recruitment of women, and requiring all institutions that receive government aid to do a certain percentage of their business with female-owned (or minority-owned) businesses.

When an employer hires a woman today, he or she might be required to finance her pregnancy (the Federal Pregnancy Discrimination Act [which treats pregnancy as a compensable disability]), feel pressured to finance maternity leaves and get into the child-care business (incurring new real estate costs, higher insurance premiums, and the costs of hiring teachers and administrators for her children).

The Government as Substitute Husband did for women what labor unions still have not accomplished for men. And men pay dues for labor unions; the taxpayer pays the dues for feminism. Feminism and government soon became taxpayer-supported women's unions.

Female-Only Clubs

Hundreds of federal programs subsidize "female-only clubs": clubs such as the "Women, Infants, and Children Club" (called the WIC program) but no "Men, Infants, and Children Club." Federal and state money subsidizes more than 15,000 women's studies courses versus 91 men's studies courses. Almost every state government uses taxpayer money to form Women's Divisions with no parallel Men's Divisions.

Feminist ideology, initially opposed to male-only clubs in the areas of male dominance, soon supported female-only clubs in areas of female dominance. Money to men was seen as taking money away from women. So while the Office of Family Planning initially provided family planning services for both sexes, by 1982, it provided money *only* for *female* clients. This attitude pushed men out of the family. While male-only clubs in areas of male dominance were being declared illegal, female-only clubs in areas of female dominance were being subsidized. . . .

All this creates a huge taxpayer subsidy to look at virtually every aspect of life from the perspective of women as defined by feminism. Feminist ideology was soon called women's studies and the women's studies graduates called their ideology education. As thousands of women's jobs became dependent on a feminist perspective, feminism bureaucratized. Like communism, feminism went from being revolutionary to dictating politically correct ideology. And, like communism, this political correctness was supported most strongly in the universities.

Politically Wooing Women

The political parties have become like two parents in a custody battle, each vying for their daughter's love by promising to do the most for her. . . .

Asay, by permission of the *Colorado Springs Gazette Telegraph*.

Ironically, when political parties or parents compete for females' love by competing to give to it, the result is not gratitude but entitlement. . . . But here's the rub. When the entitled child has the majority of the votes, the issue is no longer whether we have a patriarchy or a matriarchy—we get a victimarchy. And the female-as-child *genuinely* feels like a victim because she never learns how to obtain for herself everything she learns to expect. Well, she learns how to obtain it for herself by saying "it's a woman's right"—but she doesn't feel the mastery that comes with a lifetime of doing it for herself. And even when a quota includes her in the decision-making process, she still feels angry at the "male-dominated government" because she feels both the condescension of being given "equality" and the contradiction of being given equality. She is still "the other." So, with the majority of the votes, she is both controlling the system and angry at the system.

While both parties are needy of the female vote, the Democratic party cannot live without it. So the Democratic party, in particular, keeps its child a child because it fears losing her. And the female in transition who wants the option of independence without losing the option of government as substitute protector keeps voting to keep its protector protecting.

In the meantime, many men's alienation from the Democratic party makes that party even more female dependent. As one voter, Eric D. Sherman, put it:

> My family and I are voters of the "traditional Democratic constituency" who have just become Republicans.
>
> The Democratic party . . . has consistently:
>
> —favored discrimination against men in employment, university admissions, divorce, and child custody.
>
> —supported absurd laws (such as those on "marital rape" and "sexual harassment") which allow the conviction of innocent men on the sole basis of uncorroborated . . . accusations by women. . . .

The Democratic party seems intent on reducing American men to second-class citizens.

Government As Husband

The income of a *middle-class* man provides a mother with three options (full-time work; full-time children; combination of both). But if the man is poor, it doesn't. So the *government* provides the woman with *more* than what a poor man provides— enough so that she "marries" the government rather than the poor man: the government becomes a substitute husband. The man who is poor becomes disposable.

The problem is not that women and children are fed, but that men are excluded from the lives of women and children. The lack of an MIC program (for *Men*, Infants, and Children) makes WIC a federally financed females-only club. (And every state supplements the federal money with state money.)

At least programs with names such as *Women*, Infants, and Children make the sexism apparent; names like Aid to *Families* with Dependent Children hide the sexism. Yet to receive AFDC— or numerous other awards to "families"—men must meet much more stringent standards than women. For example, the AFDC's "hundred hour rule" allows a mother to work one hundred hours a month and still receive her aid money. But a father who works a hundred hours a month receives *no* aid money. Even if a father is starting a new business and is *losing* money, he still gets no aid.

In contrast, *if a mother is doing the same, she gets all her aid*. This obviously violates the Fourteenth Amendment's provision for all citizens to receive equal protection of the law. Yet no one challenges it.

Paying only the woman is the law's way of keeping a man who is without money "in his place"—out on the streets—until he becomes a wallet. If he fails, he remains on the streets; if he succeeds, he gets to compete with other men for a woman's love—and with AFDC and WIC. Of course, he must earn not only what AFDC and WIC pay her, but enough to also support himself.

Males Need Not Apply

The social scene now finds that it is not females, but males, particularly middle-class whites, who are being denied equal rights. Decades ago, stores and companies often put up "Help Wanted" signs that read, "Irish, Colored, and Italians need not apply." Were such signs to prevail today, they would read instead, "White males need not apply." Ask any business, police or fire department, or school if such is not the case. . . .

Political activists declared 1992 the Year of the Woman. In fact, we have lived through several *decades* of women. Their names are household words in virtually every field of endeavor. . . .

It doesn't take a misogynist to recognize that women now have highly organized networks to help them achieve their goals. Whether the "Sisterhood," National Organization of Women (NOW), or various professional associations such as those of female professors or woman mayors, they are at work.

Their ability to use their newly acquired power was witnessed in the nationally televised Anita Hill/Clarence Thomas [Supreme Court confirmation] hearings. Thomas won the battle [against Hill's charges of sexual harassment], but lost the war for men. . . . To use a mixed metaphor, men must be cleaner than Caesar's wife in dealing with women in the workplace, for frivolous harassment charges lurk behind every office door. The mood of females today is that males are guilty until proven innocent.

Gerald F. Kreyche, *USA Today*, March 1993.

We often hear that "the amount a woman receives on AFDC is hardly enough to support a family." True. No *one* government program provides the woman with more options than a lower-income male would provide. AFDC provides more than 10 million women with only $10 billion per year. That alone does not provide enough for a family. But that doesn't include food stamps, Medicaid, subsidized housing, school lunch programs,

WIC, or any undeclared under-the-table income.

The effect? A new nuclear family: woman, government, and child. The woman legally retains her three options until the child is 6. Then she can have another child and keep these options another six years. For the woman, there is no end. For the dad, there is no beginning. . . .

In the meantime, a father's absence in the family is the single biggest predictor of a child's deterioration. Why? A father's absence appears to damage what might be called the child's "social immune system." When the child's social immune system is damaged, it is more vulnerable to drug abuse, delinquency, teen pregnancy, etc. Thus when a government subsidy deprives the child of its dad and destroys the child's social immune system, the government is really subsidizing child abuse. Which means *we* are subsidizing child abuse.

Why do we tolerate this? Our instinct to protect women from immediate harm is stronger than our instinct to provide long-term protection to any given child. This derived from our Stage I [the past] survival heritage (if a woman survived, she could always have another child). Our laws evolved from that heritage, but Stage II [present and future] survival depends on laws which allow children to have dads—and allow dads to have children. Why? The next generations' children will need that sense of stability and internal security to solve the world's problems with love rather than war.

Who Pays?

ITEM. The child was over three. The judge assessed that good baby-sitters were available, poverty was hurting the child, and the child would benefit if the mother worked. The judge ruled the mother should work.

The feminist response to the judge's decision was that the mother's "right to choose" was being violated, not that the judge had wrongly assessed the best interests of the child. The mother's choice was considered primary; the best interests of the child secondary. Yet one rationale for a woman's "right to choose" in abortion cases has always been the importance of "a child having a decent life."

Since most tax money is paid by men, her "right to choose" is the choice to obligate mostly men to pay for her choice. When he adds this to his obligation to support his own wife and children, he is often forced to take a job he likes less because it pays more—which produces the stress that leads to his earlier death.

In essence, a woman's choice can kill a man. If it were only her body, it would be only her business, but his earlier death means his body is also at stake. And the child's life is at stake if it lives in poverty.

When political parties are dependent on keeping woman-as-child, we encourage women to develop the psychology of the entitled child: an ever-sharper eye for seeing only the discrimination against her, not the discrimination *for* her. For example, feminists claimed that Social Security was discriminating against women because the average woman receives slightly less per month than the average man. They neglected to mention that the average man pays in more per month.

They also neglected to mention the real discrimination: Men as a group pay *twice* what women pay into Social Security but women receive more than 150 percent of what men receive in total retirement benefits from Social Security. Men *as a group* also receive less than women in any given year. But no men's movement suggests that, as a result, men should be charged only about 33 percent of what women are charged for Social Security (because as a group they pay twice as much in and receive a third less). . . .

How Men Succeed

Feminism introduced women not only to succeeding in the workplace but to suing the workplace—and in almost the same breath. Men who succeeded rarely learned this one-two punch. When Thomas Watson, Sr., was fired from National Cash Register in 1914, he started a little company of his own. He called it IBM. When Henry Ford II fired Lee Iacocca from his job as president of Ford Motor Company, Ford told Iacocca, "I just don't *like* you." Some feminists might have sued. Iacocca succeeded. . . .

Making Life "Fair"

People who succeed do not expect every company to reward fairly; they *screen for* companies which will recognize their contribution. And if they aren't being recognized, they change employers, they don't sue employers.

People who succeed monetarily *and spiritually* don't think of men as being the sex that has the power as much as being the sex most willing to pay the price of power. They know there are few privileges without responsibilities and, if a responsibility doesn't give them some leverage for a privilege, they avoid it; they don't take it on and then gripe about it.

By giving women training to sue a company for a "hostile environment" if someone tells a dirty joke, we are training women to run to the Government as Substitute Husband (or Father). This gets companies to fear women, but not to respect women. The best preparation we can give women to succeed in the workplace is the preparation to overcome barriers rather than to sue: successful people don't sue, they succeed.

"Many young men in the sixties tried to accept initiation from women [and the women's movement] . . . but only men can change the boy to a man."

Men Need to Become More Manly

Robert Bly

In the following viewpoint, excerpted from his controversial book, *Iron John*, Robert Bly claims that today's men have become soft—out of touch with their masculinity—as a result of being cut off from their fathers and other older men. Bly relates a male's discovery of his own "deep masculinity" through an old fairy tale retold by the Brothers Grimm. In this story, a hairy wild man named Iron John is brought up from the bottom of a pond and imprisoned by a king. The king's son loses a golden ball to the wild man, who will only give it back if the boy releases him from the cage. According to Bly, the boy separates from his mother by stealing the cage key from under her pillow, and begins the work of becoming a man by courageously going off with Iron John into the forest. Bly, a lecturer, author, and National Book Award–winning poet, has become a central figure in a growing men's movement that aims to recover an older, preindustrial form of masculinity.

As you read, consider the following questions:

1. Who does Bly blame for men's lost masculinity?
2. How does Bly support his belief that only men can make a man?

Iron John (excerpted from pp. 1-4, 14-22), ©1990 by Robert Bly. Reprinted by permission of Addison-Wesley Publishing Co., Inc.

We talk a great deal about "the American man," as if there were some constant quality that remained stable over decades, or even within a single decade.

The men who live today have veered far away from the Saturnian, old-man-minded farmer, proud of his introversion, who arrived in New England in 1630, willing to sit through three services in an unheated church. In the South, an expansive, motherbound cavalier developed, and neither of these two "American men" resembled the greedy railroad entrepreneur that later developed in the Northeast, nor the reckless I-will-do-without culture settlers of the West.

Even in our own era the agreed-on model has changed dramatically. During the fifties, for example, an American character appeared with some consistency that became a model of manhood adopted by many men: the Fifties male.

The Fifties Male

He got to work early, labored responsibly, supported his wife and children, and admired discipline. Ronald Reagan is a sort of mummified version of this dogged type. This sort of man didn't see women's souls well, but he appreciated their bodies; and his view of culture and America's part in it was boyish and optimistic. Many of his qualities were strong and positive, but underneath the charm and bluff there was, and there remains, much isolation, deprivation, and passivity. Unless he has an enemy, he isn't sure that he is alive.

The Fifties man was supposed to like football, be aggressive, stick up for the United States, never cry, and always provide. But receptive space or intimate space was missing in this image of a man. The personality lacked some sense of flow. The psyche lacked compassion in a way that encouraged the unbalanced pursuit of the Vietnam war, just as, later, the lack of what we might call "garden" space inside Reagan's head led to his callousness and brutality toward the powerless in El Salvador, toward old people here, the unemployed, schoolchildren, and poor people in general.

The Fifties male had a clear vision of what a man was, and what male responsibilities were, but the isolation and one-sidedness of his vision were dangerous.

The "Soft Male"

During the sixties, another sort of man appeared. The waste and violence of the Vietnam war made men question whether they knew what an adult male really was. If manhood meant Vietnam, did they want any part of it? Meanwhile, the feminist movement encouraged men to actually look at women, forcing them to become conscious of concerns and sufferings that the

Fifties male labored to avoid. As men began to examine women's history and women's sensibility, some men began to notice what was called their *feminine* side and pay attention to it. This process continues to this day, and I would say that most contemporary men are involved in it in some way.

There's something wonderful about this development—I mean the practice of men welcoming their own "feminine" consciousness and nurturing it—this is important—and yet I have the sense that there is something wrong. The male in the past twenty years has become more thoughtful, more gentle. But by this process he has not become more free. He's a nice boy who pleases not only his mother but also the young woman he is living with.

In the seventies I began to see all over the country a phenomenon that we might call the "soft male." Sometimes even today when I look out at an audience, perhaps half the young males are what I'd call soft. They're lovely, valuable people—I like them—they're not interested in harming the earth or starting wars. There's a gentle attitude toward life in their whole being and style of living.

Unhappy Men

But many of these men are not happy. You quickly notice the lack of energy in them. They are life-preserving but not exactly life-giving. Ironically, you often see these men with strong women who positively radiate energy.

Here we have a finely tuned young man, ecologically superior to his father, sympathetic to the whole harmony of the universe, yet he himself has little vitality to offer.

The strong or life-giving women who graduated from the sixties, so to speak, or who have inherited an older spirit, played an important part in producing this life-preserving, but not life-giving, man.

I remember a bumper sticker during the sixties that read "WOMEN SAY YES TO MEN WHO SAY NO." We recognize that it took a lot of courage to resist the draft, go to jail, or move to Canada, just as it took courage to accept the draft and go to Vietnam. But the women of twenty years ago were definitely saying that they preferred the softer receptive male.

Incomplete Development

So the development of men was affected a little in this preference. Nonreceptive maleness was equated with violence, and receptive maleness was rewarded.

Some energetic women, at that time and now in the nineties, chose and still choose soft men to be their lovers and, in a way, perhaps, to be their sons. The new distribution of "yang" [masculine, active] energy among couples didn't happen by accident.

160

Young men for various reasons wanted their harder women, and women began to desire softer men. It seemed like a nice arrangement for a while, but we've lived with it long enough now to see that it isn't working out.

"Brad is a pussycat. Unfortunately, I'm in the market for a human being."

©Haefeli/Punch/Rothco. Reprinted with permission.

I first learned about the anguish of "soft" men when they told their stories in early men's gatherings. In 1980, the Lama Community in New Mexico asked me to teach a conference for men only, their first, in which about forty men participated. Each day we concentrated on one Greek god and one old story, and then late in the afternoons we gathered to talk. When the younger men spoke it was not uncommon for them to be weeping within five minutes. The amount of grief and anguish in these younger men was astounding to me.

Completing the Journey

Part of their grief rose out of remoteness from their fathers, which they felt keenly, but partly, too, grief flowed from trouble in their marriages or relationships. They had learned to be receptive, but receptivity wasn't enough to carry their marriages through troubled times. In every relationship something *fierce* is needed once in a while: both the man and the woman need to have it. But at the point when it was needed, often the young man came up short. He was nurturing, but something else was required—for his relationship, and for his life.

161

The "soft" male was able to say, "I can feel your pain, and I consider your life as important as mine, and I will take care of you and comfort you." But he could not say what he wanted, and stick by it. *Resolve* of that kind was a different matter.

In *The Odyssey*, Hermes instructs Odysseus that when he approaches Circe, who stands for a certain kind of matriarchal energy, he is to lift or show his sword. In these early sessions it was difficult for many of the younger men to distinguish between showing the sword and hurting someone. One man, a kind of incarnation of certain spiritual attitudes of the sixties, a man who had actually lived in a tree for a year outside Santa Cruz, found himself unable to extend his arm when it held a sword. He had learned so well not to hurt anyone that he couldn't lift the steel, even to catch the light of the sun on it. But showing a sword doesn't necessarily mean fighting. It can also suggest a joyful decisiveness.

The journey many American men have taken into softness, or receptivity, or "development of the feminine side," has been an immensely valuable journey, but more travel lies ahead. No stage is the final stop. . . .

Iron John

The moment the boy leaves with Iron John [in the Brothers Grimm fairy tale] is the moment in ancient Greek life when the priest of Dionysus accepted a young man as a student, or the moment in Eskimo life today when the shaman, sometimes entirely covered with the fur of wild animals, and wearing wolverine claws and snake vertebrae around his neck, and a bear-head cap, appears in the village and takes a boy away for spirit instruction.

In our culture there is no such moment. The boys in our culture have a continuing need for initiation into male spirit, but old men in general don't offer it. The priest sometimes tries, but he is too much a part of the corporate village these days.

Among the Hopis and other native Americans of the Southwest, the old men take the boy away at the age of twelve and bring him *down* into the all-male area of the kiva. He stays *down* there for six weeks, and does not see his mother again for a year and a half.

What Is Missing?

The fault of the nuclear family today isn't so much that it's crazy and full of double binds (that's true in communes and corporate offices too—in fact, in any group). The fault is that the old men outside the nuclear family no longer offer an effective way for the son to break his link with his parents without doing harm to himself.

The ancient societies believed that a boy becomes a man only through ritual and effort—only through the "active intervention of the older men."

It's becoming clear to us that manhood doesn't happen by itself; it doesn't happen just because we eat Wheaties. The active intervention of the older men means that older men welcome the younger man into the ancient, mythologized, instinctive male world. . . .

In the absence of old men's labor consciously done, what happens? Initiation of Western men has continued for some time in an altered form even after fanatics destroyed the Greek initiatory schools. During the nineteenth century, grandfathers and uncles lived in the house, and older men mingled a great deal. Through hunting parties, in work that men did together in farms and cottages, and through local sports, older men spent much time with younger men and brought knowledge of male spirit and soul to them.

Wordsworth, in the beginning of "The Excursion," describes the old man who sat day after day under a tree and befriended Wordsworth when he was a boy:

> He loved me; from a swarm of rosy boys
> Singled me out, as he in sport would say,
> For my grave looks, too thoughtful for my years.
> As I grew up, it was my best delight
> To be his chosen comrade. Many a time
> On holidays, we wandered through the woods . . .

Much of that chance or incidental mingling has ended. Men's clubs and societies have steadily disappeared. Grandfathers live in Phoenix or the old people's home, and many boys experience only the companionship of other boys their age who, from the point of view of the old initiators, know nothing at all.

During the sixties, some young men drew strength from women who in turn had received some of their strength from the women's movement. One could say that many young men in the sixties tried to accept initiation from women. But only men can initiate men, as only women can initiate women. Women can change the embryo to a boy, but only men can change the boy to a man. Initiators say that boys need a second birth, this time a birth from men. . . .

Absent Dads

So what can be done? Thousands and thousands of women, being single parents, are raising boys with no adult man in the house. The difficulties inherent in that situation came up one day in Evanston when I was giving a talk on initiation of men to a group made up mostly of women.

Women who were raising sons alone were extremely alert to the dangers of no male model. One woman declared that she re-

163

alized about the time her son got to high-school age that he needed more hardness than she could naturally give. But, she said, if she made herself harder to meet that need, she would lose touch with her own femininity. I mentioned the classic solution in many traditional cultures, which is to send the boy to his father when he is twelve. Several women said flatly, "No, men aren't nurturing; they wouldn't take care of him." Many men, however—and I am one of them—have found inside an ability to nurture that didn't appear until it was called for.

An Accidental Break

Even when a father is living in the house there still may be a strong covert bond between mother and son to evict the father, which amounts to a conspiracy, and conspiracies are difficult to break. One woman with two sons had enjoyed going each year to a convention in San Francisco with her husband, the boys being left at home. But one spring, having just returned from a women's retreat, she felt like being private and said to her husband: "Why don't you take the boys this year?" So the father did.

The boys, around ten and twelve, had never, as it turned out, experienced their father's company without the mother's presence. After that experience, they asked for more time with their dad.

When the convention time rolled around the following spring, the mother once more decided on privacy, and the boys once more went off with their father. The moment they arrived back home, the mother happened to be standing in the kitchen with her back to the door, and the older of the two boys walked over and put his arms around her from the back. Without even intending it, her body reacted explosively, and the boy flew across the room and bounced off the wall. When he picked himself up, she said, their relationship had changed. Something irrevocable had happened. She was glad about the change, and the boy seemed surprised and a little relieved that he apparently wasn't needed by her in the old way. . . .

The traditional initiation break clearly is preferable, and sidesteps the violence. But all over the country now one sees hulking sons acting ugly in the kitchen and talking rudely to their mothers, and I think it's an attempt to make themselves unattractive. If the old men haven't done their work to interrupt the mother-son unity, what else can the boys do to extricate themselves but to talk ugly? It's quite unconscious and there's no elegance in it at all.

A clean break from the mother is crucial, but it's simply not happening. This doesn't mean that the women are doing something wrong: I think the problem is more that the older men are not really doing their job.

The traditional way of raising sons, which lasted for thousands and thousands of years, amounted to fathers and sons living in close—murderously close—proximity, while the father taught the son a trade: perhaps farming or carpentry or blacksmithing or tailoring. As I've suggested elsewhere, the love unit most damaged by the Industrial Revolution has been the father-son bond.

There's no sense in idealizing preindustrial culture, yet we know that today many fathers now work thirty or fifty miles from the house, and by the time they return at night the children are often in bed, and they themselves are too tired to do active fathering.

The Industrial Revolution, in its need for office and factory workers, pulled fathers away from their sons and, moreover, placed the sons in compulsory schools where the teachers are mostly women. D. H. Lawrence described what this was like in his essay "Men Must Work and Women as Well." His generation in the coal-mining areas of Britain felt the full force of that change, and the new attitude centered on one idea: that physical labor is bad.

Lawrence recalls that his father, who had never heard this theory, worked daily in the mines, enjoyed the camaraderie with the other men, came home in good spirits, and took his bath in the kitchen. But around that time the new schoolteachers arrived from London to teach Lawrence and his classmates that physical labor is low and unworthy and that men and women should strive to move upward to a more "spiritual" level—higher work, mental work. The children of his generation deduced that their fathers had been doing something wrong all along, that men's physical work is wrong and that those sensitive mothers who prefer white curtains and an elevated life are right and always have been.

Father Hunger

During Lawrence's teenage years, which he described in *Sons and Lovers*, he clearly believed the new teachers. He wanted the "higher" life, and took his mother's side. It wasn't until two years before he died, already ill with tuberculosis in Italy, that Lawrence began to notice the vitality of the Italian workingmen, and to feel a deep longing for his own father. He realized then that his mother's ascensionism had been wrong for him, and had encouraged him to separate from his father and from his body in an unfruitful way.

A single clear idea, well fed, moves like a contagious disease: "Physical work is wrong." Many people besides Lawrence took up that idea, and in the next generation that split between fathers and sons deepened. A man takes up desk work in an office,

165

becomes a father himself, but has no work to share with his son and cannot explain to the son what he's doing. Lawrence's father was able to take his son down into the mines, just as my own father, who was a farmer, could take me out on the tractor, and show me around. I knew what he was doing all day and in all seasons of the year.

When the office work and the "information revolution" begin to dominate, the father-son bond disintegrates. If the father inhabits the house only for an hour or two in the evenings, then women's values, marvelous as they are, will be the only values in the house. One could say that the father now loses his son five minutes after birth. When we walk into a contemporary house, it is often the mother who comes forward confidently. The father is somewhere else in the back, being inarticulate. This is a poem of mine called "Finding the Father":

> My friend, this body offers to carry us for nothing—as the ocean carries logs. So on some days the body wails with its great energy; it smashes up the boulders, lifting small crabs, that flow around the sides.
>
> Someone knocks on the door. We do not have time to dress. He wants us to go with him through the blowing and rainy streets, to the dark house.
>
> We will go there, the body says, and there find the father whom we have never met, who wandered out in a snowstorm the night we were born, and who then lost his memory, and has lived since longing for his child, whom he saw only once . . . while he worked as a shoemaker, as a cattle herder in Australia, as a restaurant cook who painted at night.
>
> When you light the lamp you will see him. He sits there behind the door . . . the eyebrows so heavy, the forehead so light . . . lonely in his whole body, waiting for you.

"Robert Bly and his followers celebrate their gathering to seek a 'new vision' of masculinity. But Bly's ideas of 'masculine' and 'feminine' are cut from the same old sexist cloth."

Men Do Not Need to Become More Manly

Fred Pelka

Like many self-realization programs, the men's movement offers to help its followers get more in touch with themselves—in this case, more in touch with their masculinity. Because Robert Bly's *Iron John* has practically become the trade manual of the growing men's movement, Fred Pelka takes issue in the following viewpoint with what he considers the book's—and the movement's—romanticized notion of history and its barely concealed hatred of women. That kind of message, Pelka explains, although it is popular with many of today's identity-seeking men, is not so much an effort to deal with the ills of modern society as it is an attempt to escape from them into a mythical past. Pelka is a contributing editor at *On the Issues: The Magazine of Substance for Progressive Women.*

As you read, consider the following questions:

1. What is the significance of fathers in the men's movement, according to the author?
2. Where does Pelka say that Bly searches for models of masculinity? What does he say is wrong with those models?
3. Where does the author say the men's movement is heading?

Fred Pelka, "Robert Bly & Iron John," *On the Issues: The Magazine of Substance for Progressive Women,* Summer 1991. Reprinted with permission.

"For generations our institutions, and our parents, have warned us and shamed us away from our wildness—Our intuition, exuberance, and tears. Now, soul and spirit suffer in great measure. At gatherings of men . . . the healing often begins with the telling of ancient stories of male initiation. . . ."

So says a flyer for "Initiation in the Masculine Soul—A Day for Men," featuring keynote speaker Robert Bly. For $100 ($85 if I register early) Bly, through the telling of myths and fairy tales, will take me "places that our parents never thought of."

Introducing Robert Bly

Robert Bly, acclaimed poet, winner of the National Book Award, and leader of a burgeoning men's movement, travels the country speaking to mostly white and almost entirely male audiences about "male grief" and the myriad difficulties inherent in being a contemporary man. He commands a huge following and has been referred to as "this year's Joseph Campbell," especially since the broadcast of the Bill Moyers PBS profile, "A Gathering of Men."

Bly's thought is set down in *Iron John, A Book About Men*, many weeks at the top of the *New York Times* best-seller list. The book—an exegesis of one of Grimms' fairy tales—"is the result," according to the publisher, "of 10 years' work with men to discover the truths about masculinity."

"I want to make it clear . . . ," Bly says, "that this book does not seek to turn men against women." Bly argues, however, that men need to turn *away* from women, to liberate their "mother-bound souls." What Bly wants, in the words of *Boston Globe* reviewer Suzanne Gordon, is "a patriarchy that is kinder and gentler." And in making his case for the sanctity of male bonding, Bly romanticizes history, trivializes sexist oppression and lays the blame for much of men's "grief" on women.

Soft Men

Bly begins *Iron John* with an examination of men in America, and he is straightaway disturbed by what he sees. "When I look out at an audience, perhaps half the young males are what I'd call soft." "Soft" males are the "Sensitive New Age Guys" lampooned by Christine Lavin—men who cry freely and work at food co-ops, men who have, according to Bly, "renounced violence." The problem, says Bly, is that these "soft" men have somehow surrendered their self-esteem, their playfulness and zest for life. They are afraid "to show a sword," to stick up for themselves. They have lost touch with a host of inner characters—"The Warrior," "The King" and especially "The Wild Man." As a result, they are indecisive and subject to uniquely masculine strains of "anguish" and "grief."

To explain all this, Bly describes how fathers traditionally distance themselves from their children, leaving boys to be raised by women. Much of the emotional resonance Bly generates among his audiences has to do with the anger and grief that come with having a distant or abandoning father. Bly often describes his own father's alcoholism and frequently uses the jargon of the Adult Children of Alcoholics (ACOA) movement.

Conspiring Mothers

Were Bly to leave it at that, his book would be little more than a plea for men to be better parents. Unfortunately, he doesn't stop there. It isn't just that fathers are absent, he says: The mothers who parent in their stead are incapable of providing their male children with that special "energy" that passes from father to son. Even worse, many mothers are conspiring and destructive to the sensitive male egos entrusted to their care. They are encouraged in this by man-hating feminists. "The emphasis placed in recent decades on the inadequacy of men, and the evil of the patriarchal system, encourages mothers to discount grown men," deflating their boys' role models. "Between 20 and 30 percent of American boys," according to Bly, "now live in a house with no father present, and the demons have full permission to rage."

SYLVIA

Nicole Hollander

Reprinted with permission.

"Bly's historical analysis and his descriptions of contemporary life," says Gordon, in one of the few critical reviews of *Iron John* to appear in the mainstream press, "are difficult to reconcile with the realities women experience daily." Gordon asks, "Who are these soft men?" noting the absence of "softness" among the decision makers in Washington and Baghdad, and no great diminution in the male violence that is so much a part of women's lives. However "soft" they might be, men still hold the overwhelming preponderance of economic, social and political power, not only in American and Western society, but everywhere on earth. And "renouncing violence" doesn't mean that "soft men" don't continue to share in the benefits all men derive from living in a sexist culture.

Bly, however, doesn't see it that way. "We now live in a system of industrial domination, which is not patriarchy." Apparently, the feminists won without even knowing it. Bly adds that "When the mythological layer collapses, and the political kings fall, then the patriarchy, as a positive force, is over. The sun and the moon energies can no longer get down to earth."

A Romanticized Past

This statement is instructive in several ways. First, it tells us that, like most reactionaries, Bly has a romanticized vision of the past, of the once-upon-a-time when life was so much better than it is in the degenerate present. For Bly, this was the era of the positive patriarchy, of kings, when warriors fought for the higher causes of chivalry and blissful male bonding, when fathers worked with their sons and taught them how to hunt and farm far from the baleful influence of grasping mothers. Second, the reference to "sun and moon energy" lets us know that Bly's analysis is a mythological one, as is his understanding of history. He sees myth and fairy tales as unerring signposts on everyman's psychological journey; metaphoric ciphers on how to live the good life. And so Bly often expresses himself in fairy tale terms, often with unintentional humor. "The Iron John story proposes that the golden ball lies within the magnetic field of the Wild Man, which is a very hard concept for us to grasp." Indeed. Or as Jungian scholar Marie-Louise von Franz, often quoted by Bly, puts it: "Fairy tales are the purest and simplest expression of collective unconscious psychic processes."

But some fairy tales are purer and simpler and more unconscious than others. If we use myths to govern our social and personal lives, then the choice of which myth to use is of utmost importance. One has to examine the values represented by these myths, the purposes served, and who exactly benefits from the telling of any particular myth or story.

"Iron John" is taken from the Brothers Grimm, and speaks to Bly of a "third possibility for men," somewhere beyond being too "soft" and too hard. "Though it was first set down by the Grimm brothers around 1820," Bly tells us, "this story could be 10 or 20,000 years old," which presumably gives it its Jungian legitimacy.

In fact, the Grimms' *Nursery and Household Tales* are of dubious authenticity. Many scholars see the *Tales*, heavily edited by Wilhelm Grimm, as reflecting a moral code formulated not in pre-historic or even pre-industrial times, but rather in the context of the hypernationalistic middle class of 19th-century Germany. The Grimms, according to folklorist Ruth Bottigheimer, stress "diligent work, gender specific roles, a generally punitive stance towards girls and women, and a coherent world view conducing to stability in the social fabric." Germanic scholar Maria Tatar recounts how the ideologists of the Third Reich hailed the collection, especially such anti-Semitic tales as "The Jew in the Thorn Bush," as "a sacred book," and how the Allies removed it from German classrooms during de-Nazification. Wilhelm Grimm himself was a member of the Christian-German Society, which Bottigheimer describes as "a reactionary group . . . its program was anti-Philistine, anti-Semitic, and anti-woman."

Bly offers no reason, other than their supposed age, as to why he prefers the *Household Tales* for his analysis, but it is striking how much Bly's own arguments resemble the Grimms', in their attitude toward women. In the Brothers Grimm, mothers (especially stepmothers) are generally wicked, cruel and "unnatural." In Bly, mothers co-opt their children into conspiracies, the aim of which is to isolate, sometimes even destroy, their fathers. "The mother looks to the son for emotional satisfaction, and her fantasies in this regard may have deepened in recent years." (Bly is silent on just how he knows what women fantasize, or that "much of the rage" that feminists feel is really "disappointment over . . . their own fathers.") "Your father is convinced that he is an inadequate human being," he tells his all-male audiences. "Women have been telling him that for 30 or 40 years." Consequently, boys end up being "bound" to their mothers, and "more than one American man today needs a sword to cut his adult soul away from his mother-bound soul." A boy raised by his mother "will probably see his own masculinity from the feminine point of view"—which is "fascinated with it," but also "afraid of it." "We are aware," he adds, "of a disturbing rise in the number of sons who report sexual abuse by mothers, as well as by fathers, uncles and older brothers; but the culture still does not take seriously the damage caused by psychic incest between mother and son."

Fuzzy Language

There is much that is disturbing in this equation of "psychic incest" with sexual abuse: as if the alleged harmful effects of a female-headed household are somehow equivalent to rape by a parent or sibling. We see this same fuzzy language when Bly discusses "male mothers." "You mean, 'mentors'?" Moyers asks, the journalist refining the terminology of the poet. For Bly, "psychic incest" is equivalent to actual sexual abuse; a man spending time with a boy is equivalent to a woman giving birth; contemporary "male grief" is equivalent to several millennia of women's oppression. And though he mentions the sexual abuse of girls, Bly never admits that the vast majority of sexual and domestic violence is committed by men upon women and children, and that boy victims of incest and domestic violence are most often abused by other males.

Bly offers no evidence to support his contention that vast numbers of men suffer from a sort of post-female parenting syndrome. Instead, he tells us that certain dark "forces in contemporary society recently have encouraged women to be warriors, while discouraging warriorhood in boys and men." Hasn't the man ever heard of Rambo? Does he watch CNN? Even Moyers, in an interview uncritical to the point of being obsequious, stops Bly when he describes how his mother conspired to isolate his father.

"It seems to me," says Moyers, "you and your mother didn't push your father out; your father removed himself through alcoholism," to which Bly replies, "It's possible." Rather than pursue this point, the interview breaks away to another fairy tale.

Good Energy?

Most of the other myths and stories that Bly cites are as anti-female as the Brothers Grimm. Bly's comments on "Zeus" and "Hermes energy," for example, refer to a mythology in which women are seen as the root of all evil: The Pandora of Hesiod is analogous to Eve in the creation myths of the Bible. Women in Homer appear most often as temptresses like Helen, nags like Hera, dutiful (but conniving) wives like Penelope, or slaves, whores and victims. I need only remember the myths of the Thunder God's many rapes to dampen any enthusiasm for "Zeus energy," or that Odysseus, whose bonding with his son Telemachus is much praised by Bly, ordered the boy to butcher their female slaves as punishment for the crime of being raped.

It's also difficult to follow the distinctions Bly makes between "The Warrior" and "The Soldier," "The Wild Man" and "The Savage." Bly says that healthy male aggression is unjustly condemned and that "The physical warrior disintegrated into the soldier when mechanized warfare came on." Though Bly is vague on just who or what today's "warrior" is supposed to conquer, he does give us the occasional clue. Bly sees the lover and the warrior "mingling," and offers the axiom: "No sword, no eros."

One wonders about Bly's vision of classical and medieval warfare. Anyone who has read Thucydides' account of the wars between Athens and Sparta, or Tacitus's description of the mass rapes and murders committed by the Roman legions, can have little doubt that war, even among pagans, has always meant atrocity and murder. Similarly, Bly's notion that aggression is somehow purified by a cause "beyond" oneself is simply wrong. It is always the religious and political zealots who make the most brutal soldiers, as has been demonstrated in every ideological struggle from the Thirty Years' War to today's purges, genocides and jihads.

Sublimated Misogyny

It's obvious that Bly's notions of history come from poems and fairy tales, not always the most accurate of sources. At times his idea of what past life was like is ludicrous, even comical, and it is apparent that Bly is always talking about, and to, male elites. "We know from Shakespeare's *Romeo and Juliet*, and other Renaissance accounts, that it was not at all unusual for a young man at that time to take two or three years off, and spend it learning to be a lover. We spend those years in graduate school instead." In Bly's world view, war, warriors, kings, the patriarchy, all are sanitized and benevolent, painted in fairy tale colors. Even illness and death are romanticized, as when Bly discusses how Keats died at age 26. Things are different, he says, "for those of us who have agreed to live longer," as if Keats's death of tuberculosis was a matter of choice, perhaps coming out of the poet's desire to be poignant.

It is distressing, but not surprising, that Bly's barely sublimated misogyny strikes such a chord among so many men. Bly and his followers celebrate their gathering to seek "a new vision" of masculinity. But Bly's ideas of "masculine" and "feminine" are cut from the same old sexist cloth, and his anger and distrust of women seem hardly cause for celebration.

There is, indeed, a need for a pro-feminist men's movement, for men to join in the struggle to end rape, domestic violence, and the political, sexual, social and economic oppression of women. But rather than move forward to a new definition of masculinity that does not include the oppression of half the human race, Bly would have men look backward, through the prism of myth, fairy tale and pop psychology, to recover the positive patriarchy and "the male mode of feeling," to cut loose the inner life from the outer reality. At first glance Bly might appear apolitical, if elitist and obscure. In fact, he is riding the crest of a new wave of anti-feminist backlash.

As W.H. Auden, a poet Bly quotes, once wrote: "No fairy story ever claimed to be a description of the external world and no sane child ever believed that it was."

> *"Often the man who sincerely wants to build close friendships finds that other men shy away from him because they perceive him as 'too needy.'"*

Men Need to Form Close Male Friendships

Terry A. Kupers and Larry Letich

In Part I of the following viewpoint, Terry A. Kupers explains that men lack close same-sex friendships because of cultural values that encourage men to be emotionally self-sufficient, homophobic, and status-conscious. Only by forming male friendships will men be able to break out of these cultural constraints, Kupers insists. Their example, he says, will help others to do the same. Kupers, a psychiatrist practicing in Oakland, California, is the author of *Revisioning Men's Lives: Gender, Intimacy and Power*. In Part II, Larry Letich argues that male isolation is economic as well as cultural since in today's increasingly white-collar marketplace any trust between men is the first casualty in an often ruthless battle for the few top jobs. Like Kupers, however, Letich believes that friendship is not only possible but necessary, and he gives pointers on how to fight the "guerrilla war" of winning a male friend. Letich is an author who writes on men's issues and progressive politics.

As you read, consider the following questions:

1. According to Kupers, how and why are men taught to maintain distance from one another?
2. How are men kept from making friends with each other, according to Letich?

From "Menfriends" by Terry A. Kupers. Reprinted from TIKKUN MAGAZINE, A BI-MONTHLY JEWISH CRITIQUE OF POLITICS, CULTURE, AND SOCIETY (March/April 1993). Subscriptions are $31.00 per year from TIKKUN, 251 W. 100th St., 5th Fl., New York, NY 10025. Larry Letich, "Do You Know Who Your Friends Are?" *Utne Reader*, May/June 1991.

I

Why all the fuss about men's friendships? Is it only about men needing buddies? Is it merely that men are realizing they need each other to ward off the loneliness and envy that ensue when women get together with each other and leave them out? Or is there also some potential for progressive social change in men's soul-searching about friendship?

Discussions of men's friendships traditionally begin with the way men have learned to distance each other and keep their cards close to their chests as they climb up the hierarchy in a dog-eat-dog world. Then, there is the issue of homophobia [fear of homosexuality]. And, of course, it's all true. There was that list of rules for boys on the schoolyard, including "Never walk away from a fight," "Never let the other guy know he hurt you," and "Don't do anything that will lead other guys to think you're gay." And the rules did serve to prepare us for survival in that dog-eat-dog world. So, as adults, we don't touch each other (except in those exuberant post-touchdown moments), we don't linger too long in an affectionate glance and we certainly don't get too tearful in male company. . . .

Barriers to Friendship

There is a vicious cycle that makes it very difficult for men who want to change. Many of us would like to cross the lines that define and constrict traditional masculinity, the lines one does not cross if one wants to avoid being perceived as unmanly. It would help to have the support of other men in the crossing. But men are not very good at being close and supportive with each other. In fact, we tend to distance ourselves from a man who seems unmanly. Often the man who sincerely wants to build close friendships finds that other men shy away from him because they perceive him as "too needy." So the crossing can be very lonely.

The difficulties men have being friends are aggravated by the cyclical dynamic. Since men are socialized to believe one can judge a man's worth in relation to the men he befriends, association with someone who appears not to be "one of the guys" can be the undoing of a man who is trying to climb up the ladder. There is always the risk that, if a man relaxes his guard, and displays too much tenderness, or if he is too willing to cop to his foibles, then he will be mocked by other men. Consider the man who objects vociferously to sexual harassment or gay-bashing and is told: "Come on, don't take everything so seriously, it's only good clean fun." But men tend to remain silent about their critical concerns. After all, it would not look good if a man who is vying for promotion were to sound off at work about how distasteful he finds men's obsession with their place in hierarchies

175

(including, by implication, the structure of authority and remuneration in his office). So men cultivate the habit of hiding their disdain for traditional male posturing.

Breaking the Barriers

Friendship could be the key to breaking the vicious cycle. If men who, as a matter of principle, refuse to take part in traditional manly "fun" were better able to build friendships with like-minded men, the crossing of those lines would not be so lonely. Take, for instance, the line at work that divides the loyal company man who stays late from the "less committed" (in other words, unmanly) one who has to get home to be with the kids. The "family man" begins to feel like a failure in comparison with others. Perhaps he does not get the promotion he coveted, or is laid off. His self-esteem sinks precipitously. Perhaps, merely as a result of the renewed conviction that others love him for the values he holds dear, he can return to work and continue to live out his principles. His friends might even help him devise new ways to seek promotion, ways that do not contradict his principles.

There might even be a ripple effect, a burgeoning challenge to what many men already believe is wrong with contemporary notions of masculinity. Perhaps, if men begin to know each other better and express feelings and needs more readily with each other, the cycle could be made to work in reverse: Men who are inclined to cross the lines, with the support of like-minded male intimates, could begin to change gender relations in the workplace. Of course, straight men would need to form alliances—and friendships—with the many women and gays who are already active in that struggle. And in the process of transcending the limitations of men's friendships with men, we would find many other opportunities to improve our gendered social relations.

II

"You gotta have frieeends," sang Bette Midler. But most men past the age of 30 don't have friends—not really. They have colleagues and work buddies, golf partners and maybe a "couple" friend or two, where the bond is really between the wives. If they say they *do* have a best friend, often it turns out to be an old friend whom they see or speak to once every few years.

Sadly, for most men in our culture, male friendship is a part of their distant past. One man spoke for many at a recent men's conference in Montclair, N.J., when he lamented, "I haven't made a new friend in 25 years."

Why is this so? All sorts of theories are thrown around, from "homophobia" to the absurd idea that men are biologically geared to competitiveness, which precludes friendship. But the major reason for the shortage of true friendship among men in America is that our culture discourages it.

Friendship Is Discouraged

Male friendship is idealized in the abstract (think of *Butch Cassidy and the Sundance Kid* and numerous other "buddy movies"), but if a man manages to have any true emotional attachment to another man, a lot of subtle pressures are placed on him to eliminate it. The most obvious time this happens is when a man gets married (especially if he's still in his 20s). Think of the impression that comes to mind from a thousand movies and TV shows about the guy who "leaves his wife" for the evening to "go out with the guys." Invariably, the other guys are shown as both immature *and* lower-class, losers who'll never amount to anything in life. The message is clear—no self-respecting middle-class man hangs out regularly with his friends.

The "Male Mystique"

The male mystique was spawned in the early days of the modern age. It combines Francis Bacon's idea that "knowledge is power" and Adam Smith's view that the highest good is "the individual exerting himself to his own advantage." This power-oriented, individualistic ideology was further solidified by the concepts of the survival of the fittest and the ethic of efficiency. The ideal man was no longer the wise farmer, but rather the most successful man-eater in the Darwinian corporate jungle.

The most tragic aspect of all this for us is that as the male mystique created the modern power elite, it destroyed male friendship and bonding. The male mystique teaches that the successful man is competitive, uncaring, unloving. It celebrates the ethic of isolation—it turns men permanently against each other in the tooth and claw world of making a living. As the Ivan Boesky-type character in the movie *Wall Street* tells his young apprentice, "If you need a friend, get a dog."

Andrew Kimbrell, *Utne Reader*, May/June 1991.

In fact, friendship between men is rarely spoken of at all. Instead, we hear about something called male bonding, as if all possible non-sexual connection between men is rooted in some crude, instinctual impulse. More often than not, male friendship, reduced to male bonding, is sniggered at as something terribly juvenile and possibly dangerous.

This denigration of male friendship fit well into Ronald Reagan-

and Margaret Thatcher–style capitalism. The decline in blue-collar jobs and the great white-collar work speed-up of the 1980s made no man's job safe. And money—not the richness of a man's relationship with family, friends, and community—became even more so the universally accepted value of a man's worth.

In this system, men (at least those men without golden parachutes) are put in the position of constantly, and often ruthlessly, competing with all other men for the limited number of positions higher up the ladder—or even to hold on to their jobs at all. Men are encouraged not to trust one another, and are frankly told never to band together. (For example, in most places it is a serious faux pas, and often a dismissable offense, simply to tell a fellow worker what you make for a living; supposedly it is "bad for morale.") Naturally, this keeps men—and women, too—constantly knocking themselves out for the next promotion rather than demanding real changes, like cutting the CEO's million-dollar salary down to size.

The Emotional Wreckage

Given the kind of sterile, high-pressure work environments men are expected to devote themselves to, it's not surprising that the ideal American man is supposed to feel little or no passion about anything. As Robert Bly has pointed out, the most damaged part of the psyche in modern man is the "lover," meaning not just the ability to make love, but the ability to love life, to feel, to be either tender or passionate. But passion—and with it the capacity for intimacy—is absolutely essential for friendship.

It's also not surprising that our society's ideal man is not supposed to have any emotional needs. Since few men can actually live up to that ideal, it's considered acceptable, even laudable, for him to channel all his emotional needs in one direction—his wife and children. A man who has any other important emotional bonds (that are not based on duty, such as an ailing parent) is in danger of being called neglectful, or irresponsible, or weak, because forging emotional bonds with others takes time—time that is supposed to be spent "getting ahead."

Small wonder that the only friendships allowed are those that serve a "business" purpose or those that can be fit effortlessly into one's leisure time. Maintaining one's lawn is more important than maintaining one's friendships. In keeping with this, there are no rituals and no respect given a man's friendships. When was the last time you heard a grown man talk proudly about his best friend?

Despite all these obstacles, it *is* possible to develop a real male friendship—the kind men remember from their childhood, high school, college, or military days—after the age of 30. My best friend today, with whom I share a deep and abiding bond, is a man I met five years ago when I was 30. But to forge real male friendships requires a willingness to *recognize* that you're going against the grain, and the *courage* to do so. And it requires the sort of conscious, deliberate campaign worthy of a guerrilla leader. Here are step-by-step guerrilla tactics to forge, maintain, and deepen male friendships in a hostile environment:

1. First, you have to want it. Sounds simple and obvious, but isn't. You have to want it badly enough to work at getting it, just as you would a job or a sexual relationship. Right away, this causes anxiety, because it goes against the male self-sufficiency myth. You have to remind yourself *often* that there's nothing weird or effeminate about wanting a friend. Let your wife and children know about your quest. It's good for your sons, especially, to know what you're trying to do. They might even have some good suggestions!

2. Identify a possible friend. Men in men's groups and others who seem in some way to be questioning society's view of masculinity and success are possible candidates. Don't look for men so upstanding and "responsible" they never have a second to themselves. Stuart Miller, author of the book *Men & Friendship*, suggested in an interview reconnecting with your old friends from childhood or adolescence.

3. Be sneaky. Once you've identified the guy you want to make your friend, do you say, "Hey, I want to be your friend, let's do lunch?" No. One of you will probably soon get threatened and pull away. Instead, get involved in a project with him, preferably non-work-related. For my best friend Mike and me, it was a newsletter we were working on. You need structured time just to be together, feel each other out, and get used to each other without the pressure of being "friends."

4. Invite him to stop for a beer or a cup of coffee. Ask personal questions. Find out about his wife, his children, his girl-friend, his job. Find out what's really bugging him in his life. Look for common likes and dislikes. And risk being personal about yourself as well. Do this several times, each time risking a little more honesty.

5. Call just to get together after a few months of this. Arrange to get together at least once a month, even if only for a few hours. Expect to always be the caller and arranger, especially in the beginning.

6. Sit down and talk about your friendship. It may take some time to reach this point. But while it's typical for men to leave things unsaid, this step is crucial. In a society that treats friendships as replaceable, you have to go against the tide by declaring the value of this special friendship between you. Only then will it survive life's stresses, such as a serious disagreement or one of you moving away.

"Men are again understanding the need to talk about their feelings and develop deeper relationships with their own gender."

Men Are Already Forming Close Male Friendships

Alan Buczynski, Mike Yorkey, and Peb Jackson

Alan Buczynski argues in Part I of the following viewpoint that despite popular notions to the contrary, men can and do communicate their emotions to one another; even ironworkers, who he says are not the most articulate of men, are able to express affection for one another in their own gruff ways. Buczynski, who has a degree in English, is an ironworker in the Detroit area. In Part II, Mike Yorkey and Peb Jackson describe the Christian men's movement, a branch of the broader men's movement. Like the popular movement, it offers a safe setting in which groups of men meet and establish close, meaningful, same-sex friendships. Yorkey is editor of *Focus on the Family*, the journal of the Focus on the Family organization, which is committed to restoring traditional Christian and conservative family values. Yorkey joined his first men's group in February 1992. Jackson is senior vice president of the international ministry for Focus on the Family.

As you read, consider the following questions:

1. What example does Buczynski give to illustrate how ironworkers communicate their feelings?
2. How do Christian men's groups foster caring relationships between participants, and between the participants and their families, according to Yorkey and Jackson?

I

"I just don't get it." We were up on the iron, about 120 feet, waiting for the gang below to swing up another beam. Sweat from under Ron's hard hat dripped on the beam we were sitting on and evaporated immediately, like water thrown on a sauna stove. We were talking about the "men's movement" and "wildman weekends."

"I mean," he continued, "if they want to get dirty and sweat and cuss and pound on things, why don't they just get *real* jobs and get paid for it?" Below, the crane growled, the next piece lifting skyward.

I replied: "Nah, Ron, that isn't the point. They don't want to sweat every day, just sometimes."

He said, "Man, if you only sweat when you want to, I don't call that real sweatin'."

Although my degree is in English, I am an ironworker by trade; my girlfriend, Patti, is a graduate student in English literature. Like a tennis ball volleyed by two players with distinctly different styles, I am bounced between blue-collar maulers and precise academicians. My conversations range from fishing to Foucault, derricks to deconstruction. There is very little overlap, but when it does occur it is generally the academics who are curious about the working life.

Patti and I were at a dinner party. The question of communication between men had arisen. Becky, the host, is a persistent interrogator: "What do you and Ron talk about?"

I said, "Well, we talk about work, drinking, ah, women."

Becky asked, "Do you guys ever say, 'I love you' to each other?" This smelled mightily of Robert Bly and the men's movement.

I replied: "Certainly. All the time."

I am still dissatisfied with this answer. Not because it was a lie, but because it was perceived as one.

The notion prevails that men's emotional communication skills are less advanced than that of chimpanzees, that we can no more communicate with one another than can earthworms.

Ironworkers as a group may well validate this theory. We are not a very articulate bunch. Most of us have only a basic education. Construction sites are extremely noisy, and much of our communication takes place via hand signals. There is little premium placed on words that don't stem from our own jargon. Conversations can be blunt.

Bly's approach, of adapting a fable for instruction, may instinctively mimic the way men communicate. Ironworkers are otherwise very direct, yet when emotional issues arise we speak to one another in allegory and parable. One of my co-workers, Cliff, is a good storyteller, with an understated delivery: "The old man got home one night, drunk, real messed up and got to roughhousing with the cat. Old Smoke, well she laid into him, scratched him good. Out comes the shotgun. The old man loads up, chases Smoke into the front yard and blam! Off goes the gun. My Mom and my sisters and me we're all screamin'. Smoke comes walkin' in the side door. Seems the old man blew away the wrong cat, the neighbor's Siamese. Red lights were flashin' against the house, fur was splattered all over the lawn, the cops cuffed my old man and he's hollerin' and man, I'll tell you, I was cryin'."

Now, we didn't all get up from our beers and go over and hug him. This was a story, not therapy. Cliff is amiable, but tough, more inclined to solving any perceived injustices with his fists than verbal banter, but I don't need to see him cry to know that he can. He has before, and he can tell a story about it without shame, without any disclaimers about being "just a kid," and that's enough for me.

Ron and I have worked together for nine years and are as close as 29 is to 30. We have worked through heat and cold and seen each other injured in the stupidest of accidents. One February we were working inside a plant, erecting steel with a little crane; it was near the end of the day, and I was tired. I hooked onto a piece and, while still holding the load cable, signaled the operator "up." My thumb was promptly sucked into the sheave of the crane. I screamed, and the operator came down on the load, releasing my thumb. It hurt. A lot. Water started leaking from my eyes. The gang gathered around while Ron tugged gently at my work glove, everyone curious whether my thumb would come off with the glove or stay on my hand.

"O.K., man, relax, just relax," Ron said. "See if you can move it." Ron held my hand. The thumb had a neat crease right down the center, lengthwise. All the capillaries on one side had burst and were turning remarkable colors. My new thumbnail was on back order and would arrive in about five months. I wiggled the thumb, an eighth of an inch, a quarter, a half.

"You're O.K., man, it's still yours and it ain't broke. Let's go back to work."

Afterwards, in the bar, while I wrapped my hand around a cold beer to keep the swelling and pain down, Ron hoisted his bottle in a toast: "That," he said, "was the best scream I ever heard, real authentic, like you were in actual pain, like you were really *scared*."

If this wasn't exactly Wind in His Hair howling eternal friendship for Dances With Wolves, I still understood what Ron was saying. It's more like a 7-year-old boy putting a frog down the back of a little girl's dress because he has a crush on her. It's a backward way of showing affection, of saying "I love you," but it's the only way we know. We should have outgrown it, and hordes of men are now paying thousands of dollars to sweat and stink and pound and grieve together to try and do just that. Maybe it works, maybe it doesn't. But no matter how cryptic, how Byzantine, how weird and weary the way it travels, the message still manages to get through.

II

Anyone watching Morrie Driesenga lead a Wednesday morning men's group in Holland, Mich., would never guess that this retired salesman once tried to fill the spiritual void in his life with alcohol. Today, Morrie credits the special friendships he built with other men for helping him break those destructive patterns.

"I had grown up in the church, but I made wrong choices," he says. "My new life began when I literally dropped to my knees and said, 'Help me, Lord.' After I quit drinking, it was my friends' quiet encouragement and warm handshakes that helped me to stay sober."

When Morrie was elected to the board of elders, he invited the pastor out for a cup of coffee. "What can you teach me about prayer?" he asked, and within weeks, Morrie began meeting with the pastor and two other men every Wednesday for breakfast.

"We always begin with Scripture," Morrie says, "and then the leader asks individuals how we can best pray for them. That makes it easy for us to open up about what's going on in our lives."

Morrie is just one of many men who are gathering in churches, homes, workplaces—even restaurants—on a regular basis. Men's groups have been around since Jesus' disciples met in the Upper Room and broke bread with the Master, but in recent years, the trend has accelerated. Men are again understanding the need to talk about their feelings and develop deeper relationships with their own gender.

"Men have very few friends whom they feel they can reveal everything to," says Steve Largent, the NFL's all-time pass receiver who now works for Focus on the Family. "A lot of men don't have *anybody*—not even their wives—whom they feel comfortable to talk with. By developing relationships with other men, they can open up and express themselves freely."

The momentum behind the Christian men's movement—driven by the Spirit of God—has picked up in recent years. Several ministries have been effective: Career Impact, Priority Living, Christian Business Men's Committee and AbbaFather, to name a few. The latter ministry is the outreach of Rev. Gordon Dalbey, author of *Healing the Masculine Soul*. Men's souls have been torn, he says, between a women's movement that requires they abdicate masculinity to gain sensitivity and a deluge of Rambo-like media portrayals. Only by holding up Jesus Christ as the model for authentic manhood can men attain genuine masculine virtues, says Dalbey.

The Christian men's movement takes several guises. Some are "men-only" Bible studies, with time set aside at the end for prayer. Others are less structured; guys eating out together, chatting over food, discussing their relationships with their families or the progress of their spiritual growth. Some men attend once-a-year retreats; others prefer a large-group setting at weekly breakfast meetings.

At Cherry Hills Community Church in Denver, more than 300 men squeeze into an auditorium every Tuesday morning at 7 a.m. to hear executive pastor Bob Beltz talk about biblical masculinity. "We started with six men in 1980, and our group has slowly grown," says Dr. Beltz. "Now we just can't fit anyone else in the room."

But another trend is three or four men meeting in an "accountability group." Why would a self-reliant man submit to one? It means giving permission to raise tough questions, such as:

- "How is it *really* going with your wife?"
- "How are you spending your free time?"
- "What's your thought life like?". . .

Said one husband, "When your wife asks those questions, it often feels as though she's nagging. But when someone else sits down across from you and asks the same questions, it shows he cares for you."

Craig Wierda, who meets with three other men in Michigan, is surprised at how quickly he adapted to the closeness. "Once men experience the caring atmosphere, they go with it," he says. "Men for years have been islands, not wanting other people to get close. We haven't had anybody share what's inside because we live in a culture that says we have to go it alone."

It's almost second nature for men to keep their feelings bottled up. Many were raised by fathers who told them never to let their guard down, lest they reveal a weakness. Others make an unconscious choice to keep friendships at an arm's-length level. Some never heard their father say, "I love you."

One time, at an Adventures in Fatherhood retreat in California's Sierra Nevada mountains, several dozen fathers and their sons gathered around the evening campfire. A father stood up and described how he had never heard his father tell him that he loved him. He added that his father had never heard those three simple words from *his* father.

Then the father called his 17-year-old son to stand beside him. "Son, I'm going to break a generations-long tradition in our family. I'm here to tell you that I love you." With that, he gave his son a bear hug.

While a lot of men would find it hard to be that expressive, Dick Savidge, director of pastoral care at Cherry Hills Community Church, says, "We are starting to redefine masculinity.". . .

A Los Angeles women in a Bible study group with a half-dozen other women said all of them shared the same concern: Although they knew their husbands attended church and made the right noises, *they had no idea where their men were with God.* Each expressed regret that their husbands weren't in accountability groups. They so loved what they were experiencing that they hoped their husbands would share with other men and thus be encouraged to grow spiritually.

Perhaps that's why Dr. Howard Hendricks, professor emeritus at Dallas Theological Seminary, once said, "A man who is not in a group with other men is an accident waiting to happen."

Bruce Hosford, a Seattle real estate developer, has taken that advice to heart: he belongs to *three* small groups.

For a while, one of his groups was real small: just he and Denny Rydberg, director of University Ministries, which serves the University of Washington campus. "Denny and I have lots in common, and we would meet for lunch each week. We called it the 'Ultimate Small Group' and checked in with each other to see what's going on in life."

In recent years, Hosford and Rydberg have expanded the group to five. "Since the first of the year, we've gone through a half-dozen psalms, and sometimes we'll raise tough questions such as homosexuality. Believe me, that makes for some interesting discussions. We always have a timekeeper, though, and we always spend the last 10 minutes praying for each other."

Hosford, 43, also meets once a week with several University of Washington students in their early twenties. "It's amazing how open these college guys are: the struggles of living in a frat house, the dating scene, and the difficulties of being a follower of Christ at a large public university. These guys are willing to be vulnerable, and that is not typically male."

Accountability groups often help in unexpected ways. Anthony Munoz, the NFL All-Pro offensive tackle for the Cincinnati Bengals, used to meet weekly with six close church friends. A couple of years ago, Anthony was in the middle of contract negotiations with the Bengals.

"Things were going slow between me and the club, and I had this group to bounce things off," remembers Munoz. "One of the guys owned a small company, and he shared with me the management side of business. Not only was that beneficial, but I really grew a lot during that time."

For Morrie Driesenga, meeting with other men has been a real blessing, too.

"It's an old cliche, but we truly have cried together and laughed together as we've talked—and prayed—about our families, our frustrations and our praises. When any of us are out of town, we know we're missing a special time."

"Although it is not possible to know exactly what proportion of couples share [parenting] equally, even conservative estimates suggest that it is on the rise."

Men Are Becoming Better Fathers

Kathleen Gerson

Kathleen Gerson, author of the following viewpoint, reports that men are playing a greater, if still somewhat deficient, role as parents. Gerson examines a variety of social and economic factors influencing this shift in male roles and finds, among other things, that it is men's desire for increased involvement with their children that tips the balance in favor of shared parenthood. Gerson is associate professor of sociology at New York University and the author of *No Man's Land: Men's Changing Commitments to Work and Family*.

As you read, consider the following questions:

1. What are the categories of men the author delineates? What is the percentage of "involved fathers" in Gerson's sample? Why does she consider their involvement a significant development?
2. What causes some men to assume equal parenting responsibilities with the mother, according to Gerson? What is their percentage of her sample?

Successful revolutions, by their nature, can never remain confined to one social group. For the last 30 years, as women of all ages and family statuses have streamed into the workplace, rearranging the balance of their ties to employment and child rearing, men have been experiencing a quiet revolution of their own. While men who provide the sole or major economic support to their families have not disappeared, their ranks have dwindled. Even generous estimates suggest that no more than a third of American households now depend solely or primarily on a male earner.

Today men are facing new expectations and new choices about their commitments to society, family, and work. No longer certain what goals they should pursue, much less how they should pursue them, many men have found themselves in a no-man's land, searching for new meanings and definitions of maturity. Amid these social upheavals, some men have held steadfastly to traditional definitions of manhood while others have sought greater autonomy and freedom from family commitments, a pattern that social critic Barbara Ehrenreich has called the male "flight from commitment." In interviews I conducted with 138 men from diverse social and economic backgrounds, 36 percent defined their family and work commitments in terms of primary breadwinning, and 30 percent chose to eschew parenthood or to avoid involvement with children they had brought into the world [whom I call "autonomous men"].

Toward More Family Involvement

However, about 33 percent had moved toward more rather than less family involvement over the course of their lives. These men developed an outlook on parenthood that included caretaking as well as economic support. They represent a growing group of fathers, most of whom are married to work-committed women and have an egalitarian approach toward marriage and family commitments, who are changing diapers, pushing strollers, cuddling their children, and generally sharing in the pleasures and burdens of child rearing. Such men, whom I call "involved fathers," are demonstrating a capacity, a willingness, and an enthusiasm for parenting not seen in their fathers' and grandfathers' generations.

An involved father, however, is not necessarily an equal father. Though men's domestic participation has increased in recent years, this involvement has not kept pace with women's rapidly rising commitment to paid employment. A persistent "housework gap" has left most women with more work and less leisure time than their male counterparts. According to some estimates, women average two to three fewer hours of leisure per day than do married men. When the time spent performing paid

187

work, housework, and child care is added together, men work an average of 88 fewer hours a year than do women. . . .

It may be tempting to focus on the fact that, even among men who support equality, their involvement as fathers remains a far distance from what most women want and most children need. Yet it is also important to acknowledge how far and how fast many men have moved toward a pattern that not long ago virtually all men considered anathema. One recent survey found that 73 percent of a group of randomly selected fathers agreed strongly that "their families are the most important facet of their lives"; 87 percent agreed that "dad is as vital as mom in

raising kids." The challenge is to create the social and cultural arrangements that would enable men to uphold these beliefs more easily. . . .

Men Who Care

As men looked for commitments beyond the workplace and became involved with women who desired and expected help in child rearing, they found unexpected pleasure in parenting. Spending time with their children became as important to them as contributing money. Becoming an involved father, however, meant trading some historically male advantages for the chance to ease some historically male burdens. As Carl, a utilities worker, explains:

> Work's a necessity, but the things that really matter are spending time with my family. If I didn't have a family, I don't know what I would have turned to. . . . I look at my daughter and think, "My family is everything."

Indeed, it is a man's participation in caring for his children, not the shared breadwinning that typically accompanies it, that determines whether a man is an involved father. The type and degree of activity varied greatly among the involved fathers, but they all emphasized sharing and flexibility in parenting and domestic tasks. Lou, a sewage worker and father of a young girl, and Theodore, a planner who is married but not yet a father, sound remarkably similar despite differences in class and life stage:

> Patricia and I know how the other works. If one of us has a bad day, the other person will pick up the slack. If it's getting Hannah ready, teaching her writing, spelling, or such, it's whoever is in a better frame of mind that day that handles it. We feed off each other's vibes. If we both have bad days, then whoever had the better day takes care of her.

> One thing I learned: you can't take domestic jobs and say, "You do this, and I do that.". . . I think the same way with children. It's not going to be, "You're the one who changes the diapers while I burp the child." You do it together. If she's too tired, then I'll do it; and if I'm too tired, then she'll do it.

Autonomous men could make work choices without taking the economic needs of children into account. Primary breadwinners faced pressure to maximize their economic contribution, but they could also make choices about work without concern for spending time at home. Men who wished to care for their children, however, faced hard choices between freedom and commitment, career and parenthood, time spent with children and time spent making money or pursuing leisure. In the past, such trade-offs appeared to be the dilemma of employed mothers; today they confront any adult who tries to be both a committed parent and a committed worker. . . .

Involved fathers felt these conflicts more acutely than other

189

men precisely because they defined "good fathering" in terms of active involvement. Flexible about what they would do, their commitment not to rule anything out did not necessarily include a commitment to rule everything explicitly in. The stress on fluid, interchangeable responsibilities left unresolved the question of how much time they would commit and how much responsibility they would assume. They could use this vagueness to avoid certain tasks. Indeed, most were able to limit or pass on some of the costs of child rearing.

One way to limit the demands of parenthood and still play a significant role in child rearing is to keep the family small. Many involved fathers pushed for this, sometimes amid a wife's ambivalence. In addition, most (over three-fourths) of these households relied on paid or unpaid help from an additional caretaker. Involved fathers knew this help was essential for their own well-being, but they tended to view paid baby-sitters, housekeepers, and even relatives as substitutes for their wives (or, in some cases, ex-wives) and not for themselves. Since even the most involved fathers did not consider their responsibilities at work to be negotiable, the wife's decision to remain employed (or her absence from the home altogether) triggered the search for a "substitute mother." Frank, a bank vice president, pointed out how he "helped" his wife, a public relations officer, in caring for their young daughter:

> My participation is very extensive. I thoroughly enjoy my daughter's company. I regularly take her out on my own to allow Sharon time without the interruptions of a young child. And when she has got to go out of town on business—often for as much as a week or ten days at a time—I'm perfectly capable of stepping into her shoes.

Some fathers, however, became genuinely equal—and, in rare cases, primary—parents. Nearly 40 percent of involved fathers (or 13 percent of my entire sample) went beyond being mothers' helpers, reflecting a limited but growing trend. Although it is not possible to know exactly what proportion of couples share equally, even conservative estimates suggest that it is on the rise. In her study of dual-earning couples, for example, Arlie Hochschild found that about 20 percent shared what she called the "second shift" equally. . . .

Beyond Helping

If most involved fathers resisted equal participation, a substantial minority did not. These "equal parents" shared what mothers' helpers eschewed. Ernie, a physical therapist, shared responsibility for making arrangements for the care of his young daughter:

> I wanted to be there for the good times and the bad times. I wanted to share in making decisions, which was good for my

wife, too. I don't want her to decide on a nursery school; let's decide together. . . . How can I say I want children and not take that kind of responsibility?

Equal fathers also shared the "dirty work" of child care and housework. Lloyd, a sewage worker, had three children and drew few boundaries in dividing daily tasks with his wife, a chiropractor:

> We've always shared breadwinning and caretaking right down the middle. That's from washing the floor, changing diapers, washing clothes, cleaning the house. I don't draw any lines as to what is men's work and women's work; work is work.

In rare but significant cases, a father's contribution exceeded his partner's. Rick, a high school teacher who had once considered a legal career, assumed the lion's share of caretaking when his wife, a librarian, returned to a more highly structured, nine-to-five job shortly after the birth of their first daughter:

> For those first five years, I got the kids dressed and fed and everything. I always got up in the night with the first one. Always. It was 99 percent me with the older one. With the second one, it was shared. We have experimented and continued to do so—not really much thinking of it as an experiment anymore.

By rejecting the path of least resistance, these men illuminate the unusual circumstances that allow and promote equality and even primary parenting for men. . . .

Career Reasons

When Mothers Are More Committed than Fathers to Work. When a man's partner becomes more committed to a career than he does, neither parental equality nor a reversal of parental duties is assured. . . . Nevertheless, I found that in those rare instances when a reversal of occupational trajectories did occur among parents, a more equal arrangement became more likely. There is good reason to believe this dynamic occurs across a broad spectrum of couples. One study found, for example, that when a woman's career commitment is high, her share of domestic labor drops substantially. A comparison of nonemployed wives with those who worked 50 hours a week and earned at least $25,000 a year showed that the employed women's share of domestic labor dropped from 75 percent to 56 percent as their husbands and children took on more. While just being employed may not make much difference for married women's domestic burden, full-time employment in better paying jobs clearly does.

But the calculus of decision making involves more than money. I found that the relative degree of work commitment and satisfaction between parents was more decisive than strict economic accounting. Thus the percentage of equal fathers and mothers' helpers who earned about the same as their partners is roughly equal (44 percent to 38 percent), but equal fathers were more likely to be involved with a woman who faced better long-term career prospects (28 percent compared with only 7 percent for mothers' helpers). When a father's dissatisfaction with work combined with a mother's growing commitment to it, their job trajectories converged to make equality or primary parenting by a man more attractive—certainly not guaranteed, but more likely.

When Fathers Take Advantage of Flexible Work. Lack of job flexibility provides a genuine reason as well as a justification for unequal participation. Whatever their desires, most fathers are constrained by rigid work schedules, which make equal parenting less attractive, easier to avoid, and often out of the question. In a Census study of child-care arrangements for dual-earning couples with children under five, when both parents worked during the day, only 4 percent of mothers reported that their husbands were the primary caretakers when they were at work. When both parents worked at night, however, 31 percent relied on their husbands as primary caretakers. . . . Caretaking by fathers is more likely to occur when at least one parent works an unconventional shift.

Personal Reasons

Without the motivation to become more involved with his children, a father's job flexibility bears little relation to his parenting. But I found that the proper motivation enhanced the chances that an involved father would use a flexible work schedule to become an equal parent. This was especially so when his partner's work schedule was more rigid. For Rick, the teacher, shorter hours at the workplace and summers off allowed him more family time than his wife, a librarian, could muster. For many years he was the primary parent; now that the children are in school, he and his wife share child care "about equally."

For some, flexible work schedules had the unintended consequence of promoting equality or primary caretaking by a man. Others consciously chose to reject a nine-to-five schedule so that they could be more involved. Todd, a construction worker, opted for the evening shift so that he could spend his days with his newborn daughter while his wife pursued her dancing career:

> I take care of her in the morning and until I have to leave for work. I wake up with the morning ahead of me, and that's important with a little one. Even if I'm pretty tired when I get up, all I have to do is look at that little face, and I feel good.

Flexible work schedules could exact costs. They sometimes came at the expense of other work rewards, such as opportunities for advancement and a higher income. Equal fathers were willing to pay this price in order to spend more time with their children. In these cases, flexible work provided the opportunity for equal parenting. . . .

Single Dads

Although divorce typically separates fathers from their children, fathers can become more involved if they retain joint or sole custody. Of course, men seek custody precisely because they wish to participate in rearing their children. Nevertheless, retaining custody can have unintended as well as planned consequences.

Both one-parent families headed by men and joint-custody divorces remain rare, but the size of both groups is growing. The percentage of male custodial households has grown from 1.9 percent in 1970 to 3.1 percent in 1989. The number of divorces that produce joint-custody arrangements is harder to ascertain, but it is clearly growing at a much faster pace than male custody alone. The number of divorced fathers in my study is small (only 14), but 43 percent of them retained joint or sole physical custody, albeit not always legally.

Whatever the path, retaining some form of custody held unforeseen consequences for fathers who, though involved, were formerly able to rely on a woman to do a large share of the parental work. Divorce shattered some men's belief that a woman would always be there.

The loss of a female partner may also have more felicitous consequences. It forced once-complacent fathers to confront the previously unnoticed tasks of child rearing. Fathers who did not have a woman to rely on had little choice but to develop what some call "maternal thinking." These divorced men came to realize how much their freedom and independence had depended on their former wives' presence. They learned what their ex-wives already knew: involved parenting requires personal sacrifices. Like other equal fathers, custodial fathers were likely to search for less demanding and more flexible jobs. Roger, a businessman and divorced, custodial father of two, found himself making unexpected work sacrifices to accommodate his new job as a primary parent:

> The boys remained with me from the beginning, and I needed stability. I couldn't start a new job and rearrange my home schedule, so I stayed. I was making enough money, the hours fit, and it was convenient. I could be home at five-fifteen, have dinner on the table by six-fifteen. I was bored, but it was convenient for what else I was dealing with at the time. It's a seesaw. You've got to keep things balanced. . . .

[For the future,] the challenge is to build social institutions that support the best aspects of change (such as the expansion of equality, choice, and family involvement) and discourage the worst (such as the abandonment of children and the overburdening of women). We need to build policies that respect diversity, encourage responsibility, and create equal opportunity.

Women's movement into the labor force has made it clear that the home and the workplace are interacting rather than separate spheres. Yet conflicts between work and family have typically been viewed as a woman's problem. The current organization of the workplace makes it difficult for any parent, regardless of gender, to combine employment and parenting. Work poses obstacles to men's family involvement too, and to ignore these obstacles is to leave the problem unfairly resting on women's shoulders.

In addition, the historical bargain between employers and families has broken down. When employers paid their male workers enough to support a homemaking wife, they could argue that children's needs were not their concern. Since employers are now less likely to pay men a family wage that subsidizes female caretakers, the time has come to admit that most families depend on either two earners or one parent. What does this mean in practical terms? At the least, it means no longer penalizing employed fathers or mothers for providing the care and attention children need. Even more, it means offering workers greater flexibility in how they choose to balance work and family contributions over the course of the week, the year, and the career. Caretaking demands ebb and flow in unpredictable ways that cannot be addressed via rigid work schedules and career tracks. We need to create a more flexible boundary between family and work.

If involved parenting remains a formal option that few feel entitled to take without great sacrifice to their careers, the most ambitious or work-committed among us—women as well as men—will resist involved parenthood and reject the programs that exist on paper but punish those who utilize them.

"The reasons for a contemporary American man to assume the responsibilities of social fatherhood appear . . . problematic."

Men Are Not Becoming Better Fathers

Wade C. Mackey and Ursula White

In the following viewpoint, Wade C. Mackey and Ursula White argue that while much attention has recently focused on the meaning of fatherhood, little concern has been given to the experiences of fathers themselves. Fatherhood is an institution in decline in America, the authors assert, partly because there are no economic, social, or psychological incentives for a man to work hard to provide for his family. In fact, Mackey and White explain, the would-be father faces stiff competition from a federal government that in 1987 offered more money and services to women with children than nearly 30 percent of single men could provide. Mackey, author of *Fathering Behaviors*, is professor of anthropology at El Paso Community College in El Paso, Texas. White is professor of psychology at El Paso Community College.

As you read, consider the following questions:

1. According to the authors, how has the definition of fatherhood changed over time?
2. What do the authors say undermined the economic, social, and psychological incentives for fatherhood?
3. Why do Mackey and White say that men who are able to equal the state's support of the family may still opt out of their role as fathers?

From "The Abrading of the American Father" by Wade C. Mackey and Ursula White, *The Family in America*, July 1993. Copyright ©1993 by The Rockford Institute. Reprinted with permission.

The contemporary meaning of fatherhood has recently received a great deal of attention, both in and out of academia. Because a preponderance of the attention has been directed at the shifting expectations that others have held for him, much less effort has been expended upon analyzing fatherhood from the father's own perspective. Even less thought has been devoted to considering how current social policies might affect the father's life, as he himself experiences it.

The history of scholarly inquiry into fatherhood in the United States can be divided into three unequal intervals of inquiry: (I) up to the mid-1970s, (II) the mid-1970s to the mid-1980s, and (III) the mid-1980s to the present. Until the mid-1970s, the behavioral sciences typically defined the father as a breadwinner, a psychological support for the mother, and an ancillary child caretaker. The father was generally believed to influence the social, emotional, and cognitive development of the child less than the mother. Research surveys that did deal with fathers were, and continue to be, heavily based upon *mothers'* reports.

The 1970s brought a major shift in thinking about fatherhood, as writers in both academic and popular presses increasingly came to expect that the father's responsibilities and obligations were (or should be) comparable to those of the mother. The philosophy of egalitarian parenting gained prominence among writers and among university researchers. Some authors at the time argued that paternal deprivation was a serious problem. Others suggested that paternal involvement had been and was actually higher than believed, but that such involvement was typically unnoticed and under-reported. Despite the expectations for increased paternal involvement, however, actual behavior among fathers gave no indication of any meaningful reorienting or shifting which would meet the newly enhanced expectations of others. The limited observational data then available were typically from clinical observations of children without siblings in middle-class, Caucasian families. More complex families with two or more children of later developmental stages seldom received attention.

Elusive Fatherhood

When paternal behavior failed to change in the expected ways by the mid-1980s, a subtle change in polemics and evaluations occurred. The focus shifted from "fathering" to "husbanding" behaviors. That is, the model "father" was newly conceptualized as performing—in an egalitarian mode—traditional female domestic tasks. Framed a little differently, the "good" father became the husband who lightened the domestic load of his wife. The emphasis thus changed from a direct father-to-child interaction which (ideally) benefitted the child to a husband-to-wife relationship wherein the child (ideally) would benefit indirectly from the released time and energy of the mother and from her increased sense of well-being.

IN THE "WHAT'S WRONG WITH AMERICA" DEPARTMENT...

MOTHER   FATHER   PROVIDER

IF THE AMERICAN PEOPLE CAN PUT MEN IN SPACE OR FIGHT A WAR IN THE GULF, CERTAINLY THEY CAN TAKE CARE OF EVERYONE'S CHILDREN!

Asay, by permission of the *Colorado Springs Gazette Telegraph*.

In the decades following World War II, the father-child relationship became embedded in a rapidly changing familial context. Following the aberrant "baby boom," the American birth rate continued its centuries-long decline until, in 1972, the birth rate dropped below the replacement value of 2.1 lifetime births per woman and has stayed below that mark to the present. The divorce rate also rose to a comparatively high level and has remained there. More specifically, the divorce rate in the United States is approximately 5 per 1,000 population versus 1.1 per 1,000 population for a sample of 127 countries worldwide. The percentage of American divorces involving one or more children has, however, remained fairly consistent since 1960 when it was 60 percent until 1987 when it was 55 percent. Births to single mothers accounted for a progressively larger percentage of all births during these decades. In 1987, births to single mothers constituted 24.5 percent of all births. In contrast, births to single mothers accounted for only 4 percent of all births in 1960, 10.7 percent of all births in 1970, and 18.4 percent of all births in 1980.

As a consequence of high divorce and illegitimacy rates, the proportion of children living with their biological fathers from birth to age 18 has progressively declined. At base, the traditional nuclear family of mother, father, and child(ren) has been gradually giving way to the household defined by mother and child(ren).

When viewed economically, this displacement looms large. With the earning potential of the father separated from the mother-child(ren) household, the man's discretionary income would tend to increase, and the mother and child(ren)'s access to resources would concomitantly decrease. The "feminization of poverty" thereby became a polemic as well as a social reality. To allay or soften the negative consequences for mothers and children of the loss of father's resources, new government programs were created and old ones were expanded. "Entitlements" were redefined. By the 1980s, a series of these entitlements was increasingly available to very poor children (typically fatherless children) to provide them with a maintenance, if sub-optimal, lifestyle: food, shelter, health care, fuel, and education.

While the humanitarian objectives of these governmental interventions have received wide public support, both tacit and vocal, the size and magnitude of the programs may have also generated a social dynamic which has less universal acclaim and certainly has less visibility. With the advent and expansion of entitlement programs to alleviate mother-child deprivation, the state has emerged as a competitor with the father as the key provider for his family. The possible consequences of this latent, yet quite real, competition deserve attention.

Pointless Paternity

Human emotions, in general, and those emotions that guide parents, in particular, are delicate and sensitive. Nonetheless, in order to develop a clearer, less [farsighted] understanding of fathering, a cautious examination of those emotions is necessary. To that end, motivations may be considered in three somewhat artificial classes: economic, sociological, and psychological.

The relationship between the economic returns children bring and birth rates is rather clear. When children bring net economic benefits, birth rates are high. When children bring high net economic costs and few economic benefits, birth rates are low. Furthermore, the less that the nuclear family serves as an economic unit, the more couples will choose to divorce. When couples anticipate that familial dissolution will mean economic hardship, that perception seems to serve as a domestic "glue."

The United States is certainly not exempt from the economic pressures driving down fertility throughout the industrialized world. Having a child brings many economic burdens and few economic benefits for American parents, unless that child makes parents eligible for benefits through entitlement programs. As already noted, the American fertility rate, currently at approximately 1.9 lifetime births per woman, is below replacement level.

In contemporary America there appear to be few social pressures on young men to become fathers. The uncoupling of the generations has minimized any (grand)parental pressures which young men might have felt in the past. Furthermore, the man who has repudiated or has never assumed the role of social fatherhood seldom encounters social opprobrium because of his decisions.

No Remaining Reasons

Almost by default, psychological incentives appear to be those most likely to motivate a contemporary American man to enter (and stay in) the father role. A man may thus seek the following psychological benefits through fatherhood: (1) validation of his masculinity, (2) perpetuation of his name or bloodline, (3) expression of affection toward his children, and (4) pride in creating a home where his children can flourish and become independent. Although these psychological benefits receive ample attention in popular culture, their strength in actually energizing the father's behavior has not yet been unequivocally validated. Indeed, popular culture may camouflage rather than clarify the realities of a father's psychic world. For example, even though the siring of a child may corroborate virility and extend the bloodline one more generation, there is no . . . mandate that the biological father should become the social father. Further, a marriage followed by a divorce would allow a man's name to continue one more generation. Note also the probability that any affectional bonding from father to child would occur only when the father is physically close to his child over time. Single motherhood and divorce both dramatically reduce the likelihood of such physical proximity. Moreover, a larger percentage of children (2.9 percent) were living with *neither* parent than with the father alone (2.6 percent) in 1987.

The reasons for a contemporary American man to assume the responsibilities of social fatherhood appear even more problematic [because the costs of raising children may outweigh the benefits]. Although the presence of children seems to reduce marital disruption, it may, paradoxically, also lower the quality of marital life.

But perhaps the psychological satisfactions or rewards which accrue to the father who seeks, through his own labor, to provide a home for his children deserve closer scrutiny.

[Consider] the state as provider versus father as provider.

Major categories of state aid through entitlement programs include cash (Aid to Families with Dependent Children [AFDC]), food (food stamps; Women, Infants, and Children [WIC] benefits; and free-lunch, free-breakfast programs in schools), medical care (Medicaid), fuel (fuel allowances), education (Head Start, Pell grants), and housing (public housing). According to average figures from national data for the model year 1987, a person who qualified for all of these entitlements could receive cash, goods, and services worth between $10,227 and $14,613. Note that none of these benefits is taxable. Also note that state and local programs, which are *not* included in this analysis, spend 67 percent as much as do the federal programs (in 1987).

However, if a man's earning capacity is used to develop a benchmark comparison for the value of government entitlements, a somewhat different mosaic emerges. The range computed above (from $10,227 to $14,613) represents disposable income. Employees must pay Social Security taxes plus federal taxes (plus state and local taxes, depending on the locale).

If the federal taxes (including Social Security but *not* including any state or local taxes) are added to the base salary, then a man would have to earn between $10,958 and $16,087 in salary to match the state's programs. If he works at minimum wage ($3.35 in 1987) for 52 weeks at 40 hours per week, a man will earn only $6,968 and so will not even come close to matching the benefits available through entitlement programs. The salary required to match benefits through state programs exceeds the income of at least 12 to 23 percent of family households in 1987, and it exceeds the income of 17 to 30 percent of single men in 1987. Since single men are those who are eligible to marry single women, the 17 to 30 percent of all single men whose incomes are below the level required to match entitlement benefits are those who feel most acutely the effects of trying to compete with the state as a provider.

Redundant Roles

We need to consider, then, those men who are at or near the threshold at which the disposable income portion of their earning power is matched or exceeded by the cash, goods, and services of government entitlement programs. To the extent that a man feels satisfaction in providing for his children, then the erosion of his role as provider would simultaneously remove that motive for accepting the responsibilities of social fatherhood. In other words, to the degree that the state is a more reliable, more generous provider than the father, then to that degree a man would feel less reason to accept his role as father. In other words, the less his rewards in *his* providing, the less *his* incentive to stay.

Mothers, of course, likewise feel the effects of these financial incentives. On the one hand, a mother can live with a man who provides semi-reliable, marginal income, who requires her loyalty to him and her willingness to engage in a series of mutual negotiations on priorities. On the other hand, a mother can turn to the state, which can provide a larger, more dependable income without mandating any reciprocity from her. In the calculus of human relationships, the possibilities for reliable income without dependence upon any man create incentives for a woman to jettison the father of her children. Research indicates that women who receive entitlement packages from the government have disproportionately lower rates of marriage.

This generalized social dynamic has a negative feed-back loop. Entitlements have a one-way ratchet: programs are easier to initiate than to terminate. Accordingly, with a (mythological) "middle-class" childhood as a benchmark, the state would always be under social and political pressures to "up the ante" or raise the threshold of an appropriate, if sub-optimal, set of entitlements. To fund the incremental entitlements, the state would have to raise taxes. Increased taxation on wages and salaries, but not on entitlements, systematically adds to the proportion of men who are not economically competitive with governmental programs as providers.

The difficulties of trying to craft government policies which will help without displacing fathers are, of course, not new. Allowing severe deprivation of children is not in the American tradition. However, any social or economic policies which systematically separate parents from children are probably not in the best interests of those children. . . .

Any tacit assumption that low-income American fathers will willingly and indefinitely absorb the costs of their own children while also supporting (through their taxes) other men's children is without any empirical foundation. There are no precedents either to sustain or to refute the assumption. However, while taxes are quite difficult to avoid, the responsibilities of social fatherhood are less difficult to avoid.

The historical pattern of (known) societies in which men—fathers or maternal uncles—provide for and protect their kith and kin is not the only imaginable pattern for the future. A humanitarian state may prove to be equal or superior to a father or maternal uncle as a provider. Children can certainly survive and prosper without a social father. But in the long-term competition among cultures, a society predicated on mother-child(ren) households may not be competitive with familial systems based on father-mother-child(ren) families. There are absolutely no known precedents for the construction of a successful society without social fathers.

Periodical Bibliography

The following articles have been selected to supplement the diverse views presented in this chapter.

Sherman Alexie	"White Men Can't Drum," *The New York Times Magazine*, October 4, 1992.
Brad Andrews	"A Singular Experience," *Newsweek*, May 10, 1993.
Christopher N. Bacorn	"Dear Dads: Save Your Sons," *Newsweek*, December 7, 1992.
John Byrne Barry	"Daddytrack," *Utne Reader*, May/June 1993.
Aaron Bernstein	"When the Only Parent Is a Daddy," *Business Week*, November 23, 1992.
Sharon Doubiago	"Enemy of the Mother: A Feminist Response to the Men's Movement," *Ms.*, March/April 1992.
Andrew Ferguson	"America's New Man," *The American Spectator*, January 1992.
David Gates	"White Male Paranoia," *Newsweek*, March 29, 1993.
Nancy R. Gibbs	"Bringing Up Father," *Time*, June 28, 1993.
Mark Stuart Gill	"Boning Up," *Rolling Stone*, March 19, 1992.
Gerald F. Kreyche	"Time to Cry 'Auntie!'" *USA Today*, March 1993.
Tom McGrath	"Who Are You Calling a White Male?" *Salt*, September 1993.
Wayne E. Oates	"A Long Friendship," *The Christian Century*, January 19, 1994.
William J. O'Malley	"The Grail Quest: Male Spirituality," *America*, May 9, 1992.
Jean Seligmann et al.	"It's Not Like Mr. Mom," *Newsweek*, December 14, 1992.
Don Shewey	"Stepbrothers: Gays and the Men's Movement," *The Sun*, May 1993. Available from 107 N. Roberson St., Chapel Hill, NC 27516.
Society	Special issue on "The Proper Study of Men," September/October 1993.
Chilton Williamson Jr.	"Men Unlimited," *Chronicles*, February 1994. Available from 934 N. Main St., Rockford, IL 61103.

How Does Work Affect the Family?

MALE/
FEMALE
ROLES

Chapter Preface

"More likely to hit, push, kick, threaten, swear, and argue"; more apt to provoke "negative reactions from peers [and] earn lower grades"; and "twice as likely . . . to smoke, drink alcohol, and use marijuana."

These statements—which would seem to describe gang members or maladjusted youths from inner-city families—are actually descriptions by several psychologists of a growing population of mostly middle-class kids raised in some kind of substitute care while their parents work. These kids have behavioral problems, argues Pennsylvania State University psychologist Jay Belsky, because they experienced the work-related absences of their employed mothers at too young an age, thereby breaking the secure mother-infant attachment that children need to properly develop emotionally. Belsky worries that this interruption of the crucial mother-infant bond is a growing phenomenon, noting that 53 percent of all mothers with children under one year of age returned to the workforce in 1990. The subsequent break in these kids' emotional development, argues Barbara Hattemer, president of the International Foundation for the Preservation of the Family, may produce "individuals who remain dependent on others—both other people and other things such as drugs, alcohol, or deviant and violent behavior patterns."

Nothing could be further from the truth, insists University of Pennsylvania professor of psychology Diane Eyer, whose book *Mother-Infant Bonding: A Scientific Fiction* is devoted to exploding attachment theory. As an example of the flimsiness of the research she says is advanced to support the importance of mother-infant bonding, Eyer cites a study that used goats as subjects and another that gave high scores to women who had not been out since their babies were born, Contrary to these "fictions," Eyer claims, "For years, reliable studies have been telling us *not* that a child requires full-time care from a biological mother but that children generally thrive when they have good, stable relationships with several . . . adults." Such relationships are actually made possible by placing children in nonparental care, argues Smith College psychology professor Faye J. Crosby. "As a result of contact with children and adults outside the family," Crosby maintains, kids in day care develop an "interpersonal resourcefulness and resilience" that will better enable them "to confront the twenty-first century."

On the topic of how work affects the family there is little agreement, except that, as Hattemer puts it, how the next generation is raised will one day determine "the personality of the culture." The following chapter debates this decisive, and divisive, issue.

"No one really assumes a basic and immutable incompatibility between being a paid worker and being a parent."

Working Parents Help Their Children

Faye J. Crosby

Much of the debate over the way Americans are bringing up the next generation springs from the fact that more and more women are entering the workforce and leaving the traditional home behind. In the following viewpoint, Faye J. Crosby explains that this new state of affairs, usually portrayed as harmful to the children of working parents, is actually conducive to the development of well-adjusted, achievement-oriented sons and daughters. Crosby, professor of psychology and chair of the psychology department at Smith College in Northampton, Massachusetts, is a well-known writer on gender issues.

As you read, consider the following questions:

1. What new ideas are the children of working parents, especially working moms, imbued with, according to Crosby? How does the author suggest that these new attitudes are beneficial?
2. What are the results of graduated challenges, according to Crosby?
3. Why does the author feel that questions about whether mothers should work or stay home are unproductive?

[M]any researchers] have identified benefits that children reap from having a mother employed outside the home. To those benefits they mention I have added a few of my own. Here's the list generated more by life than by science.

Increased Contact

Men certainly do not do their share of the laundry, cooking, shopping, cleaning, and general household maintenance. They do not even do their share of child care. But the child of a working mother has at least a little better chance than most children to see Dad in an apron. Such children may also have more opportunity than others to become intimately acquainted with Granny and Grandpa in Kansas City and Aunt Lucille in Berkeley.

When asked what effect their employment had on the father-child relationship, for example, 58 percent of the young mothers in a sample of middle-class Caucasians replied that the effect was unequivocally positive. Even a higher percentage of men in the sample agreed. Another study, this time of Chicano families, found that maternal employment was strongly associated with a shift in the family toward egalitarian child-care patterns. When the mother worked, the father shed some of the trappings of patriarchy.

Rigid separations between work and home are harder to maintain when mother works at the office as well as in the kitchen. When I was a child, I saw the inside of my father's office about twice a year. We did have a constant flow of his business associates through the house, and most dinners when he was home included conversations about the day at work. My mother was a helpmate to my father in his work and had no office of her own. Our children see the inside of my office several times a week. Tim's first trip to the office, in a little yellow jumpsuit, occurred when he was one week old. He has been coming to work with me ever since. In fact, the building where I currently work has a machine that dispenses chocolate milk, and Tim's comment when I told him about writing this book was: "Tell them about how the best part of your working is the chocolate milk."

That the children see my office more than my husband's office has to do, in our case, with the fact that his office is out of town—110 miles out of town. But even if we worked in the same location, the children might still know more about my work day than about his. Typically the children in two-career families are drawn more into the work life of the mother than of the father. This, in any event, was what Lisa Silberstein found in her study of dual-career couples.

Greater Resourcefulness and Resilience

Sandra Scarr, Edward Zigler, Kathleen McCartney, and other researchers have found that children who attend high-quality child-care centers show benefits in their intellectual and emotional development as a result of contact with children and adults outside the family. Interpersonal resourcefulness and resilience are the hallmarks of some children in other [nonparental] care. Child care is a positive experience for many girls and boys. As high-quality centers increase, this becomes more frequently true.

Children can be very stereotyped in their thinking. One might expect some children to resent their mothers' involvement in a job or career. Yet, at least one study shows that children of jugglers [parents who hold a job and take care of the home and family] are proud of them. The question arises: Are the children of jugglers also more supple—less stereotyped in their thinking—than others?

Measurable Improvements

Studies of working mothers with young children indicate that these mothers are more verbally attentive to their daughters than at-home mothers are, and that infants of working mothers, even as young as five months, show higher rates of exploration and accompanying verbalization. Discouraging clinginess and, conversely, demanding independent and mature behavior have also been associated with higher intelligence scores and higher level of achievement in school. In a study conducted by the National Assessment of Educational Progress, 100,000 daughters *and* sons of working mothers in grades four, eight and eleven were found to have significantly higher reading scores than their classmates. Researchers engaged in the study speculated that working mothers tend to be better educated than at-home mothers and that children of working mothers attend nursery school at an earlier age than do the children of at-home mothers.

Anita Shreve, *Remaking Motherhood: How Working Mothers Are Shaping Our Children's Future*, 1987.

A respectable amount of research has now accumulated on the sex-role attitudes of the children of housewives and of the children of employed women. The research shows rather compellingly that children lose some of the rigidity of their sex-role stereotyping when they have mothers who play the provider role as well as the nurturer role. Employed mothers in two-parent families have children who are more egalitarian in terms of gender than are the children of other mothers. Less research has documented the effects of having a father who is involved in the day-to-day minutiae of family life; the little there is also suggests that children of men who are highly involved in child

207

care retain less rigid sex-role ideologies than do other children.

How you view a liberal sex-role ideology in your children is, of course, likely to depend on what you yourself believe. In the early 1970s the standard textbook on the sociology of the family contained these grim words: "a child whose father performs the mothering functions both tangibly and emotionally while the mother is preoccupied with her career can easily gain a distorted image of masculinity and femininity." Perhaps some people have retained such views, but most parents today recognize the value of a flexible sex-role ideology. Especially in view of the challenges presented to the contemporary adolescent's sense of identity, children who are free of overly rigid and confining sex-role stereotypes may be better equipped than other children to negotiate the traumas of teenage years. Most likely, too, flexible children are well equipped to confront the twenty-first century.

Positive Self-Regard

Learning how to get about in the world not only can make a child more tolerant; it can increase his or her self-confidence. Some of the classic investigations of [what drives children to achieve] demonstrated the importance of graduated challenges. Without challenges, children did not develop a striving for excellence. Children who faced tasks where they had a good chance, but not a certainty, of succeeding developed the need and capacity for achievement [David McClelland showed].

Challenges must, of course, be at the right level. Challenges that are too great stunt growth. There is nothing that disrupts emotional growth so much as having inappropriate adult demands foisted on us too early. Six year olds are not capable of carrying adult responsibilities. It is wrong of adults—whether or not the adults work outside the home—to give children too much responsibility. Everyone needs a childhood, and if you do not have one when you are young, you will take one when you are older.

[A family therapist raised the question "What about the children?" after a speech I gave on juggling to a group of psychotherapists. She] has my agreement that those actions and responsibilities which foster self-confidence and boost self-esteem in the adolescent can crush the younger child. I agree that the good parent age grades the challenges he or she gives to the children. The parent who is too busy or preoccupied to spend time fitting the challenge to the child's development stage may do damage to her child.

Where the therapist and I part company is the point at which she assumes that employed mothers are any less attentive to age grading than at-home mothers. I know of no evidence whatsoever to support such a view. Indeed, research invalidates her assumption. One intricate study brought 100 mother and child pairs into the laboratory and observed them as they played a co-operative game. The interactions were coded on a number of di-mensions. The researchers rated the mothers on the extent to which they were accepting, protective, indulgent, and ready to discipline the child. The employed mothers were just as warm in their interactive style as the at-home mothers.

Money Benefits

The last major benefit—and it is, in my book, the most impor-tant—concerns finances. There are 12.5 million children in this country who live with a mother and no father. Many of these children depend entirely on their mother's income for survival. For these children, having a working mother allows them to have the basic necessities.

Even when there is a father in the family who brings in money, the mother's money also matters to children. Just as people are accustomed to thinking of men as babysitting for their own chil-dren, people are accustomed to thinking of women as helping out with family finances. Such a point of view has become quaint. Even as long ago as 1977, wives who were employed full time year around contributed about four dollars to the family coffers for every six dollars brought in by their husbands. Looking at all families at that time, wives' earnings accounted for one-quarter of family earnings. In 1978, the average income of a family in which the husband was the sole earner leveled at just above $16,000. For the dual-earner families in that same year, average family income exceeded $22,000. Two years later, the median in-come of a family in which both husband and wife earned money reached $27,700, about one-quarter higher than the median fam-ily income of the traditional family. Recent government figures show that the wealthiest fifth of our citizens includes a dispropor-tionately large number of dual-income families.

Figures and facts change stereotypes and myths only slowly. Our tendency to discount the women's financial contribution to the family's welfare perpetuates maternal guilt. Why do we ask employed women how they can choose between their jobs and their children when we do not ask men the same question?

My friend Emily is married to a successful psychiatrist, Clark. Clark earns an astonishing amount of money each year. So does Emily, but Emily's astonishing earnings have held at about half the size of Clark's over the last decade. A few years ago Emily was offered a job in a city at a little distance from home. The job would have increased her earnings so that she would have earned 75 percent and not 50 percent of Clark's earning. Emily did not take the job. She claimed that her decision was financial.

"What I had to figure," said Emily, "was the tax angle. First, you have got to start with Clark's salary. He pushes us close to the top bracket. Then I push us over. So, an increase of X thousand dollars is really only an increase of one-half of X thousand. Then, of course, I subtract from that my transportation costs and added costs of the housekeeper for the extra hours I'm gone."

Emily was a feminist. She had written a book on women and working. Yet even she said, without batting an eyelash: "You've got to start with Clark's salary." Why? Why not start with hers and figure his as the add on? And why not charge the housekeeper, at least in part, to his long hours at work? Why only to hers?

It has taken me years to come to see myself as a financial provider, but I am glad to be at that point. So are my children. They are normal kids. They like the things money can buy—basics such as clothing, food, and shelter as well as extras, like chocolate milk from the machine.

Questioning Old Assumptions

Back in the days of June Cleaver, housewifely motherhood constituted the feminine ideal. Motherhood was assumed. Today labor force participation is taken as a given, and motherhood has become a question. Childlessness is on the increase. In the late 1970s, 2.7 million women were childless. In 1987, 4.5 million were. Delayed childbearing is increasing, too. Among women who decide to have children, the desire for large families has all but vanished. And, for fear of jeopardizing their careers, many bright-eyed young women today seem to opt, at least temporarily, to be child free.

The ambitious young career women might appear to have values that differ dramatically from those of the family therapist who had asked, "What about the children?" In one fundamental way, however, they are agreed. Both doubt that a mother can work for money outside the home and simultaneously assume responsibility within. For both the frosty therapist and the career-track yuppies, the basic question is: Should a woman juggle work and children or shouldn't she?

The should-she–shouldn't-she question has some curious aspects. While motivated in large part by a very legitimate concern for the health and well-being of growing children, it also assumes certain sexual scripts and precludes others. The same question is not asked of men. Presumably, then, no one really assumes a basic and immutable incompatibility between being a paid worker and being a parent. Apparently, people make the assumption of incompatibility in the case of female parents. This assumption is in turn tied to the belief—newly popular among those who hear women speaking in a different voice than men—that women are affiliative and men are not.

The should-she–shouldn't-she question strikes an odd note in another way as well: It derived from a limited vision and further impedes progress toward a larger view. Martha Minow has written: "The critics often repeat in new context versions of the old assumptions they set out to contest." As long as we persist in asking whether she should or should not juggle, we will persevere in our old ways.

> *"The plight of the middle-class child is often centered on a massive deficit in parental time and attention."*

Working Parents Harm Their Children

Sylvia Ann Hewlett

In the following viewpoint, excerpted from her influential book, *When the Bough Breaks*, Sylvia Ann Hewlett catalogs some of the developmental problems experienced by the children of working parents. These problems, Hewlett argues, are the result of a parenting gap caused in part by "the retreat of the traditional mother." Sylvia Ann Hewlett is a prominent writer and economist who has served with the United Nations Association and the Council on Foreign Relations.

As you read, consider the following questions:

1. What specific problems does Hewlett find today's children are having as a result of the "parental time deficit"? What evidence does she offer to support her observations?
2. What are some of the origins of the "parental time deficit," according to the author? Why is the role of women central to Hewlett's description of this deficit?
3. Does Hewlett believe that money can solve the problems of "mainstream" kids?

On April 21, 1989, ABC-TV's newsmagazine *20/20* was devoted to examining a group of teenagers who seem to have it all and yet are hooked on drugs and alcohol. They live in Pacific Palisades, California, one of the country's wealthiest suburbs. In this lush community of big homes, fast cars, and swimming pools, youngsters seem intent on self-destruction.

The parents of these kids work hard at "making it" in a highly materialistic culture, and they're often generous with their children to the point of indulgence. What they don't give them, however, is enough time and attention. . . .

The Parent Gap

Clearly, the problem goes beyond a resource deficit. Even if we were to eliminate poverty and vastly improve the benefits and services provided to families with children, it would still be difficult to touch the more complex problems that routinely derail children in contemporary society. Becky Kraus [a hypothetical troubled child] does not like eating rice and beans for supper, but she is not poor in any ordinary sense. Nor can her problems be solved by the simple application of large doses of money. Better social supports would help at the margin—an after-school program, for example, would reduce the emotional toll of being a latchkey kid—but in the main, Becky's enormous load of pain, her poor performance at school, her inability to make sense of the future are all wrapped up in her parents' divorce, her absentee father and stressed-out mother. She feels that both her parents missed out on her childhood, leaving her exposed and rudderless, coping more or less badly with the difficult business of growing up in the 1980s.

Becky's experiences—and those of the teenagers interviewed on *20/20*—highlight a burgeoning parenting deficit that is increasingly threatening the well-being of children. The root causes range from the massive increase in the amount of time adults spend in the workplace to spiraling rates of divorce and single parenthood. Over the last twenty-five years the proportion of mothers in the paid labor force has tripled and the number of children growing up without a father has increased by a factor of two. The central consequences for youngsters have been little contact with parents and large quantities of time badly spent. By and large the vacuum left in children's lives by the retreat of the traditional mother has not been filled with attentive fathers, quality child care, expanded educational programs, or any other worthy activity. Hundreds of thousands of kids like Becky have been left to fend for themselves in a society that is increasingly inhospitable to children.

Children in the mainstream of our society are at risk in a variety of ways. Compared to a previous generation, these children are more likely to: underperform at school; commit suicide; need psychiatric help; suffer a severe eating disorder; bear a child out of wedlock; take drugs; be the victim of a violent crime. According to a 1990 study by the National Commission on the Role of the School and the Community in Improving Adolescent Health, even privileged youngsters are overwhelmed "by drugs, pregnancy, bad grades and bad jobs."

Drawing by R. Chast; ©1989 The New Yorker Magazine, Inc.

A central fact about contemporary middle-class children is that they are not doing well in school. No matter how you judge performance, whether you compare American students with students in other countries, or compare this generation of children with their parents, or simply ask whether these youngsters are learning enough to become viable members of society, it is hard to be complacent about educational standards among American youth. . . .

A dramatic measure of the failure of the U.S. educational system is our track record on the illiteracy front. Since the early 1960s the United States has dropped from eighteenth to forty-ninth place among nations in terms of the proportion of the population that is literate. Today approximately 6 percent of the adult population has not attained "basic literacy" (a fourth-grade reading level), and fully 20 percent—36 million people—are functionally illiterate in that they cannot read or write at the eighth-grade level, which is thought to be the minimal educational requirement for most jobs. Functional illiteracy among minority youth may run as high as 40 percent. Standards in some high schools are so low that hundreds of thousands of functionally illiterate young people graduate every year. William Brock, Secretary of Labor in the Reagan administration, estimated that 700,000 high school graduates "get diplomas each year and cannot read them." He calls it an "insane national tragedy."

In 1987 almost half this nation's seventeen-year-olds could not correctly determine whether 87 percent of 10 is greater than, less than, or equal to 10; nor could they determine the area of a rectangle. According to Elizabeth Ehrlich, some 35 percent of American eleventh-graders write at or below the following level: *"I have been experience at cleaning house Ive also work at a pool for I love keeping thing neat organized and clean. Im very social Ill get to know people really fast."*

Such an impressive level of educational failure has serious repercussions in the labor market. In 1987 New York Telephone had to test 57,000 people before it could find 2,100 who were well educated enough for entry-level jobs as operators or repair technicians. One-third of the nation's large corporations now provide courses in reading, writing, and arithmetic for those who need it, and the army gives courses to bring recruits up to ninth-grade reading levels. Xerox's chairman, David Kearns, estimates that U.S. industry spends $25 billion a year on remedial education for workers.

Evidence of Decline

In 1983 the National Commission on Excellence in Education told us that "for the first time in history, the education skills of one generation will not surpass, will not equal, will not even approach, those of their parents." The clearest evidence of educational decline is the pronounced drop in the SAT scores of college-bound high school seniors.

Between 1963 and 1981, mean scores on the mathematical portion of the test fell 32 points, while mean scores on the verbal portion fell 51 points. There has been some modest improvement since 1981, but scores started to dip again in 1987. The total recovery [to 1990] has amounted to less than 13 points. Average SAT scores remain 70 points below those of 25 years ago. . . .

We are not just talking about a deficit in math and writing skills—American students seem to absorb very little factual knowledge during their years in school. Geography is a particularly weak area. A 1987 study by James Kilpatrick of five thousand high school seniors in eight major cities found that "25 percent of the students tested in Dallas could not identify the country that borders the U.S. on the south. In Boston, 38 percent of the students could not name the six New England states. . . . And 40 percent of those in Kansas City could not name three countries in South America."

Where Are We?

Students are also less well informed than their parents were when they were young. According to a series of *New York Times* surveys, forty years ago 84 percent of college students knew that Manila was the capital of the Philippines; today only 27 percent know the correct answer to that question. Senator Bill Bradley (D-N.J.) is among those worried: "This news is not only shocking; it is frightening. . . . When 95% of college students cannot locate Vietnam on a world map, we must sound the alarm. We cannot expect to be a world leader if our populace doesn't even know where the rest of the world is."

Only 72.6 percent of American students who enter ninth grade earn a high school diploma four years later, a figure that slipped five percentage points between 1968 and 1990. Most policy makers see this as a national disgrace in an age when our economic competitors have near-universal secondary school education. In Japan, for example, 90 percent of seventeen-year-olds graduate high school. Equally worrisome is the fact that only about 60 percent of college students graduate. A 1989 federal study found a sharp decline in the proportion of students completing higher education in both two- and four-year colleges. Only 18 percent of the class of 1982 had earned a degree or diploma four years after high school, compared with 45 percent ten years earlier.

Emotional Problems

Not only is a large proportion of American youth growing up badly educated and ill prepared for the world of work, but a significant number of youngsters are failing to cope on psychic and emotional fronts.

Suicide among adolescents has increased dramatically over the past quarter-century (in contrast with suicide among adults, which has remained stable). The suicide rate for teenagers ages fifteen to nineteen tripled between 1960 and 1986, going from 3.6 to 10.2 deaths per year per 100,000 persons in that age range. The rate for younger adolescents is considerably lower, but it too has been climbing, going from 1.2 to 2.3 deaths per 100,000 between 1978 and 1986. Teen suicide is a highly disturbing phenomenon. Each of these deaths has an enormously demoralizing effect on family and community. Parents, grandparents, siblings, friends, and fellow students are left coping with guilt, anxiety, and unanswered questions. It should be remembered that suicide is only the extreme expression of emotional problems present among a much larger number of young people who either attempt suicide or self-destruct slowly through substance abuse or violent behavior. In 1986, 10 percent of teenage boys and 18 percent of teenage girls attempted suicide.

A wealth of less dramatic evidence indicates that the emotional well-being of children and adolescents has deteriorated over the past three decades. According to a 1990 American Medical Association report, today's youngsters "are having trouble coping with stresses in their lives and more have serious psychological problems" than a generation ago. State surveys on the number of schoolchildren needing help for chronic emotional problems point to a growing problem among grade-school students. Elementary-school teachers identified twice as many needy children in 1986 as in 1970. And more teens seek psychiatric help than ever before. Between 1971 and 1990 the number of adolescents admitted to private psychiatric hospitals has increased fifteenfold, a particularly striking statistic given that the teen population has shrunk over the last twenty years. Experts in the field point out that these disturbing trends are not due to a national epidemic of crazed kids; rather, family turmoil—provoked by divorce, disappearing fathers, mothers at work, and lengthening work weeks—has left many parents too overburdened to set limits or impose controls on their children. For example, the pressures on newly divorced mothers are often so severe that according to a study by E. Mavis Hetherington, "parenting breaks down and becomes inconsistent and erratically punitive." The children retaliate, venting their pain and frustration on the only available parent. One divorced woman [in the study] said that the constant harassment felt "like being bitten to death by ducks."

Eating Disorders

Obesity, which very often has emotional roots, is also on the rise and is now a major disorder among American children. Twenty-seven percent of youngsters aged six to eleven are now defined as obese, up from 18 percent just twenty-five years ago.

217

Obesity causes severe psychological and social problems and is linked to a set of physical ailments that range from hypertension, respiratory disease, and diabetes to orthopedic malfunctions.

If a quarter of American children are obese, some 10 to 15 percent of all teenage girls have some type of eating disorder, and a minority of these—approximately 2 to 5 percent—suffer from a serious form of anorexia (self-induced near-starvation) or bulimia (binge eating coupled with self-induced vomiting and purging). Both disorders can have serious physical, psychological, and social consequences. Anorexia and bulimia took off in the 1970s, and since that time the incidence of these disorders has increased by a factor of three.

Laurel Mellin, director of the Center for Adolescent Obesity in San Francisco, sees these eating disorders as intimately linked to family dysfunction. "Mother's increasing presence in the work place, father's failure to pick up the residual fifty percent of parenting . . . and marital instability" all contribute to a situation where "children are not likely to receive the balance of warm nurturing support and effective limit-setting that protects them from exhibiting various forms of distress, including eating and weight problems." Findings of a 1987 study by the Select Committee on Children, Youth and Families showed that 46 percent of adolescents with eating disorders came from "chaotic families.". . .

The Parental Time Deficit

The problems that plague mainstream kids seem to be different as well as much more complicated than those that beset disadvantaged kids. If a poor child comes down with measles, suffers a hearing loss, or fails to learn to read, the difficulty can often be resolved by spending more public money on health care or education. In affluent homes, problems of academic underperformance, suicide, and obesity cannot be clearly or directly linked to material deprivation. The plight of the middle-class child is often centered on a massive deficit in parental time and attention.

The huge jump in the number of mothers at work, the escalation in job-related stress, the expanding work week, the sharp increase in divorce and single parenthood, and the abandonment of children by their fathers all play a part in explaining why so many mainstream American kids are in distress. In millions of homes around the nation, these trends translate into a significant decline in the quantity and quality of time parents spend caring for their children.

Parents are devoting much more time to earning a living and much less time to their children than they did a generation ago. Stanford economist Victor Fuchs has shown that parental time available to children fell appreciably between 1960 and 1986:

"On average, in white households with children there were ten hours less per week of potential parental time . . . while the decrease for black households with children was even greater, approximately twelve hours per week." A prime cause of this falloff in parental time is the enormous shift of women into the paid labor force. In 1960, 30 percent of mothers worked; by 1988, 66 percent of all mothers were in the paid labor force. This dramatic increase has eaten into the amount of time mothers are able to devote to their children.

University of Maryland sociologist John Robinson has shown that the more hours mothers are employed, the fewer hours they can give to "primary-care activities" such as playing with and talking to children; dressing, feeding, and chauffeuring children; and helping with homework. According to Robinson, employed mothers spend an average of six hours each week in primary child-care activities—just under half the average time logged by nonemployed mothers and roughly twice that of fathers (employed or nonemployed). In single-parent households, children typically receive two or three fewer hours per week of primary care from their mothers, and three fewer hours from their fathers, than do children in two-parent homes. Robinson points out that wage labor not only eats into primary care but also influences the amount of contact parents have with their children. The data show that the amount of "total contact time"—defined as time parents spend with children while doing other things— has dropped 40 percent during the last quarter-century. This drop is significant because many of the things parents do with children, whether it's visiting Grandma or shopping for groceries, play an important role in building strong parent-child relationships and in giving families a shared identity. Studies that focus on [what Deborah Fallows calls] "all-out, undisturbed, down-on-the-floor-with-the-blocks time" fail to provide an accurate gauge of parent-child interaction precisely because they do not recognize the importance of just being together.

In harried dual-worker or single-parent families, even time-honored rituals such as eating family dinners or taking summer vacations are being squeezed. During the 1980s the length of the average family vacation declined 14 percent, and the number of families that eat their evening meals together has dropped 10 percent.

Many parents are uncomfortable with this loss in family time. A national survey commissioned by the Mass. Mutual Insurance Company found that nearly half the parents who responded were concerned about not having enough time to spend with their families. The majority believed that "parents having less time to spend with their families" is the single most important reason for the decline of the family in American society.

*"In about half of the infants placed in day care
while their mothers worked, the researchers
identified social-emotional problems."*

Day Care
Harms Children

J. Craig Peery

Many researchers believe that a secure mother-infant attachment is necessary for a child's proper emotional development.
In the following viewpoint, J. Craig Peery argues that day care
disrupts this essential bond, resulting in emotional impairment
and behavioral problems in children. Worse still, Peery explains,
are the serious diseases and even sexual abuse that many of the
children of working mothers face in day care. Peery, professor
of human development at Brigham Young University in Provo,
Utah, was formerly special assistant for child and family issues
to the chairman of the U.S. Senate Committee on Labor and
Human Resources.

As you read, consider the following questions:

1. What, according to Peery, are the possible results of weak
   attachment, especially in peer group relationships?
2. What diseases are children exposed to in day care, according
   to the author?
3. Peery lists a series of propositions in favor of day care. Since
   he refutes propositions two through four, what may we
   conclude is his opinion about number one, "The Problem"?

From "Children at Risk" by J. Craig Peery, *The Family in America*, February 1991. Copyright
1991 by The Rockford Institute. Reprinted with permission.

Amid a surge of enthusiasm for government-sponsored day care, federal day-care legislation has been signed into law [the 1990 Act for Better Child Care, which includes the Child Care and Development Block Grants to fund state-provided child care]. Those vocally supporting day care come largely from a coalition of feminists, day-care providers, and university academics who do research and training. The debate rarely includes an analysis of *how children ought to be raised in order to promote optimal development*. Those advocating day care focus on a number of adult considerations quite outside the world of childhood. Because they dismiss consideration of what is *best* for children, many who are now framing public policy may reach conclusions with disastrous results for children. Thoughtful parents and prudent policymakers need to exercise care to avoid being entangled in this inappropriate thinking. An examination of the arguments used by those championing expansion of government-funded day care is instructive.

Day-Care Delusions

Reasons for promoting day care can be summarized in four propositions:

1. *The Problem.* Most women are working outside the home; more will be working all the time; working mothers must leave their children in order to work; and that means:
2. *The Solution.* Someone other than the mothers must take care of the children of working mothers (pay for these caretakers, many advocates propose, should be federally subsidized).
3. *Don't Worry About The Solution.* The supposedly overwhelming conclusion of research evaluating day care is that quality day care is not harmful; in fact, it is helpful to disadvantaged children.
4. *The Opposition.* Anyone who questions any of the first three propositions is guilty of obsolete thinking (or trapped in the 50's, or is still living with Ozzie and Harriet, etc.).

An example of this day-care mantra may be found in the first paragraph of an advocacy article by developmental psychologists Deborah Phillips and Carolee Howes:

> The majority of children younger than age 6, including more than half of those younger than 1 year of age, were in need of child care while their mothers worked. This demographic fact had a profound effect on the major issues addressed in child care research. The question of whether or not children should be in child care has become obsolete. We have also been able to move beyond this question because 20 years of research on child care allayed our worst fears that nonmaternal care is inevitably harmful to children. To the contrary, the overwhelming message was that children in good quality child care show

no signs of harm and children from low-income families may actually show improved cognitive development (K.A. Clarke-Stewart & G. Fein, 1983; M. Rutter, 1981; E.F. Zigler & E.W. Gordon, 1982).

We might have looked at any statement promoting day care, since the arguments are very uniform. This particular paragraph is written by individuals who would generally be considered as thoughtful, well-informed scholars.

However, the assumptions and assertions of the day-care lobby will not bear scrutiny. Proposition #4, concerning *The Opposition*, can be summarily dismissed as at best a value judgement, at worst, a kind of intellectual name-calling.

The Burden of Proof

But what about proposition #3? What are the results of separating young children from their parents by putting them in day care? Indicative of our moral concern about child-rearing practices, research investigating the impact of nonparental child care has burgeoned. In hundreds of studies, not one even remotely suggests that separating children from parents is an *optimal* approach. But then day care is neither contrived nor promoted as something advantageous for the child. Day care is seen rather as the solution to an adult problem (see proposition #1: women are working). Also remember the appropriate framework for this analysis is *not*, "Can those who question the wisdom of government-funded day care prove day care is harmful?" Rather the appropriate question is, "Can *pro*ponents of day care establish it is beneficial to children?" If day care exposes children to conditions of risk or if there is evidence of harm, proposition #3 fails.

But who can Americans trust to supply the facts about how day care affects children? Both advocates and critics seem to have experts willing to testify at the day-care trial. Phillips and Howes, quoted above, are experts who cite research which demonstrates "overwhelmingly" that "children in good quality child care show no signs of harm."

It is worth examining the research they cite. As one examines these sources, one soon realizes that research does not give day care a clean bill of health. But we do get some real insight into how day-care advocates think. Too often, day-care advocates insist that research must "prove harm" before they recognize concerns about day care as legitimate. Even when harm is proved, day-care advocates usually defend the day-care system or call for more funding so "quality" can be raised. Day-care advocates do not usually look out for the best interests of the child.

For example, the Clarke-Stewart and Fein article cited by Phillips and Howes is a very detailed technical review of early childhood programs. It does include considerable information regarding outcomes of early day care, and on the whole the authors are favorable in their assessment of day care. However, they are also well aware of the potential for problems. They concede that "for children less than 1 year of age, there may be some effect on the mother-child relationship, an effect which *may* be negative, especially if the mother's work responsibilities absorb much of her emotional energy and if the family situation does not alleviate those pressures."

What Children Need

I cringe when I hear politicians and other public figures say that the "key" to curing social ills ranging from violent crime to racism is *education*. . . .

A mother provides exactly that type of "education" that *is* the key to "social problems" that plague us: an education in daily living. . . . Parents who expect day-care to fill this role are playing with fire. As one might expect, small children who are deprived of the all-important, formative relationship with a mother seem to exhibit less capacity to relate to others. "The attachment relationship that a young child forges with his mother forms the foundation stone of personality," says psychologist Brenda Hunter. "The young child's hunger for his mother's presence is as great as his hunger for food, and her absence inevitably generates a powerful sense of loss and anger." For a mother to cavalierly surrender [this] awesome vocation to some anonymous day-care worker (whose interest in her child is primarily monetary) is strange enough. But to do so in order to pursue a career is genuinely bizarre. It is essentially a decision to work so that you will be able to pay someone else to raise your child.

Brian Robertson, *Human Life Review*, Fall 1990.

Clarke-Stewart and Fein do identify the *"optimal"* attachment pattern in infants, namely secure attachment to parents characterized by "trust and enjoyment in the interaction." Yet Clarke-Stewart and Fein acknowledge that there is considerable evidence of a disruption in this optimal pattern for infants placed in day care. "Children in day care," they acknowledge, "are more likely than children at home to position themselves farther away from mother, to spend less time close to or in physical contact with mother, and to ignore or avoid mother after a brief separation." These are symptoms of insecure attachment that (according to psychological theory) indicate impaired emotional development. Infants, in particular, do not have the mental or emotional capacity to develop adequately without hourly parental support. Day care disrupts this bond. When a baby needs changing, feeding, play time, comfort or rocking, the need is crucial and immediate. . . .

Another reference cited by Phillips and Howes is *Day Care*, edited by E.F. Zigler and E.W. Gordon. This volume is a compilation of many articles, some dealing with history, some with the policy and politics of day care. Two articles in particular discuss the effects of day care on children. . . . Here are some quotes from that [first] article as [psychologist M.] Rutter summarizes the research findings of others:

- "Children who experienced day care from infancy were rated as significantly less cooperative with adults, more physically and verbally aggressive with peers and adults, and more active; there was a tendency for them to be less tolerant of frustration.". . .
- "For teenage boys . . . diffused mothering [experiencing day care as young children] tended to result in 'fearless aggressive nonconformity' to parental requirements with outgoing, active, social interests which showed a peer-group orientation."

Rutter suggests that children from troubled family backgrounds may be more vulnerable to day-care stresses. But he believes more research needs to be done on family backgrounds.

The other article in *Day Care* devoted to evaluation risks is by E.A. Farber and B. England, who report their own research on the developmental consequences of out-of-home care for infants in low-income families, precisely the population that daycare advocates say need care most. In about half of the infants placed in day care while their mothers worked, the researchers identified social-emotional problems, as judged within attachment theory. "At 12 months, the 47 percent of the infants in the Early Work group who were not securely attached were all in the anxious-avoidant group," write Farber and England. Infants with an "anxious-avoidant attachment" to their mothers respond to their mothers in an anxious and avoidant manner. Farber and England found that by age 18 months, 50 percent to 70 percent of the infants placed in day care demonstrated insecure attachments to their mothers. By two years of age, children placed in day care in earliest infancy displayed less enthusiasm, were less compliant, and less persistent on task, and had higher negative affect than infants who had been cared for by nonworking mothers.

Intellectual Dishonesty

Exactly how any day-care advocates can read this research, *let alone cite it* as proof that "children in good quality child care show no signs of harm," is almost beyond comprehension. Why do day-care proponents use such misleading tactics? It appears most day-care advocates are so convinced of proposition #1 (women must work outside the home) and proposition #2 (day care is necessary for the children of working mothers) that they are completely converted to day care as a "necessity" to alleviate perceived adult problems. Consequently, they become intellectually dishonest and distort the research findings. Why else would day-care advocates continually ignore the consistently negative effects and conditions of risk inherent in day care, while disseminating *disinformation?*

Even in research cited by day-care advocates, evidence abounds of risks in day care for social and emotional disruption. Dozens of additional studies confirm these findings. Few conclude that day care is benign. The negative findings continue to roll in, and they are very consistent with those that have been accumulating for the past 20 years. Here is a brief catalogue:

- Level of infant stimulation in day care is low and lacks variety.
- Day care during infancy is associated with "deviations" in the expected course of emotional development.
- Infants placed in 20 or more hours of day care per week avoid their mothers and are insecurely attached; sons have attachment problems with both mothers and fathers.
- Children placed in day care receive less adult attention, try to communicate less, receive and display less affection, are more aggressive, and are less responsive to adults.
- Compared with children who were cared for by their mothers as preschoolers, third-graders who were placed in day care as preschoolers are viewed more negatively by their peers, have lower academic grades, and demonstrate poorer study skills.
- Compared with children who go home to their mothers after school, suburban third-graders who are in day care after school provoke more negative reactions from peers, earn lower grades, and score lower on standardized tests.

Health Risks

However, even as grim as these findings are, social-emotional trauma is only a part of the day-care risk. There is a large and growing body of evidence that day care is a breeding ground for infectious diseases. The mere act of separating an infant from his mother may suppress the immune system and make the child more vulnerable to disease. Putting a number of young children together increases exposure to disease. Compared to children cared for at home in a six-month period, children in day-care homes are 25 percent more likely to contract infections, while those in day-care centers get nearly 50 percent more infections and are nearly three times as likely to need hos-

225

pitalization. Medical costs for children in day care are close to 100 percent to 200 percent higher.

It has long been known that attending day care increases incidence of upper respiratory tract infections (colds). Recently, increased lower respiratory tract infection (e.g., bronchitis and pneumonia) resulting in hospitalization has specifically been linked to attendance at day-care centers.

Gastrointestinal infections causing diarrhea are very common in both day-care centers and family day care. Outbreaks not only typically involve from one-third to one-half of the children in a center, but the disease spreads to the day-care workers and then to the homes of the children and the workers. Even with physicians actively involved and training the staff and the children in hygiene, major outbreaks recur regularly.

As a matter of fact, virtually all agents which cause illness in children are more common in day-care centers. Children in day care are routinely exposed to and contract respiratory tract infections, gastrointestinal infections, skin infections, and invasive bacterial disease. Among the most serious of these are those caused by the bacterium Haemophilus influenza type b. An estimated 10,000 cases of meningitis and another 5,000 nonmeningitic infections are caused by this organism each year in the United States. Three percent to 7 percent of Haemophilus influenza meningitis cases result in death, while another 25 percent to 40 percent of these children sustain permanent morbidity. The vast majority of these meningitic infections (95 percent) occur in children under 5 years of age. The disease is spread by sneezing (respiratory droplet) or by direct contact, and children under 2 years of age are particularly vulnerable because their immune systems are immature and because new vaccines afford little protection to children this young. Children in day care are at 50 percent to 100 percent increased risk for contracting these fatal and maiming diseases for each year in day care. . . .

Sexual and Physical Abuse

Among the darkest of the day-care risks is that of sexual abuse. The national media have in the mid-1980s covered the longest running criminal trial in U.S. history: the case of purported sexual abuse in the McMartin Pre-School in California. Although those accused were acquitted, the testimony given by the children was blood-curdling, including accounts of teachers having sex with each other in front of the children, fondling the children, and torturing animals to frighten the children, so they wouldn't tell their parents. Individuals with mental illness, including sexual perversions directed toward children, are sometimes drawn to the day-care setting. When parents turn their children over to strangers, there is no way to be completely sure the caregivers are not maliciously or unnaturally motivated. Day-care centers in many states have been closed because of increasingly frequent allegations of physical and sexual abuse. Complaints about physical and sexual abuse in Texas day-care facilities nearly doubled between 1980 and 1984.

Approximately 1 percent of all licensed (and therefore state-approved and presumed safe) day-care facilities in Michigan were accused of either sexual or physical abuse between 1982 and 1986. In a study of 48 children who had been sexually abused in this Michigan sample, Kathleen Faller found the following grim patterns: Day-care centers accounted for 75 percent of the sexual abuse; 25 percent came from day-care homes; half of the facilities where sexual abuse occurred were state licensed! . . . Of course, the short-range consequences of such abuse include masturbation, sleep problems (nightmares, insomnia, etc.), physical illness, eating disorders, emotional disturbances, behavioral problems, school difficulties, and phobias. The long-term damage to such children almost always casts shadows on their adulthood, and some kind of intensive, professional therapy (even decades after the occurrence) is usually necessary to overcome the detrimental effects of sexual abuse. In Colorado, an organization for parents, Public Awareness About Child Care, was developed after "an avalanche of information [was produced] about children killed or hurt by those licensed or hired to care for them."

Mounting Evidence

As the evidence against day care mounts, more and more child development experts are concerned. Most frequently the experts consulted in the media are psychologists and educators, who are usually unaware of the risks of illness and of sexual and physical abuse. However, even among psychologists and educators, concern is being expressed. Professor Jay Belsky at Pennsylvania State University (involved in day-care evaluation for nearly two decades) has become convinced that negative results from day care cannot be explained away. Belsky, considered neutral in his attitude toward day care in the early 1980's, has been attacked by day-care advocates for his shift toward a more negative opinion of day care. But Belsky looked objectively at the growing mass of negative findings, including his own research. He observed, "The data changed, the data looked different, and I see lots of people ignoring the data and explaining it away."

Dr. Burton White, a nationally known expert on parent education, maintains "continuing resistance to people other than family raising children as a routine policy." White believes that the child-care industry is "a total disaster area," with "no feasible way of turning it into a model industry." He feels the comparison between how children ought to be raised and the kinds of conditions found in day care creates an unbridgeable gap. "The gap is so large, in my perspective, that I continue to feel totally uncomfortable with it." White concludes, "After more than 30 years of research on how children develop well, I would not think of putting an infant or toddler of my own into any substitute-care program on a full-time basis, especially a center-based program. . . . I urge you not to delegate the primary child-rearing task to anyone else during your child's first three years of life."

Inherently Dangerous

Clearly, a child in day care is a child at risk. The research results identifying these risks are consistent. Nor is it appropriate to consider only short-term risks. Day care causes young children to be aggressive, less responsive to adults, and more peer-centered. But researchers have established that adolescents who are not responsive to parents and adults and who are peer-centered are much more likely to use drugs and alcohol, commit delinquent acts, adopt morally permissive attitudes, engage in sexual intercourse, abort unborn children, earn lower grades, or drop out of school. What little research there is on the long-range effects of day care points precisely to these disturbing outcomes.

For parents with children in day care, the issue is damage control, not optimal development. The research on day care has set the red lights blinking. How much risk and potential damage to children are we willing to accept? This is not just an ivory tower debate: real children are subject to real danger. A national day-care policy could put over 10 million children at risk in a grisly experiment, virtually without controls. Harvard's Jerome Kagan once remarked, "I think they [children raised in day-care environment] will be different, but I can't say how." Based on what we currently know, the differences will be lamentable.

Quality day care may be less damaging than bad day care. But "real world" day care is usually not nearly as good as that provided in financially subsidized university settings where many of the negative findings about day care have been found. In order to get "quality" child care that approaches parental care, someone must be hired to be a "parent." Urie Bronfenbrenner, from Cornell, reminds us it is impossible to pay someone enough to get them to do for children what parents will do for free. Quality really isn't the issue; day care itself is inherently dangerous.

"The findings . . . suggest that day-care infants are not more anxious, insecure, or emotionally disturbed overall."

Day Care Does Not Harm Children

Susan Faludi and Rosalind C. Barnett

In Part I of the following viewpoint, taken from a 1993 adaptation of her original 1988 article, Susan Faludi makes a still-pertinent argument in favor of day care. Faludi categorically refutes findings of day care hazards; she points out that there are, in fact, many benefits for children who spend at least part of their day in outside care. Faludi, a Pulitzer Prize-winning reporter for the *Wall Street Journal*, is the author of the controversial book *Backlash*. In Part II, Rosalind C. Barnett addresses concerns about day care's effects on the quality of infant-mother attachment—a bond that many believe is essential for a child's psychological development. Barnett argues that attachment theory is based on psychoanalytic principles and lacks scientific or cross-cultural evidence. Barnett is a research associate at the Massachusetts-based Wellesley College Center for Research on Women.

As you read, consider the following questions:

1. What positive aspects of day care does Faludi find, especially for low-income children?
2. If day care is not necessarily harmful, how does Faludi account for its bad reputation?
3. What do Faludi and Barnett say is the result of negative reports on day care?

From "The Kids Are All Right" by Susan Faludi, *Mother Jones*, 1988. Reprinted with permission from *Mother Jones* magazine, ©1988, Foundation for National Progress. Rosalind C. Barnett, "Evaluating the Effects of Maternal Employment on Infant-Mother Attachment," *Research Report from the Wellesley College Center for Research on Women*, Spring 1991. Reprinted with permission.

I

What should be most curious to anyone reviewing the voluminous research literature on day care is the chasm between what the studies find and what people choose to believe. Despite a pervasive sense that day care is at best risky for children and at worst permanently damaging, much of the research indicates that if day care has any long-term effect on children at all, it has made them somewhat more social, experimental, self-assured, cooperative, creative. At the University of California at Irvine, K. Alison Clarke-Stewart, professor of social ecology, found that the social and intellectual development of children in day care was six to nine months ahead of that of children who stayed home.

Day Care Bonuses

The research on day care points to other bonuses, too. Day-care kids tend to have a more progressive view of sex roles. Canadian researchers Delores Gold and David Andres found that the girls they interviewed in day care believed that housework and child care should be evenly divided; the girls raised at home still believed these tasks are women's work. We are reminded constantly by the press that children in day care turn out to be too "aggressive." But researchers point out that what is being billed as aggression could as easily be labeled assertiveness, not at all a bad quality in a child.

Media Hype

As for the supposed and much-publicized day-care child abuse "epidemic," a three-year, $200,000 study by the University of New Hampshire's Family Research Laboratory found in 1988 that if there is an "epidemic" of child abuse, it's in the home—where children are almost twice as likely to be molested as in day care. And, ironically, the researchers found that children were *least* likely to be sexually abused in day-care centers located in high-crime, low-income neighborhoods (there tends to be more supervision in these centers). Despite frightening stories in the media, the researchers concluded that there is no indication of some special high risk to children in day care.

Although many of the celebrated tales of day-care workers molesting children have turned out to be tall tales, we continue to believe their message. "The consequences of all the negative play in the press about the McMartin case were really quite dramatic," says Abby Cohen, managing attorney of the Child Care Law Center, referring to the 1984 sex-abuse scandal at the McMartin Pre-School in Manhattan Beach, California. "Because, unfortunately, up until then there hadn't been very much play about child care, period. So it was terribly detrimental that the first real wide attention to it was in such a negative light."

230

For children of poverty, day care may be their ticket out of the ghetto. The studies find that the futures of low-income kids brighten immeasurably after a couple of years in day care. The Perry Pre-School Project of Ypsilanti, Michigan, followed 123 poor black children for 20 years. The children who spent one to two years in preschool day care, the researchers found, stayed in school longer, were not as prone to teenage pregnancy and crime, and improved their earning prospects significantly. A New York University study of 750 Harlem children came up with similar results: The children enrolled in preschool were far more likely to get jobs and pursue education beyond high school.

Equivocal Research

Presented with the evidence, some day-care critics will concede that preschool may have a negligible negative effect on toddlers, but then they move quickly to the matter of infants. So 3-year-olds may survive day care, they say, but newborns will suffer permanent damage. Their evidence comes from two sources. The first is a collection of studies conducted in the 1940s, '50s, and '60s in France, England, and West Germany. These studies concluded that infants who were taken from their mothers had tendencies later toward juvenile delinquency and mental illness. But there's a slight problem in relying on these findings: The studies were all looking at infants in orphanages and hospital institutions, not day-care centers.

Science or Social Control?

In the 1950s, psychologists told women who wished to work outside the home that maternal deprivation would cause their children to become neurotics at best, sociopaths at worst. The women's movement temporarily dismantled such notions, but a backlash was inevitable. As women poured into the workplace throughout the 1970s, challenging men's power both at the office and in the home, [mother-infant] bonding not so coincidentally became the hot new theory, reminding women that they alone were responsible for the fate of their children.

Diane Eyer, *Glamour*, July 1993.

The other source frequently quoted is the much-celebrated turnabout by Pennsylvania State University psychologist Jay Belsky, once a leading supporter of day care. In 1982 Belsky had reviewed the child-development literature and concluded that there were few if any significant differences between children raised at home and those in day care. Then in September 1986 he announced that he had changed his mind: Children whose mothers work more than 20 hours a week in their first year, he said, are at "risk" for developing an "insecure" attachment to their mothers. Belsky's pronouncement provided grist for the anti-day-care mill—and was widely reported. What did not receive as wide an airing, however, is the evidence Belsky cited to support his change of heart. Two of the studies he used flatly contradict each other: In one of them, the study's panel of judges found the infants in day care to be more insecure; in the other, the panel found just the opposite. The difference in results was traced to the judges' own bias against day care. In the study where the judges were not told ahead of time which babies were in day care and which were raised at home, the judges said the children's behavior was indistinguishable. In the study where they did know ahead of time which babies were in day care, they concluded that the day-care children were more insecure.

Popular Knowledge

It is this bias that makes our day-care terrors so intractable. If the feeling comes from the gut, if it is an internalized, strictly personal belief, then its truth must be of a higher order, unassailable by any number of studies. But what many people fail to see is how our seemingly personal perceptions of day care are not so personal after all; how they have been shaped by forces that have little to do with gut instinct. Our opinions have been hammered by years of relentless anti-day-care and anti-working-mother rhetoric from the Reagan and Bush administrations and from the media, where bashing day care seems to be a sanctioned sport. (A few headlines from well-read magazines: "'Mommy, Don't Leave Me Here!': The Day Care Parents Don't See." "When Child Care Becomes Child Molesting: It Happens More Often Than Parents Like to Think." "Creeping Child Care . . . Creepy.")

Other cultural forces are at work here, too. We suffer a compulsion to replicate our childhoods, no matter how unpleasant those early years might have been. If our mothers stayed home, that must be the "healthy" way. What we forget is that it's only been since the 1940s that public opinion has so insistently endorsed the 24-hour-mom concept. The Victorians may have kept their women at home, but not for the sake of the children. "An educated woman," writer Emily Davies advised mothers in the 1870s, "blessed with good servants, as good mistresses generally are, finds an hour a day amply sufficient for her domestic duties." An early version of quality time.

The Next Generation

The paranoia may ease once the younger generation reaches adulthood; they are not freighted with the same cultural assumptions about child care as those weaned in the 1950s. When I brought up the matter of child rearing to teenagers at Lowell High School in San Francisco, they all seemed to favor day care more than their parents do. How come? "Well," one 17-year-old girl reasoned, in what turned out to be a typical response, "I went to day care when I was little and I had a really good time."

II

One of the most dramatic social changes since the early 1980s has been the increased participation of mothers of young children in the labor force. Almost one of every two women with a child under one year of age is now employed full-time. The rapid increase in the number of women with infants returning to work has sparked concern about the effects on children of infant day care. The specter of anxious children insecurely attached to their mothers has surfaced, catapulting the issue of infant-mother attachment to the forefront of the research agenda. No issue has as much emotional weight among new mothers struggling with questions about whether or when to return to the workforce.

A Cultural Dilemma

The psychological study of child-rearing has focused almost exclusively on the mother-child relationship. Psychoanalytic theory assumes an inevitable and necessary single mother-infant relationship. . . . Other theories, especially evolutionary theory, argue that the survival of the child is enhanced by having multiple caregivers. Cross-cultural data support the view that our emphasis on mother-infant attachment reflects a cultural theory of development rather than a scientific theory of development. . . . Thus we see a focus on the question of whether substitute child care disrupts the formation of attachment.

Attachment vs. Dependence

It is important to distinguish between attachment and dependence. A child is dependent on whoever is providing care at any moment, whereas attachment develops in response to the quality of interaction with a particular person who is often, but does not need to be, the child's primary caretaker.

Social science researchers assess attachment among infants 12 to 18 months of age primarily through the use of the Ainsworth Strange Situation Test. In 1988, two developmental psychologists, Karen McCartney and Deborah Phillips, identified 25 studies concerning whether there are differences in attachment behaviors between children attending day care and children cared for at home by mothers. Of these, 14 employed the Strange Situation Test. Their results suggest that children attending day care are

233

no different from children reared at home on mother attachment behaviors as assessed through the Strange Situation.

Negative Findings

These studies examined specific attachment *behaviors*, not attachment *quality*. Attachment quality was the topic of a 1989 review by K.A. Clarke-Stewart, entitled "Infant Day Care: Maligned or Malignant?" The author reported on 17 studies of infant attachment quality. In concluding her review, the author states:

> These findings corroborate earlier findings indicating that mothers' *early* resumption of work may not impede the emergence of secure infant-mother attachments.

The findings above suggest that day-care infants are not more anxious, insecure, or emotionally disturbed overall. The resulting picture of the child in day care is one of a child fully capable of developing a secure attachment with his or her mother. Thus, based on the available evidence, there is no reason to believe that shared childrearing interferes with the development of the child's attachment with the mother.

The task now facing researchers is to identify those factors that affect the infant-mother attachment, whether the child is reared at home or in an alternate-care environment. Among the factors that seem important are the level of education of the families, their social class, the birth order and sex of child, and the age of entry into day care. The nature of fathers' involvement is also crucial. Unfortunately, the substantial literature on fathers' participation in child care and its effects on both child and mother outcomes has not been integrated into the literature on infant attachment.

The Guilt Engendered

Because issues of infant care touch upon basic values and conceptions, it is hard to form dispassionate conclusions about the effect of alternate care environments. In a 1988 review, two child psychologists, K. McCartney and D. Phillips, describe the ambivalence around this issue which persists:

> . . . despite historical, cross-cultural and developmental evidence that child care neither harms children nor erodes the mother-child bond . . . the ideal of the stay-at-home mother continues to provide the norm against which personal decisions are judged. . . .

This ideal contributes heavily to the conflict today's mothers feel.

Indeed, we live in the age of the conflicted mother, where rapid social change has left mothers and the larger society with the task of redefining motherhood to include the option of child care. The conflicted mother is a product of a short historical perspective, a narrow belief that one mothering style is best, and a romanticized construction of motherhood which is then taken to be equivalent to the natural image of motherhood. Out of these conflicts and the guilt they engender, many mothers may reduce their commitment to the labor force, opt for part-time rather than full-time employment, and in so doing jeopardize their own mental health, impair their marital satisfaction, and inadvertently weaken the infant-mother attachment.

We need to continue to ask questions and promote discussion about the effects of maternal employment on the infant-mother attachment. In so doing we will help reduce the unnecessary guilt so many working mothers now experience.

> *"The public recognizes that for the great majority of women, work is not a 'selfish' indulgence, nor is child care a luxury."*

Families Need Government-Subsidized Child Care

Sheila B. Kamerman

Citing the growth of poverty among American families and the concurrent rise in the numbers of working mothers, Sheila B. Kamerman, author of the following viewpoint, asserts the need for a coherent federal child care policy to assist today's beleaguered parents. Kamerman describes the events of 1990 that sparked the ongoing child care debate and precipitated the federal government's introduction of the 1991 Child Care and Development Block Grant and the Family and Medical Leave Bill (which became law in 1993). This legislation, though a step in the right direction, is still inadequate, the author asserts. Kamerman is professor of social policy and planning and codirector of the Cross-National Studies Program at Columbia School of Social Work in New York City.

As you read, consider the following questions:

1. How does Kamerman support her belief that many women must work?
2. What, in the author's narrative, was the result of factionalism on the development of federal family leave legislation?
3. What specific federal policy recommendations does Kamerman make?

Examine the facts of life for America's approximately eleven million children under the age of three, and the need for new measures to address their plight becomes apparent. As the 1980s ended:

- more than half the mothers of under-threes were in the labor force, up from 27 percent in 1970;
- about one in four of the under-threes were living in single-parent (chiefly mother-only) families, up from almost 8 percent in 1970;
- almost one in four of the under-threes were living in families with incomes below the poverty threshold, the highest poverty rate for any age group.

Despite all the official declarations on behalf of children, one fact stands out above all: The child poverty rate was higher throughout the 1980s than at any time since the middle 1960s, and consistently higher the younger the child. . . .

There has [also] been a dramatic change in how very young children spend their days. Ever greater numbers of the under-threes are cared for outside their homes by caregivers who are not members of their families. One-quarter of the children in this age group (approaching half of the more than five million with working mothers) are in the care of an adult other than a relative. A little more than half of this group are cared for in "family day care," largely informal and of unknown quality, while the remainder are in day care centers.

Programs serving children under age three are in the shortest supply of all child care services, despite efforts in some states to recruit family day care providers. Some highly publicized cases of maltreatment and abuse have also provoked extensive concern about the quality of available services. And the price of day care is a big worry for average working parents, who cannot easily afford the $5,000 a year estimated at the end of the 1980s to be the cost for each child under age three at good day care centers and even, in some places, for family day care.

The Child Care Debate

The new conditions affecting America's youngest children have elicited a divided and ambivalent response in different quarters of American society and public life.

On one side of the debate, the champions of liberal child policies and gender equality have sought to accommodate, even to facilitate, the changing patterns of work and family life with new government and private-sector policies. . . .

A countermovement, coming chiefly from the right, has resisted the very premise of these measures. Some conservatives—still committed, however unrealistically, to the traditional view that mothers should stay at home—have opposed new policies that make it attractive for women to be in the labor force and that impose new costs on government and business to enable women to work. . . .

"Can I call you back, J.F.? I've got a situation here."

Two incidents in October of 1990 crystallized the national debate over child care. Campaigning for governor of Massachusetts, John Silber set off a furor when he denounced the "overweening materialism" of two-career couples who use child care. Silber went on to declare: "We have a generation of abused children by women who have thought that a third-rate day care center was just as good as a first-rate home."

The same month, Chante Fernandez, a 24-year-old single mother, was arrested in Woodbridge, New Jersey, for leaving her five-year-old daughter unattended in a parked car while she worked the night shift at a local mall. But when the press disclosed that Fernandez had been unable to find any child care and was working hard to support herself and her daughter without any assistance from her former husband, public opinion rallied

238

to her side and all serious charges against her were dismissed.

Silber's comments probably would not have created so great a furor had they not touched a tender point of anxiety, quite literally engendering guilt among the many parents who are genuinely troubled about the day care their children receive. But as the support for Chante Fernandez demonstrated, the public recognizes that for the great majority of women, work is not a "selfish" indulgence, nor is child care a luxury. If some child care is "third-rate," the imperative now is to upgrade it, not to pretend that all families—least of all single-parent ones—can make ends meet with mothers at home. . . .

The Family Leave Battle

There is no specific research on the consequences of the lack of [parental] leaves for children. But the U.S. has more very young infants (under three months) in poor quality out-of-home child care arrangements than does any other major industrialized country.

This was one of many considerations to propel the movement to enact a national parental leave policy. The family leave legislation approved by the House and Senate in the spring of 1990 would have given employees the right to an unpaid leave at the time of childbirth, adoption, or a serious health condition of a child or parent, and to temporary medical leave at the time of an employee's own serious health condition, with adequate protection of the employees' employment and benefit rights.

To get the principle of family leave established, congressional sponsors of the legislation accepted a series of compromises. The original bill provided for 26 weeks of medical leave for serious injuries to employees themselves and 15 weeks of family leave; the final legislation called only for a total of 12 weeks of leave per year for all reasons combined. Originally, the bill exempted firms with 15 or fewer employees. The final bill exempted firms with 50 or fewer employees. Thus, in its final form, the benefit had been greatly watered down; still, business groups adamantly opposed it.

After President George Bush's veto, the House voted again for the legislation but fell 54 votes short of the two-thirds approval needed to override the President. Representative Pat Schroeder of Colorado pledged, "We shall override some day.". . . But while a valuable step, the limited, unpaid parental leave policy that Congress seems likely to approve will still leave millions of Americans, particularly low-income and single-parent families, without much protection. [The unpaid, twelve-week Family and Medical Leave Bill passed, virtually unchanged, in February 1993.] . . .

The United States has never had a national program for child care as such. Rather, the federal government finances child care through a variety of avenues, direct and indirect, including a miscellany of programs with child care provisions such as Aid to Families with Dependent Children (AFDC), the child care food program, child welfare services, and various tax benefits. Among all these programs, four stand out as especially important: the dependent care tax credit, Head Start, Title XX of the Social Security Act, and the new Child Care and Development Block Grant.

Federal Programs

In recent years, the dependent care tax credit has been the largest single federal source of child care funding. The credit is estimated to be worth $3.9 billion in 1990, but it provides no benefit to many of the families who need it most—those with incomes below the tax threshold. The credit is also of limited value to low- and moderate-income families who use informal family day care. These deficiencies could be partially alleviated if the credit were made "refundable"—that is, if the value of the credit were paid out even to people whose incomes are too low for them to owe taxes.

Head Start, budgeted at $1.4 billion in 1990, has been the next largest source of child care assistance, albeit mostly part-day. It is the single biggest subsidy on the "supply" side (that is, going directly to programs providing services to small children). Under the new budgetary plans, Head Start should now play an even larger role and, indeed, become the pillar of early childhood education among the poor.

Block grants to the states for social services, including child care, are made under Title XX of the Social Security Act. In recent years, about one-quarter of the total value of the grants, or $650 million in 1990, has gone to child care. The new budget agreement gives $2.5 billion over three years to the Child Care and Development Block Grant and allows the states discretion in subsidizing child care for the working poor, without as strict income limitations as under previous programs. Under another new program, Entitlement Funding for Child Care Services, states receive $1.5 billion for families who are on welfare or close to welfare eligibility levels because of their difficulty in affording child care.

The expansion of the child care grants was the subject of intense political conflict over the past several years. Popularly known as "ABC," or the Act for Better Child Care, legislation increasing aid for child care received approval by the House in March 1990 and the Senate in June, only to run up against severe differences in House-Senate reconciliation. The differences in Congress concerned, among many issues, the form of the program as well as its magnitude. The House favored earmarking funds specifically for child care; the Senate wanted to preserve a broader social service block grant enabling states to make their own decisions about funding child care versus meals for the elderly, drug treatment, and other programs.

The White House and some people in Congress favored the alternative of a tax credit for all low-income families with young children, regardless of parents' employment. In the end, during the final, bruising budget battle, the Child Care and Development Block Grant emerged as a compromise and gained the President's signature. At the level of funding approved, the block grants can scarcely be expected to have a big effect on the availability of child care. But the principle of federal responsibility has at least been affirmed. . . .

Overcoming Divisions

It will not be easy to focus policy attention on very young children in the United States. Policymakers disagree about the substantive issues, and many Americans suspect child policy proposals will disproportionately benefit black and other minority children and encourage more out-of-wedlock, minority births. These anxieties and sources of opposition, often latent and unacknowledged, should be confronted openly and answered directly. We are unlikely to make much progress unless we can show that effective family policies are consistent with widely shared values and provide broad benefits across racial and class lines.

Even if we overcome prejudice and racism, however, we face great obstacles to consensus because of the deeply conflicting moral values and cultural practices in America. Some conservatives would support family policy initiatives, but only if they are limited to traditional families. Some feminists are concerned that policies designed to improve conditions for children may have harmful consequences for women. While some conservatives object to providing paid leaves for working mothers, some feminists fear the consequences (lower wages, constricted career paths) for women who take extended leaves.

Given the diversity of values in the United States, what can be done? First, child policy must support parental choice as to whether a mother remains at home to care for her very young child or takes employment in the outside labor market. It also should support choice in the type of child care. Of course, everyone likes the idea of "choice." But real choice requires active support of alternatives, not passive acceptance of the limited options now available to most parents.

All parents—working or not—warrant support in their child rearing. But working parents deserve something more, at least in part because they are paying taxes and contributing to the future Social Security benefits of at-home parents as well. Enabling single mothers to have some time at home without job and income loss, and without having to turn to a stigmatized and inadequate welfare program, is a worthwhile policy goal, as is providing some additional support for those families who maintain traditional roles.

Child Care Goals

Thus, the goals of any policy agenda for the under-threes should be either to enable at least one parent to remain at home for some time to care for his or her baby, or to enable employed parents to stay at work with support for child care. The policies would include:

- establishment of a stronger social infrastructure for families with children, including health insurance for all children, available free to those in families with low or modest income, and adequate, affordable housing;
- stronger, family-related income support through one of several avenues: a universal, taxable child allowance (a cash benefit to families with children, based on the presence and number of children in the family), or a child tax credit that is refundable to families with incomes below the tax threshold, or a further expanded earned income tax credit;
- a universal one-year job and benefit-protected leave for working parents with prior work history at the time of childbirth (or adoption) paid for as a contributory social insurance benefit at 75 percent of salary up to the maximum wage covered under Social Security;
- a reformed, more adequate, nationally uniform AFDC as an option for poor single mothers who fail to qualify for the employment-related parenting benefit, with the requirement that now exists for teen mothers to complete high school, and an additional requirement that these young, single mothers participate in parenting classes;
- increased federal funding for good quality toddler care, both family day care and center care.

Inevitably, questions of cost will influence the debate over child policies. Clearly, we must make choices rather than pretend that the society can do everything at once. Yet we should also remember that countries not as wealthy as ours do all these things.

If it is necessary to start slowly with the under-threes, then the poor, the deprived, and the handicapped are the logical groups to target first. . . . At this point, the United States has assured our very youngest children neither adequate care outside their homes nor adequate care within them. Congressional achievements and new commitments to children should encourage us, however, to reach for the bolder alternatives.

"Able parents bear children, for the first time in history totally by choice, and then assume society, government, or corporations owe them a subsidy."

Families Do Not Need Government-Subsidized Child Care

Allan Carlson

The child care shortage is a fallacy, contends Allan Carlson, author of the following viewpoint. Equally groundless, he says, is the supposed cause of this deficit, namely, the economic need for women in the workforce. Instead of allowing the modern welfare state to take over the function of the family, Carlson explains, American parents should assume responsibility for raising their own children. Towards this end, Carlson urges tax breaks for families with dependent children and a variety of community-based, low-cost supports for the traditional family. Carlson is president of the Rockford Institute, a research and advocacy group promoting traditional, Judeo-Christian family values, and is a member of the National Commission on Children.

As you read, consider the following questions:

1. What does Carlson say is the real crisis affecting American families? How do working mothers exacerbate this crisis?
2. What does the author recommend that the voluntary sector should do that the government cannot?

Allan Carlson, "Family Questions," *Society*, July/August 1990, ©1990 by Transaction Publishers. Reprinted with permission.

The first concern of any decent community is its children. At some level, social life exists to nurture and protect children, who will perpetuate the community into the future. For the individual, children represent the fulfillment of an obligation to ancestors and a uniquely personal covenant with posterity. In short, it is fair to say that concern for children is hardly something new. Yet, judging from the column inches found in newspapers these days, and from the speeches now heard in Congress, children are, in a unique and puzzling way, the leading social policy issue of the day.

Americans have a sense that something is going seriously wrong with our children, and that childrearing . . . is more problematical and more difficult [now] than in any decade or century before. We hear about the unprecedented new demand for day care, or about early childhood intervention strategies designed to break the cycle of poverty in which many children are caught.

Now, amidst all this debate and concern, a conventional wisdom about the child care problem has emerged. This is a set of attitudes, or statements, which no one sets out either to debate or prove. . . . They are usually simply asserted and are given as self-evident truths. But like most conventional wisdoms, statements about children belie both the complexity and the real and somewhat disturbing truth about the situation and status of children in America.

The Noncrisis

Let us look at some of the statements or attitudes that are involved in this conventional wisdom, at what they say about children, about day care, and about early intervention strategies. The conventional wisdom tells us that there is a day care crisis. Corollaries of this statement are: the rising number of working mothers is an irresistible tide that will end only when nearly all mothers are in the labor force; these working mothers and their spouses prefer professional, institutionalized care for their children when they are at work; and the marketplace and the voluntary sector are incapable of meeting the demand. These are the arguments or assumptions which are driving the push for the ABC (Act for Better Childcare) bill and related measures in Congress.

But reality, as they say, is a cruel mistress, and it undercuts this sense of a day care crisis. To begin with, we need to remember that young mothers are a very diverse lot. While slightly more than 50 percent of the mothers of pre-schoolers are in the labor force, this includes a substantial number engaged in seasonal work, part-time work, or labor at home. Looked at another way, about two-thirds of mothers with pre-school children in the United States are either at home full time or working only part

244

time. Roughly 70 percent of those working full time say they would prefer to be at home or they would prefer part-time work if they could find it: again, a diverse lot.

For those in the labor market, the preferred kind of alternate care provider is a family member or a neighbor or a church, with institutionalized care of the sort that the ABC bill would provide quite low on the list of choices.

Market Forces

There are day care openings in commercial or proprietary centers in most cities in the United States. The so-called shortage of day care is found only when one seeks high-quality, low-cost, alternative care. But in an economic sense, this is the equivalent of saying that high-quality, low-cost BMWs are also in short supply. Free or below-market-priced goods are always in short supply. We live in a historically odd period where able parents bear children, for the first time in history totally by choice, and then assume society, government, or corporations owe them a subsidy, a special kind of subsidy, for the care of those children.

Asay, by permission of the *Colorado Springs Gazette Telegraph*.

A second piece of conventional wisdom is that mothers need to work in order to maintain family living standards. In truth, the picture is more complicated. Among some income categories, this is true. If we look between the years 1970 and 1985, the real after-tax income of young male wage earners steadily eroded. Now, this was due to many factors. One could look at rising taxes, or the decay of the industrial sector, which once provided high-paying jobs, primarily to men. We also could look at the rapid growth of the service sector, which disproportionately employs women. All of these factors played a role in the collapse of what I have called the family wage economy. This was the legal/cultural system that existed in the United States until the late 1960s, a system premised on the idea of one principal pay check per family. Among the blue collar population, the passing of the family wage ideal meant that the family's living standard could be maintained only by sending a second or even a third income earner into the labor market.

But at another level, this assertion rings hollow. The economic pressure is ephemeral. When one adds together the marginal income and payroll taxes on the income of a second earner, the costs of being employed (buying lunches and that sort of thing), an extra car, and the value of lost home production, such as meal preparation and the cost of alternate child care, the average mother with a preschooler may actually be worse off when she enters the labor force, although it is less apparent because we do not often "cost out" these new expenses and the lost income from abandoned home production.

This, at least, is the conclusion of work by economist Reuben Gronau of Hebrew University, and it suggests why the day care subsidy is such an important issue. If we talk about the marginal return on labor in the marketplace or on labor in the home, and recognize the relatively small sums involved at the margins, then the day care subsidy can significantly alter the economic incentives.

The Real Crisis

My criticism here of the conventional wisdom might suggest that there is no day care crisis per se. So, you ask, is there really nothing to worry about? Actually, and despite my distrust of anything called a crisis, we are in the midst of a crisis. But it takes a different and more disturbing form than the simple and indeed easily remedied problem of insufficient day care spaces. It might be defined in two ways:
- There is substantial evidence suggesting that Americans, on average, simply do not like or value children as much as they used to. The birth rate in the United States has been stuck at a historic low since the early 1980s, well below the replacement level. This derives in part from a growing level of voluntary childlessness, that is, people who choose never

to have children; and in part from a diminished family size among those who do. They will have one or two children, but rarely more. Meanwhile, the abortion rate remains at a high plateau, about 1.5 million abortions annually. The greater tragedy in the abortion question is not its legality, but rather that continued high level of demand.

- The new concentration of poverty among children, histori-cally unprecedented among modern nations, has generated surprisingly few policy consequences and little real substan-tive interest. At one level, this may simply be because the old vote and children do not. But at a deeper level, it sug-gests a diminishing interest in posterity; it reflects an obses-sion with our own lives and little concern with the future.

On the whole, the inhabitants of this nation have never been wealthier. Yet, never before have parents spent so little time with their children. Even the celebrated grandmother shortage, part of the day care crisis, it is said, is not due to the rising number of working women. The over-55 age category is the only one where the proportion of women working is actually declining. Grandmothers, too, are simply less interested in car-ing for their own grandchildren.

Whose Responsibility?

Why are these things true? An adequate explanation would be long and multi-factored. Part of the reason emerges from such cultural developments as the decaying influence of religious be-lief on personal behavior, or the triumph of "self-fulfillment" over social obligation.

Another part of the explanation probably involves the growth of the modern welfare state, at the expense of traditional institu-tions such as the family. This growth disparity is the key to the second aspect of what I would call the authentic child care cri-sis. It is the growing confusion over who is responsible for chil-dren; who do they belong to? Are they the responsibility of their parents or are they the responsibility of society, meaning in practical, modern terms, the state?

For all stages of history, one could truthfully argue that children have been a joint responsibility of both parents and some form of broader community, such as the tribe or the village or the neigh-borhood, which has exercised a shared responsibility for raising children. What is new in our time, though, are first, the degree to which the state and federal governments have expanded their claims, to the detriment of family autonomy and local commu-nity and, second, the speed of the shift in this direction.

A crisis of this sort is much more difficult to counter. It is a spiritual crisis, a cultural crisis, a moral crisis rather than one caused simply by an inadequate distribution of resources.

The alternative is to assume that personal responsibility and love for children are not dead in the hearts of Americans. It is to pursue a strategy at both the political level and the voluntary sector level that creatively disengages the state from the family, and that restores our liberties by returning functions back to the family.

Bureaucrats Butt Out

American parents don't want or need a bunch of federal bureaucrats telling them how they should raise children. They want tax relief and greater flexibility in their job options so they can spend more time with their children. . . .

The vast majority of women with pre-school age children either are not employed outside the home, or work only part-time. American families need tax credits for child care so that mothers are not driven to work outside the home out of economic necessity. The present deduction for dependent children is woefully below what it should be for today's economic reality. Most mothers who are employed outside the home greatly prefer to leave their children with relatives or in small, home-style care.

Phyllis Schlafly, *New Dimensions*, November 1990.

Concerning federal policy, this would mean a creative combination of tax deductions and tax credits, possibly including refundable tax credits, keyed to the number and age of children. It would allow all families with children to retain more of their earned income and spend it as they choose.

At the state level, it would mean reducing rather than expanding governmental policing of families through state child protection agencies. At all levels of government, it would mean leaving training in sexual ethics and family life to traditional institutions, where these subjects belong, even if they sometimes do not do it so well these days, with churches and parents, rather than with the clumsy efforts of public education.

For the voluntary sector, the challenges are more daunting, because they involve the critical moral tasks that government cannot begin to address: for example, moral or character education. Among all children, and particularly the children of poverty, the need is somehow—and I admit I do not know exactly how—to instill adherences to the virtues of duty, fidelity, and responsibility. Only in this way can we break the cycle of dependence.

In a viable community, these are virtues taught by example in homes and by the popular culture in which children grow up. In shattered or weakened communities, we need to find ways of rebuilding moral order by creating personal commitments that will last, personal commitments to marriage, to a spouse, to children.

Communities Can Help

The second area is what I would call family support, for lack of a better term. Within all American cities and towns, organizations exist that build or sustain new communities of families, that seek to pass on the knowledge of what raising children means and how to do it. They perform this task, though, in ways that arise from voluntary activity rather than state-directed activity. Few of these organizations now derive much help from the philanthropic sector. Some have risen up spontaneously, as in the case of Le Leche League [an organization that promotes breast feeding, which, it believes, encourages closer family relationships]. Others derive from a kind of lay ministry, such as Focus on the Family [an organization committed to restoring Christian and conservative family values]. In addition to such organizations, the number of home schoolers is rapidly growing, now involving well over a million children, supported by parents who, at considerable sacrifice, are finding ways of rebuilding an aspect of the meaningful family economy. And finally, there are those extra millions of Americans, the true pioneers and revolutionaries, who are now experimenting with ways of reintegrating paid labor into the home, so that children can enjoy again the presence of both parents.

In some ways, these are people who are battling back 150 years of the industrial revolution, one mark of which was the separation of adults from the home during the day. Growing interest in both handicrafts and Alvin Toffler's electronic cottage [where people work at home, connected to their businesses through computer modems] reflect new strategies for reintegrating the economy of the home into a market system.

I would also look towards organizations that focus not on the failures found in our devastated inner cities, but on our successes. These include the organizations that sponsor self-help projects, and identify people who not only survive under bad circumstances, but thrive and indeed even turn things around. One good example of such a success would be the National Center for Neighborhood Enterprise [an organization promoting community self-sufficiency through neighborhood group efforts], led by Robert Woodson.

These represent new, somewhat unorthodox directions for philanthropy, for the support of organizations, for research. It is creative thinking and funding in these areas of moral and family reconstruction that will in the end make a difference for children.

Periodical Bibliography

The following articles have been selected to supplement the diverse views presented in this chapter.

James E. Ellis, Judy Temes, and Joan O'C. Hamilton — "What Price Child Care?" *Business Week*, February 8, 1993.

Diane Eyer — "Is Mother-Infant Bonding a Myth?" *Glamour*, July 1993.

Michele Galen — "Sure, 'Unpaid Leave' Sounds Simple, But..." *Business Week*, August 9, 1993.

David A. Hamburg — "The American Family Transformed," *Society*, January/February 1993.

Keith H. Hammonds and William C. Symonds — "Taking Baby Steps Toward a Daddy Track," *Business Week*, April 15, 1991.

Diane Harris — "Big Business Takes on Child Care," *Working Woman*, June 1993.

Michele Ingrassia and Karen Springen — "Living on Dracula Time," *Newsweek*, July 12, 1993.

Richard Louv — "Should Corporations Care About Child Care?" *Business and Society Review*, Winter 1992.

Ian Miles — "Consequences of the Changing Sexual Division of Labor," *The Annals of the American Academy of Political and Social Science*, July 1992.

Annetta Miller and Dody Tsiantar — "Mommy Tracks," *Newsweek*, November 25, 1991.

David Moberg — "All in the Family: Family and Medical Leave Is Welcome but Only a Tiny First Step," *In These Times*, February 22, 1993.

Richard Pearcey — "Brenda Hunter: A Voice for Mother Love," *The World & I*, May 1992.

Frank Rodimer — "Addressing the Needs of Children," *Origins*, March 19, 1992. Available from 1312 Massachusetts Ave. NW, Washington, DC 20005.

Richard B. Stolley — "An American Tragedy," *Parenting*, October 1993. Available from 501 Second St., San Francisco, CA 94107.

Utne Reader — Special issue on child care, May/June 1993.

Daniel Wattenberg — "The Parent Trap," *Insight*, March 2, 1992. Available from 3600 New York Ave. NE, Washington, DC 20002.

The World & I — Special issue on child care, September 1991.

What Is the Future of Male/Female Relationships?

**MALE/
FEMALE
ROLES**

Chapter Preface

When then-Vice President Dan Quayle blasted television sit-com character Murphy Brown for having a child out of wed-lock, he created a public furor over the proper definition of the American family. That was in 1992. Yet the "family values" de-bate continues today because Quayle's statement, which blamed poverty and crime on the decline of the "American family," helped to highlight a widespread trend in male/female relation-ships: Compared to previous generations, fewer people are now getting married, and of those who do, a lot fewer are staying married. Even the presence of children—once the reason for ty-ing the knot and keeping it tied—has not kept the divorce rate from doubling since 1960 (producing 3.9 million single-parent families, according to 1993 U.S. Census Bureau statistics).

There has been a net decrease in the number of marriages, agrees Iris Marion Young, author of *Justice and the Politics of Difference*. But, she argues, blaming the decline of this institu-tion—presumed by some to be the repository of hard-working, law-abiding "family values"—for the growth of crime and poverty overlooks the fact that a growing number of single parents are "midlife women with steady jobs." These single parents are quite capable of instilling their children with morals, Young as-serts, pointing out that their friends can often be of help in maintaining parental authority over the children. Most impor-tant, Young says, is the fact that single-parent homes are free of "the conflict between parents . . . [that] is a frequent cause of emotional distress in children."

Adults' needs may be served by the single life, counters Barbara Dafoe Whitehead, research associate at the Institute for American Values, "but the same cannot be said for [their] children." Con-trary to the conflict-free ideal of single parenthood, Whitehead ar-gues, kids experience emotional distress as a result of having to repeatedly "come to terms with the parent's love life and roman-tic partners." By any measurable standard, these families are not doing well, Whitehead asserts: "Half the single mothers in the United States live below the poverty line" and fully 70 percent of all juvenile delinquents "come from fatherless homes," she main-tains. According to Whitehead, these figures support Quayle's concern over the demise of the traditional family, that institution she calls "the seedbed for the virtues required by a liberal state." Without the family, she says, "the entire experiment in demo-cratic self-rule is jeopardized."

The following chapter debates the future of male/female rela-tionships—and, thus, the shape of society as a whole—by exam-ining the ways the sexes are getting along today.

"As they nestle into middle age, baby boomers dissatisfied with the trials of living together and 'commitmentphobia' are returning to their parents' values."

Marriage Is Becoming More Popular

Diane Medved

In the following viewpoint, Diane Medved contends that an increasing number of men and women are giving up the swinging single life of past decades and committing themselves to the security and personal fulfillment of marriage. As the baby boomers (the post-World War II generation that has, by its sheer size, greatly influenced our culture's norms for the past three decades) get older, Medved says, they are feeling the need to have children while they can; and it is this change of priorities, she argues, that is causing many of them to choose that most stable environment for the raising of their children—marriage. Diane Medved, a psychologist in private practice in Santa Monica, California, is the author of three books, including *The Case Against Divorce*.

As you read, consider the following questions:

1. How does televised romance compare with reality, according to the author?
2. What social and personal values does Medved say the baby boom generation was brought up with?
3. What do children offer to the marriage of their parents, according to Medved? Conversely, what does she believe married parents offer to their children?

From Diane Medved, "Set Me Free: Marriage as Liberation." This article appeared in the February 1991 issue and is reprinted with permission from *The World & I*, a publication of The Washington Times Corporation, copyright ©1991.

Darlene Stanford waited a long time for the right guy to come along. But here she was, at thirty-six, her gown's ten-foot white train pausing behind her with each two-step as she strode down the garden aisle. Her groom, Michael Kelley, thirty-eight, beamed as he reached out for her hand. For both of them, this moment replaced years of frustration and anxiety with the excitement of shared dreams.

Stanford always knew she wanted a husband and children. But as the years passed without finding that perfect match, she dedicated herself without remorse to her career. Raised with the post-1960s ideals of independence and self-fulfillment, she pursued a teaching credential, and then, while working full time, followed it up with a master's degree and her doctoral coursework. Meanwhile, she fell in love, was ultimately rejected, and then invested another four years in a second dead-end relationship. Finally, she gave up.

But on a plane returning from a professional conference, she met Michael, also never married, and within six weeks they were engaged.

Now, three years and two babies later, Stanford raves about the domestic life. She's taken the last two years off to care for her infants and has no regrets about putting her career on hold: "I'm finally free at last," she grins. "Marriage and family have brought me what I never could achieve in my career—the *option* to have it all. Before, I never had a choice—I had to work to support myself, and I had to make work my consuming passion." A forelock of gray dips toward her sparkling brown eyes. "Only now do I know that before having kids, I could never fully understand the meaning of either *consuming* or *passion*."

Coming of Age

Stanford speaks for a growing number of achieving women who are confessing that life as a single person—even with a stellar career—is not what it's cracked up to be. Their experiences are surprising even to themselves, coming of age at a time when a common feminist theme was the bondage of marriage. As these largely baby-boom women now mature to middle age— with their biological clocks sounding their final alarms—they are increasingly beginning to reassess and even reverse their views on marriage. No longer do they denigrate marriage as inherently oppressive; to the contrary, they now herald matrimony as the key to their greatest liberation.

Two developments have convinced thousands of Darlene Stanfords and their mates that, given the range of possibilities for living out one's life, marriage offers the most practical and rewarding option. First, the disappointments of the singles life, often a life of wasted time, emotion, and energy, have made the

stability and security of marriage appealing. And second, a renewed understanding of marriage, one that combines new respect for its traditions with a fresh translation of each partner's
role, has established it as the logical and accessible setting for
fulfilling the goals of most men and women.

Counterculture

Despite a never-ending parade of movies, television programs,
and happily-ever-after magazine stories and romance novels
about singles, many people are coming to view the joviality of
the unattached life with a jaundiced eye. Most films suggest that
the search for a partner is studded with easy sex, giddy romance, and a neat wrap-up in ninety minutes. "Hollywood con-
veys the clear and unmistakable message that singles life is
more exciting and rewarding than married life—as evidenced by
the fact that movies about single people are more common than
movies about couples, by a ratio of at least twenty to one," notes
film critic Michael Medved, author of four books on movies,
and host of PBS's *Sneak Previews* (and who happens to be my
husband). Still, even these films overwhelmingly conclude with
a touching transition from exciting independence to perfect pair-
ing—emphasizing that a committed relationship still provides
the preferred climax.

And in reality, it's no longer tacky to openly admit a desire for
one's own connubial conclusion. In fact, it seems the efforts of
unmarried people have never before been so publicly and fero-
ciously directed toward changing their status. Personal classifieds
now generate major income for publications of all types; advertisers straightforwardly seek a "marriage minded" respondent with
whom to "share Vivaldi, racquet ball, and long walks on the
beach." Computer and video match organizations proliferate,
placing brazen come-ons in the most respectable journals. . . .

Parallel with the change in attitude toward single living is a
rise in the reputation of marriage. As they nestle into middle
age, baby boomers dissatisfied with the trials of living together
and "commitmentphobia" are returning to their parents' values.
Having explored the career track, or simply unable biologically
to postpone parenthood any longer, many boomers are having
their first children in their middle thirties to early forties. And
with parenthood comes the question of the best environment in
which to raise their progeny.

This renewed interest in parenthood has contributed to the re-
discovery of that institution once eschewed by feminists as "en-
slavement" and has fostered its adaptation to the more egalitarian and casual life-styles baby boomers have pioneered and
adopted over the years. After discarding role expectations that
left women few or no career choices and men with sole finan-

cial responsibility for the family, contemporary couples have come to preserve and even cherish many of the norms and benefits of traditional marriage. What has emerged is a picture of the ideal marriage as one with more options for both partners—and in some cases, more responsibility. . . .

Now, About Romance

While the singles life as portrayed on television and in movies is unarguably exciting, couples are coming to find that only the permanent, long-term connection of marriage is truly *romantic*.

The "New Familism"

The baby boom generation is settling down [and] getting grayer. . . . The divorce rate has leveled off. There were 4.2 million new births in 1990, the highest number since 1964. . . .

I won't pretend to know what deep changes might be taking place in the polity or the economy. But I do believe that, within the culture, a shift *is* beginning to take place. . . . It is a shift away from a calculus of happiness based on individual fulfillment and toward a calculus of happiness based on the well-being of the family as a whole. This emergent cultural ethos is what David Blankenhorn and I have called the "New Familism."

Many forces might be contributing to this shift, but I believe one of the most important is the changing life cycle of large numbers of the baby boom generation. . . . During the seventies and eighties, there was a nice fit between the life stage of many baby boomers and the values of expressive individualism. Singlehood on the one hand. Individual freedom on the other hand. . . . Today, a critical mass of baby boomers has reached a new stage in the life cycle. They've married. They are becoming parents. And they're discovering that the values that served them in singlehood no longer serve them in parenthood. What used to be a tight fit has now become a mismatch.

Barbara Dafoe Whitehead, *Family Affairs*, Summer 1992.

Martin Ellwise lived with his wife, Pamela, for three years before they married. "One of my concerns about getting married was that all the spice and romance would be lost," he admits, seven years after their wedding. "I think because we've gone through so much now, including my father's death and the birth of our two-year-old son, we have a sweeter and more meaningful relationship. With a two-year-old you can't just jump into bed whenever you have the urge, but I'm finding that I have the urge more often, and when we do get together, our lovemaking is even better than before."

The sense of shared history that years of marriage bring allows a greater range of tender connections. Ellwise continues, "Pam and I have a lot more to be romantic *about*, the longer we've been married. Now Pamela puts little notes in my briefcase about what our son said, and we have Mother's Day and Father's Day to add to our sentimental holidays." And, he says, the gravity of marriage gives their closeness more import: "The idea that we'll be together forever makes me more protective and more caring of her. She's a permanent extension of me, rather than simply a great companion for the movies or sexy afternoons."

W.H. Auden observed that "any marriage, happy or unhappy, is infinitely more interesting and significant than any romance, however passionate." Participants in a Los Angeles experimental college course, "Transition from Single to Married," taught by Milton and Esther Simon (married to each other and the parents of five daughters), learn that marriage is the only setting for true romance. They also learn that the meaning of the word *romance* has been distorted. What popular media call "romance" might be better labeled "infatuation," or "chemical reaction."

Janis Littman, a studio publicist, single and hopeful at age thirty-three, says, "I know in five minutes if the relationship is worth the effort. If I feel an initial attraction, I'll go for it. But the real test isn't the first month or two—it's how we get along after six months or a year. Unfortunately, all my relationships have fallen apart after that. And I'm jealous of my married friends who have romance, because their relationships are solid, and not fragile like mine are."

Littman's message is that "romance" in the Hollywood sense, by its sheer titillation and novelty, distracts you from the central issues of communication and personality; in contrast, the genuine romance of marriage allows the essence of a partner to shine. True, people inevitably change over time; they inescapably add to their characters, and sometimes what they add is not so appealing. Usually, however, healthy people develop on a path of self-improvement. Many marriage hopefuls are now concluding that the sharing of that process may indeed be more romantic and fulfilling than a week at a glance loaded with hot dates.

A True Mirror

In a nation where the average length of residence at a single location is a mere four years, people have few relationships that are of the sort that can help them uphold the standards they've decided to live by.

If you start to swerve from your more lofty goals; if you develop an obnoxious habit; if you become involved with something that is more deleterious than simply different—your husband or wife has a unique position, with his or her long-term perspective and commitment, from which to offer constructive advice. A psychologist can ask exacting questions but must still view your history through the filter of your recollections. A parent's vantage point became distant when you moved away and entered adulthood, and it is colored with the unique bias of paternal or maternal love. The reactions of friends are useful, but friends too view you from a position far more remote from your habits and values than does a spouse.

A spouse sees how you act with your parents and how you adjust when you're around friends. He or she is in a position to observe how your moods change from morning to mealtime. A spouse watches you make plans and mull over concerns and understands what you think and why you think it. Only a husband or wife has this singular and personal vantage point from which to act as a mirror and reflect to you who you are, what you've become, and where you want to go.

A True Friend

This was the loss Sonia Lasky, a divorcee, . . . felt most acutely: "I cry because he was more than just the kids' dad; more than my travel companion or my sex partner. He was all those things wrapped up in my *friend*. I can't stand it that I no longer have my friend. I have nobody who will tell me when I'm going off track or when my hair looks lousy or when the kids need a tutor. Because we shared every aspect of our lives, because we were headed together in the same direction, we could consult each other and know that the other one really, truly understood. Now there is no one who can completely understand."

Perhaps the most liberating aspect of marriage, note many of the new advocates of marriage, is its ability to provide a comfortable basis from which to develop personally. Judith Bardwick, author of *In Transition*, writes, "While it has become chic to emphasize the ways in which commitment, especially in permanent relationships, diminishes choice, narrows experience, and therefore truncates growth, one can argue quite the opposite. People may be far better able to grow when they are in a mutually committed relationship, because, feeling secure, they are better able to take risks. The more one trusts the relationship, the more one will protect it and, simultaneously, the more one will feel free to change within it."

Two Heads

Marriage not only provides a stable base to change within but also a "safe haven" of security from which to tackle the world at large. The frustration of commanding an office full of employees was made bearable for Heidi Ingalsbe, a social worker in

Orange County, California, because she could rely on the understanding and support of her husband, Bill.

Thinking back, Heidi explains that Bill "knew I was crazed
and nervous, and he also knew that my style is to 'unload'
when I'm under stress. So he sat back after work and held my
hand through my recounting all the day's horror stories. It was
because of his stability and calmness that I managed the week
until the supervisor returned. I wouldn't want her job for anything." She found, in addition, that Bill provided the proverbial
"second head" that is more useful than one, in helping her handle a problem with an employee. He accomplished that by using
his skills as a successful attorney to probe options from various
angles, and play the devil's advocate when helpful. "He really
saved the day for me," Heidi recalls. "He helped me avoid what
could have been serious blunders.". . .

Children

With all the talk about whether it is better for children to experience the divorce of their parents or the ongoing unhappiness in
a home where parents are at odds, one conclusion is without dis-
pute: A harmonious home with two loving parents is indeed the
best setting for raising children. Societal expectations have
shifted such that women who remain unmarried as their childbearing years dwindle may now choose single parenthood, with
little societal reproval. Few of them, however, consider this the
best option—all recognize that raising a child solo will be more
demanding and pressure filled than with the help of a mate.

Staying married for the sake of the children, renounced in some
circles as a "good" reason to stay together, has lately earned positive attention as a motivator to save a troubled marriage. A long-
term study of children of divorce by Judith Wallerstein and
Sandra Blakeslee, *Second Chances*, found that "children can be
quite content even when their parents' marriage is profoundly
unhappy for one or both partners."

However, Wallerstein's and Blakeslee's research reveals far-
reaching negative consequences of divorce. Ten years post-
divorce, both the divorced parents and the affected children were
suffering, often exhibiting "sleeper effects" that only surfaced
years after the event. In a magazine interview, Wallerstein states
point blank: "The best protection we can provide children is a
functioning, happy relationship between a man and a woman.
That's the image a child internalizes and brings into his own
adult life.". . .

Something That Matters

As the baby boomers reach mid-life, they are increasingly
asking existential questions. And the answers they are finding

make marriage look pretty good. "I used to say I never wanted to marry," laughs Mary Jo Berringer, forty-one. "That was in my 'radical feminist' phase, when men were considered the enemy. But I soon reversed myself, because I realized that I was depriving myself of some of the basics that I knew deep-down I wanted—security, family, a sense of roots." She lived with a fellow graduate student in architecture for three years, then remained unattached for four more. Finally, at age thirty, she married the man who would father her three sons. "I married him because my central values told me it was time to grow up," she admits. "I'd been an adolescent wasting my life too long. It was time to finally do something that mattered."

I overheard two forty-ish men waiting in line for concert tickets as they discussed their relationships. The first said, "Jane and I have been living together for three years, and we really love each other." The second one replied, "Yes, but I've been with Lois for three years, and not only do I love her, but I have a marriage and a twelve-month-old daughter to show for it." The second gentleman was suggesting that marriage answers the existential question by giving you something to show for your time on earth—a family that has permanent consequences and significance.

It is no longer "unhip" to value marriage and its rewards. Couples today are indeed discovering that marriage—and this includes marriage with children—far from being an institution that undermines a person's independence and fulfillment, offers the most practical and realistic means of achieving both. As single men and women of the baby-boom generation look at marriage anew, this time with a deeper and more mature sense of who they are, they are discovering, just as Mary Jo Berringer did, that "marriage is the springboard to what I want to do and become."

"Among persons who have sought marital happiness by marrying at least once, a decreased proportion seem to be experiencing it."

Marriage Is Not Becoming More Popular

Norval D. Glenn

A large percentage of Americans may say that having a happy marriage is one of the most important goals in their lives, Norval D. Glenn reports in the following viewpoint, but a divorce rate approaching two-thirds of all recent marriages suggests that these good intentions have an ever-decreasing chance of translating into the real thing. Several factors help explain the decline of marriage, Glenn theorizes, but they all boil down to a basic egotism which, the author says, is the result of too much social freedom. Glenn is Ashbel Smith Professor of Sociology and Stiles Professor in American Studies, University of Texas at Austin.

As you read, consider the following questions:

1. What different interpretations of the recent trend in marriages does the author cite? Which view does Glenn support?
2. What three changes in American society does Glenn claim are responsible for the current state of marriage?
3. How might marriage failure be self-perpetuating in American society, according to Glenn?

Norval D. Glenn "What's Happening to American Marriage?" Reprinted from *USA Today* magazine, May 1993. Copyright 1993 by the Society for the Advancement of Education. Reprinted with permission.

Since the mid-1960s, there has been a period of substantial changes in the institution of marriage in the U.S. The divorce rate doubled from 1965 to 1975, increased more slowly through the late 1970s, and leveled off in the 1980s, but at such a high level that almost two-thirds of the marriages entered into in recent years are expected to end in divorce or separation. The increase in divorce, a decrease in remarriage after divorce, and a higher average age at first marriage have lowered the proportion of adults who are married. Out-of-wedlock births have increased substantially, so that one-fourth of all births now are to unmarried mothers. The proportion of married women who work outside the home has risen steadily, the increase being especially great among those with preschool-age children.

Interpreting the Numbers

Everyone agrees that these changes are important, but different authorities and commentators disagree as to what they mean for the health and future of the institution of marriage. One point of view is that marriage is in serious trouble—that it may disappear or lose its status as the preferred way of life for adult Americans. For example, a recent book is titled *The Retreat from Marriage*, and numerous books and articles refer to a decline or deinstitutionalization of marriage.

An opposing view, held until recently by most social scientific students of marriage, is that recent changes do not indicate decline or decay, but, rather, are adaptive and have kept the institution viable and healthy. These observers point out, for instance, that the increase in divorce has come about because people are rejecting particular marriages, rather than the institution of marriage—that most divorced persons want to remarry, and about three-fourths of them do so. Some of these commentators even view the increase in divorce positively, claiming that it reflects an increased importance people place on having good marriages and a decreased willingness to endure unsatisfactory ones. Divorce and remarriage, according to this view, are mechanisms for replacing poor relationships with better ones and keeping the overall quality of marriages high.

The evidence doesn't support consistently either the most negative or most positive views of what is happening to American marriage. For instance, the notion that it is a moribund or dying institution is inconsistent with the fact that a large percentage of Americans say that having a happy marriage is one of the most important, if not *the* most important, goal in their lives. About two-fifths of the respondents to the 1989 Massachusetts Mutual American Family Values Study indicated this was one of their most important values, and more than 90% said it was one of the most important or very important. Approximately three-fourths of the high school seniors studied by the Monitoring the Future Project at the University of Michigan have stated they definitely will marry, and the proportion has not declined. When adults are asked what kind of lifestyle they prefer, a very large majority select one involving wedlock, and a substantial minority (more than one-third) choose a traditional marriage in which the husband is the breadwinner and the wife a homemaker.

Making Marriage Matter

Our society requires a change in the habits of the heart, in the ways we think about marriage and how we value it.

"Supervows" would send a powerful message. Such vows are premarital contracts in which those about to be betrothed declare that they are committing more to their marriage than the law requires. They may choose from a menu of items what they wish to incorporate in their voluntary agreement. For instance, if either spouse requests marital counseling, the other promises to participate. If one asks for a divorce, he or she promises to wait at least six months to see if differences can be worked out. Once the couple freely arrives at an agreement, the supervows become legal commitments between the spouses.

Not very romantic, demur critics. Fair enough. Shoring up marriages may well require less infatuation and more responsibility.

Amitai Etzioni, *Time*, September 6, 1993.

Even when one takes into account that what people say in response to survey questions may not always reflect accurately what they think and feel, these survey data clearly demonstrate that Americans in general have not given up on matrimony. However, there is even more compelling evidence against the most extremely positive assessments of recent changes. Although having good marriages may be as important to people as ever, or may have become even more important in recent years, my research indicates that the probability of attaining them has declined to a large extent.

The Happiness Report

Those who argue that marriages in this country in general are doing quite well often cite data showing that a high and rather stable percentage of married persons give positive responses when they are asked about the quality of their unions. In fact, since the early 1970s, the reported quality of marriages has gone down, though not very much. Most years since 1973, the General

Social Survey conducted by the National Opinion Research Center at the University of Chicago has asked people to rate their marriages as very happy, pretty happy, or not too happy. The percentage of those who cited "very happy" fell by 5 percentage points from 1973–76 to 1988–91, dropping from 68 to 63%.

The indicated over-all happiness quality of American marriages still would be quite high if these ratings were to be taken at their face value, but they should not be interpreted that way. Many people are reluctant to admit to an interviewer—and perhaps even to themselves—that their marriages are less than satisfactory. Therefore, an unknown, but possibly substantial, proportion of the marriages reported to be "very happy" are not of very high quality, whereas virtually all those reported to be less than very happy are seriously deficient.

What is important about the indicated trend in marital quality is not that it has been slightly downward, but that it has not been steeply upward. If, as some commentators have claimed, the increase in divorce resulted only from people becoming less willing to stay in unsatisfactory marriages, the average quality of intact marriages should have climbed in tandem with the divorce rate. The fact that it didn't means that the probability of marriages remaining satisfactory must have declined substantially.

During 1973–76, about 60% of the persons who had first married 3–5 years earlier were still in their first marriages and reported them to be "very happy." By 1988–91, it had declined to about 54%. For persons who first married 12–14 years earlier, the decline was greater, from 54 to 38%, while for those who married 20–24 years earlier, it dropped from 50 to 36%. There were declines of around 10 or more percentage points at most other lengths of time since the first marriage.

Looking More Closely

Those who view recent changes in American marriage positively may not find these data very alarming. To them, what is important is the kind of marriage a person eventually attains, not the success of his or her first union. From this perspective, the percentages of ever-married persons who were in marriages of any order (first, second, or subsequent) that they reported to be "very happy" are even more significant.

The changes from 1973–76 to 1988–91 show a distinct downward trend in the probability of being in a successful marriage. Among persons who have sought marital happiness by marrying at least once, a decreased proportion seem to be experiencing it. This indicates that the increase in divorce and the other changes in marriage since the mid-1960s have not been solely or primarily a matter of people becoming more willing and able to go from poor marriages to better ones.

Still, one might suspect that there has been one positive aspect of the changes of the past few years—namely, a decreased tendency for people to be in poor marriages. However, the proportion of ever-married persons who were in marriages they reported to be less than "very happy" increased from 1973–76 to 1988–91 at all lengths of time after the first marriage up to 20 years—the changes being in the range of 3 to 5 percentage points. Only among persons who married 20–29 years earlier was there a slight decrease in the percentage of persons in the less satisfactory unions.

The Effects of Failure

Most of the decrease in the probability of being in a very happy marriage resulted from an increase in the probability of being divorced or separated. For instance, at 12–14 years after the first marriage, the percentage divorced or separated at the time of the surveys went from 8 to 18%, and at 20–24 years, it rose from 8 to 19%.

The most important consequences of the increase in marital failure have been on the offspring. An enormous amount of evidence, from sources varying from in-depth clinical studies to large-scale surveys, indicates moderate to severe short-term negative effects on the well-being and development of most of the children of divorce. Although the causal link is less well-established, there also apparently are some important long-term effects on a substantial minority of those whose parents divorce, including difficulty in making commitments in relationships and an increased probability of various mental health problems. Equally important is evidence for harmful effects from failed parental marriages that do not end in divorce—especially from those unions characterized by high levels of tension and conflict.

The changes in matrimony also have tended to lower the well-being of adults. Although there are exceptions, in general, those who are the happiest and most fulfilled and who function the best are those in successful marriages. On average, the happily married are the happiest, by a large margin, and the less than happily married are the least happy. In other words, to be in a good marriage is the best situation, but a poor marriage is not better than no marriage at all.

The causal relationship between marital situation and well-being is not entirely clear. Happily married individuals may do best partly because those who are the happiest and best-adjusted, for whatever reasons, are more likely than others to marry and to succeed at marriage. However, most researchers who have studied the relationship between marital situation and well-being believe that it primarily is the former that affects the latter. If so, and if the strength of the effects has not diminished markedly in

265

recent years, the decline in the percentage of persons at various stages of adulthood who are happily married has been distinctly detrimental to their welfare.

Why the Decline?

One of the most likely reasons for the decline in marital success is the well-documented increase in what persons expect of marriage. The levels of intimacy, emotional support, companionship, and sexual gratification that people believe they should get from marriage have increased, while what they are willing to give very likely has declined. In other words, the motivation for marriage has become more purely hedonistic, or more selfish. This is just one aspect of a general increase in individualism in America and throughout most of the modern world.

Another likely reason is the breakdown in the consensus of what it means to be a husband or wife. Whereas, until recently, the rights and obligations of spouses were prescribed culturally and fairly well-understood by just about everyone, they have become a matter for negotiation in individual marriages. This increased flexibility in marital roles, according to its advocates, should have increased the quality of matrimony or at least the quality of the lives of married persons, and for many persons it may have done so. For others, however, it has led to discord and disappointment. The optimistic view is that we eventually will learn to deal more effectively with the new freedom and flexibility in marriage, but that remains to be seen.

Another change that was supposed to have had unambiguously positive effects, but that may not have done so, is the easing of moral, religious, and legal barriers to divorce. The reasoning of those who advocated this was that making it easier for persons to correct marital mistakes—to escape from unsatisfying, stultifying, or dehumanizing marriages—would have positive effects on human welfare. Indeed, if one concentrates only on individual cases, as therapists and marriage counselors do, one readily can see how diminishing the guilt, social disapproval, and legal penalties of divorce has improved the quality of many lives.

Freedom vs. Marriage

However, the changes that resulted in short-term benefits to many individuals may have lessened the probability of marital success and resulted in long-term losses in the well-being of the population as a whole. One spouse's freedom—to leave the marriage, to change the terms of the marital contract—is the other spouse's insecurity. That insecurity tends to inhibit the strong commitment and investment of time, energy, and lost opportunities that are conducive to marital success. The decline in the ideal of marital permanence—one of the most well-documented value changes among Americans in recent decades—also has tended to make persons less willing and able to make the needed commitments to and investments in marriage. To the extent that a person constantly compares the existing marriage with real or imagined alternatives to it, that marriage inevitably will compare unfavorably in some respects. People are hardly aware of needs currently being well-served, but tend to be keenly attuned to them not being well-satisfied. Since attention tends to center on needs not being especially well-met in one's marriage (and there always are some), the grass will tend to look greener on the other side of the marital fence. Therefore, merely contemplating alternatives to one's marriage may engender discontent.

Those authorities who have come to recognize the negative aspects of recent changes in American marriage are dividing into two camps—those who believe that the negative changes are inevitable and irreversible and that the best we can do is to try to lessen their impact, and those who believe that at least some of the changes can be reversed. The pessimists give strong arguments for their position, pointing out, for instance, that the trend to individualism that underlies many of the changes has occurred in most parts of the modern world and may characterize an advanced stage of economic development. Furthermore, the insecurity that inhibits commitment in marriage is likely to be self-perpetuating, as it leads to marital instability, which in turn leads to further insecurity.

There are signs, however, that a reversal in some of the changes already may be occurring. In recent years, there has been a strong reaction against radical individualism among many intellectuals in this country, and attitudinal survey data indicate that a similar reaction may be beginning in the general public. Marriage is just as crucial an institution as ever, and most Americans seem to know that. What has been missing is sufficient awareness of the costs of maintaining the health of the institution. It is to be hoped that Americans will recognize that the loss of personal freedom, renunciation of pleasure seeking, and acceptance of greater responsibility necessary for good marriages will benefit themselves, their children, and the entire society.

> *"A society . . .* humanely *adapted to the fact that most women work . . . would include men whose notion of manhood encouraged them to be active parents and share [the work] at home."*

Men and Women Should Share Domestic Responsibilities

Arlie Hochschild with Anne Machung

In the following viewpoint, excerpted from their influential book *The Second Shift: Working Parents and the Revolution at Home,* Arlie Hochschild and Anne Machung argue that while an increasing number of women are accepting paid employment, there has been no corresponding effort by men to share the domestic responsibilities. The authors contend that the resulting double shift that women must work—one at the office, and one at home—almost always results in marital strife. Hochschild, a professor of sociology at the University of California at Berkeley, has written extensively on gender and social issues. Machung served as research assistant to Hochschild for this study on working families.

As you read, consider the following questions:

1. What, according to the authors, is the size of the "leisure gap" between men and women? What do they say are its effects?
2. What percentage of men the authors interviewed shared the housework with their wives? Why did the leisure gap persist in some of these relationships, according to Hochschild and Machung?

She is not the same woman in each magazine advertisement, but she is the same idea. She has that working-mother look as she strides forward, briefcase in one hand, smiling child in the other. Literally and figuratively, she is moving ahead. Her hair, if long, tosses behind her; if it is short, it sweeps back at the sides, suggesting mobility and progress. There is nothing shy or passive about her. She is confident, active, "liberated." She wears a dark tailored suit, but with a silk bow or colorful frill that says, "I'm really feminine underneath." She has made it in a man's world without sacrificing her femininity. And she has done this on her own. By some personal miracle, this image suggests, she has managed to combine what 150 years of industrialization have split wide apart—child and job, frill and suit, female culture and male.

When I showed a photograph of a supermom like this to the working mothers I talked to in the course of [my] research, many responded with an outright laugh. One daycare worker and mother of two, ages three and five, threw back her head: "Ha! They've got to be *kidding* about her. Look at me, hair a mess, nails jagged, twenty pounds overweight. Mornings, I'm getting my kids dressed, the dog fed, the lunches made, the shopping list done. That lady's got a maid." Even working mothers who did have maids couldn't imagine combining work and family in such a carefree way. "Do you know what a baby does to your life, the two o'clock feedings, the four o'clock feedings?" Another mother of two said: "They don't show it, but she's whistling"—she imitated a whistling woman, eyes to the sky—"so she can't hear the din." They envied the apparent ease of the woman with the flying hair, but she didn't remind them of anyone they knew.

The women I interviewed—lawyers, corporate executives, word processors, garment pattern cutters, daycare workers—and most of their husbands, too—felt differently about some issues: how right it is for a mother of young children to work a full-time job, or how much a husband should be responsible for the home. But they all agreed that it was hard to work two full-time jobs and raise young children.

The Increase in Working Women

How well do couples do it? The more women work outside the home, the more central this question. The number of women in paid work has risen steadily since before the turn of the century, but since 1950 the rise has been staggering. In 1950, 30 percent of American women were in the labor force; in 1986, it was 55 percent. In 1950, 28 percent of married women with children between six and seventeen worked outside the home; in 1986, it had risen to 68 percent. In 1950, 23 percent of married women with children under six worked. By 1986, it had grown to 54 percent. We don't know how many women with children under the age of one worked outside the home in 1950; it was so rare that the Bureau of Labor kept no statistics on it. In 1989 half of such women did. Two-thirds of all mothers are now in the labor force; in fact, more mothers have paid jobs (or are actively looking for one) than non-mothers. Because of this change in women, two-job families in 1989 made up 58 percent of all married couples with children.

©Gail Machlis. Reprinted with permission.

Since an increasing number of working women have small children, we might expect an increase in part-time work. But actually, 67 percent of the mothers who work have full-time jobs—that is, thirty-five hours or more weekly. That proportion is what it was in 1959.

If more mothers of young children are stepping into full-time jobs outside the home, and if most couples can't afford household help, how much more are fathers doing at home? As I began exploring this question I found many studies on the hours working men and women devote to housework and childcare. One national random sample of 1,243 working parents in forty-four American cities, conducted in 1965-66 by Alexander Szalai and his coworkers, for example, found that working women averaged three hours a day on housework while men averaged seventeen minutes; women spent fifty minutes a day of time exclusively with their children; men spent twelve minutes. On the other side of the coin, working fathers watched television an hour longer than their working wives, and slept a half hour longer each night. A comparison of this American sample with eleven other industrial countries in Eastern and Western Europe revealed the same difference between working women and working men in those countries as well. In a 1983 study of white middle-class families in greater Boston, Grace Baruch and R.C. Barnett found that working men married to working women spent only three-quarters of an hour longer each week with their kindergarten-aged children than did men married to housewives.

Women's "Double Day"

Szalai's landmark study documented the now familiar but still alarming story of the working woman's "double day," but it left me wondering how men and women actually felt about all this. He and his coworkers studied how people used time, but not, say, how a father felt about his twelve minutes with his child, or how his wife felt about it. Szalai's study revealed the visible surface of what I discovered to be a set of deeply emotional issues: What should a man and woman contribute to the family? How appreciated does each feel? How does each respond to subtle changes in the balance of marital power? How does each develop an unconscious "gender strategy" for coping with the work at home, with marriage, and, indeed, with life itself? These were the underlying issues.

But I began with the measurable issue of time. Adding together the time it takes to do a paid job and to do housework and childcare, I averaged estimates from the major studies on time use done in the 1960s and 1970s, and discovered that women worked roughly fifteen hours longer each week than men. Over a year, they worked an *extra month of twenty-four-hour days a year*. Over a dozen years, it was an extra year of twenty-four-hour days. Most women without children spend much more time than men on housework; with children, they devote more time to both housework and childcare. Just as there is a wage gap between men and women in the workplace, there is a "leisure gap" between them at home. Most women work one

271

shift at the office or factory and a "second shift" at home.

Studies show that working mothers have higher self-esteem and get less depressed than housewives, but compared to their husbands, they're more tired and get sick more often. In Peggy Thoits's 1985 analysis of two large-scale surveys, each of about a thousand men and women, people were asked how often in the preceding week they'd experienced each of twenty-three symptoms of anxiety (such as dizziness or hallucinations). According to the researchers' criteria, working mothers were more likely than any other group to be "anxious."

In light of these studies, the image of the woman with the flying hair seems like an upbeat "cover" for a grim reality, like those pictures of Soviet tractor drivers smiling radiantly into the distance as they think about the ten-year plan. The Szalai study was conducted in 1965-66. I wanted to know whether the leisure gap he found in 1965 persists, or whether it has disappeared. Since most married couples work two jobs, since more will in the future, since most wives in these couples work the extra month a year, I wanted to understand what the wife's extra month a year meant for each person, and what it does for love and marriage in an age of high divorce.

The Research

With my research associates Anne Machung and Elaine Kaplan, I interviewed fifty couples very intensively, and I observed in a dozen homes. We first began interviewing artisans, students, and professionals in Berkeley, California, in the late 1970s. This was at the height of the women's movement, and many of these couples were earnestly and self-consciously struggling to modernize the ground rules of their marriages. Enjoying flexible job schedules and intense cultural support to do so, many succeeded. Since their circumstances were unusual they became our "comparison group" as we sought other couples more typical of mainstream America. In 1980 we located more typical couples by sending a questionnaire on work and family life to every thirteenth name— from top to bottom—of the personnel roster of a large, urban manufacturing company. At the end of the questionnaire, we asked members of working couples raising children under six and working full-time jobs if they would be willing to talk to us in greater depth. Interviewed from 1980 through 1988, these couples, their neighbors and friends, their children's teachers, daycare workers and baby-sitters, form the heart of this [study]. . . .

The women I interviewed seemed to be far more deeply torn between the demands of work and family than were their husbands. They talked with more animation and at greater length than their husbands about the abiding conflict between them. Busy as they were, women more often brightened at the idea of yet another interviewing session. They felt the second shift was *their* issue and most of their husbands agreed. When I telephoned one husband to arrange an interview with him, explaining that I wanted to ask him about how he managed work and family life, he replied genially, "Oh, this will *really* interest my *wife*."

It was a woman who first proposed to me the metaphor, borrowed from industrial life, of the "second shift." She strongly resisted the *idea* that homemaking was a "shift." Her family was her life and she didn't want it reduced to a job. But as she put it, "You're on duty at work. You come home, and you're on duty. Then you go back to work and you're on duty." After eight hours of adjusting insurance claims, she came home to put on the rice for dinner, care for her children, and wash laundry. Despite herself her home life *felt* like a second shift. That was the real story and that was the real problem.

Men who shared the load at home seemed just as pressed for time as their wives, and as torn between the demands of career and small children. But the majority of men did not share the load at home. Some refused outright. Others refused more passively, often offering a loving shoulder to lean on, an understanding ear as their working wife faced the conflict they both saw as hers. At first it seemed to me that the problem of the second shift was hers. But I came to realize that those husbands who helped very little at home were often indirectly just as deeply affected as their wives by the need to do that work, through the resentment their wives feel toward them, and through their need to steel themselves against that resentment. Evan Holt, a warehouse furniture salesman, did very little housework and played with his four-year-old son, Joey, at his convenience. Juggling the demands of work with family at first seemed a problem for his wife. But Evan himself suffered enormously from the side effects of "her" problem. His wife did the second shift, but she resented it keenly, and half-consciously expressed her frustration and rage by losing interest in sex and becoming overly absorbed with Joey. One way or another, most men I talked with do suffer the severe repercussions of what I think is a transitional phase in American family life.

A Question of Responsibility

One reason women take a deeper interest than men in the problems of juggling work with family life is that even when husbands happily shared the hours of work, their wives felt more *responsible* for home and children. More women kept track of doctors' appointments and arranged for playmates to come over. More mothers than fathers worried about the tail on a child's Halloween costume or a birthday present for a school friend. They were more likely to think about their children

273

while at work and to check in by phone with the baby-sitter.

Partly because of this, more women felt torn between one sense of urgency and another, between the need to soothe a child's fear of being left at daycare, and the need to show the boss she's "serious" at work. More women than men questioned how good they were as parents, or if they did not, they questioned why they weren't questioning it. More often than men, women alternated between living in their ambition and standing apart from it.

As masses of women have moved into the economy, families have been hit by a "speed-up" in work and family life. There is no more time in the day than there was when wives stayed home, but there is twice as much to get done. It is mainly women who absorb this "speed-up." Twenty percent of the men in my study shared housework equally. Seventy percent of men did a substantial amount (less than half but more than a third), and 10 percent did less than a third. Even when couples share more equitably in the work at home, women do two-thirds of the *daily* jobs at home, like cooking and cleaning up—jobs that fix them into a rigid routine. Most women cook dinner and most men change the oil in the family car. But, as one mother pointed out, dinner needs to be prepared every evening around six o'clock, whereas the car oil needs to be changed every six months, any day around that time, any time that day. Women do more childcare than men, and men repair more household appliances. A child needs to be tended daily while the repair of household appliances can often wait "until I have time." Men thus have more control over *when* they make their contributions than women do. They may be very busy with family chores but, like the executive who tells his secretary to "hold my calls," the man has more control over his time. The job of the working mother, like that of the secretary, is usually to "take the calls."

The Undesirable Chores

Another reason women may feel more strained than men is that women more often do two things at once—for example, write checks and return phone calls, vacuum and keep an eye on a three-year-old, fold laundry and think out the shopping list. Men more often cook dinner *or* take a child to the park. Indeed, women more often juggle three spheres—job, children, and housework—while most men juggle two—job and children. For women, two activities compete with their time with children, not just one.

Beyond doing more at home, women also devote *proportionately more* of their time at home to housework and proportionately less of it to childcare. Of all the time men spend working at home, more of it goes to childcare. That is, working wives spend relatively more time "mothering the house"; husbands spend more time "mothering" the children. Since most parents prefer to tend to their children rather than clean house, men do more of what they'd rather do. More men than women take their children on "fun" outings to the park, the zoo, the movies. Women spend more time on maintenance, feeding and bathing children, enjoyable activities to be sure, but often less leisurely or "special" than going to the zoo. Men also do fewer of the "undesirable" household chores: fewer men than women wash toilets and scrub the bathroom. . . .

The "Stalled Revolution"

The exodus of women into the economy has not been accompanied by a cultural understanding of marriage and work that would make this transition smooth. The workforce has changed. Women have changed. But most workplaces have remained inflexible in the face of the family demands of their workers; and at home, most men have yet to really adapt to the changes in women. This strain between the change in women and the absence of change in much else leads me to speak of a "stalled revolution."

A society which did not suffer from this stall would be a society *humanely* adapted to the fact that most women work outside the home. The workplace would allow parents to work part time, to share jobs, to work flexible hours, to take parental leaves to give birth, tend a sick child, or care for a well one. As Delores Hayden has envisioned in *Redesigning the American Dream*, it would include affordable housing closer to places of work, and perhaps community-based meal and laundry services. It would include men whose notion of manhood encouraged them to be active parents and share at home. In contrast, a stalled revolution lacks social arrangements that ease life for working parents, and lacks men who share the second shift. . . .

In a time of stalled revolution—when women have gone to work, but the workplace, the culture, and most of all, the men, have not adjusted themselves to this new reality—children can be the victims. Most working mothers are already doing all they can, doing that extra month a year. It is men who can do more. . . .

Caring for children is the most important part of the second shift, and the effects of a man's care or his neglect will show up again and again through time—in the child as a child, in the child as an adult, and probably also in the child's own approach to fatherhood, and in generations of fathers to come. Active fathers are often in reaction against a passive, detached father. But an exceptionally warmhearted man could light the way still better. In the last forty years, many women have made a historic shift into the economy. Now it is time for a whole generation of men to make a second historic shift—into work at home.

"American women are painfully and rapidly realizing that there are some things a man just won't do, and taking equal responsibility for child care is one of them."

Men and Women Should Not Share Domestic Responsibilities

Steven Goldberg

In the following viewpoint, Steven Goldberg explains that the social and economic forces of modernization have ushered many women out of the home and into the job market. This trend, Goldberg asserts, is obliterating the differences between men and women, thus destroying the harmony of male-female relationships. Men will not shoulder a greater part of the domestic burden; women will suffer under the conflicting demands of job and family; and marriage, which used to allocate responsibilities between the sexes is, Goldberg ironically concludes, the first thing to suffer. Goldberg, a sociologist specializing in cross-cultural male-female roles, is the author of several books, including *The Inevitability of Patriarchy* and *Why Men Rule*.

As you read, consider the following questions:

1. What attributes does Goldberg assign to women and men?
2. What does the author say the "masculinization of the world" is doing to women and men?

Back in the Sixties, many ridiculed the idea of lifelong marriage because they saw it as inherently undesirable. Today the idea is ridiculed because it seems virtually impossible. The divorce rate is half again as high as it is virtually anywhere else in the modern world—and it is high virtually everywhere in the modern world. And increasing numbers of people choose not to marry at all.

This will not engender social disintegration; individuals and societies have a way of stumbling through. But the increasing fragility of marriage does threaten to make the breakup of the parents and absence of the father the typical experience of the child; years of loneliness the typical experience of the older woman; and self-destructive and anti-social behavior the typical contribution of increasing numbers of men not constrained by the intimacy and responsibility of marriage.

A tendency in this direction is probably inherent in modern industrial society's decreasing dependence on physical labor, its increasing need of huge numbers of workers skilled in the intricacies of modern work life, and the entailed requirement that women be socialized, educated, and trained to join the labor force in large and increasing numbers.

In many ways, this tendency serves women well; it makes possible a choice of lives and a legal equality in areas that were formerly rewards for simple maleness. Furthermore, while no modern society can accord women's feminine, maternal, and familial roles a status as high as that accorded these roles in *some* primitive and agricultural societies, no modern society—with its requirement of reward according to perceived contribution, equal treatment by the law, and other exchanges of status for rights—can treat women as chattels, as in *other* non-modern societies.

The Cost of Socialization

However, the tendency for females to be socialized and educated to compete with males in superfamilial areas—rather than to define their primary value in terms of the traditional roles for which men cannot compete—carries a heavy cost, including a reduction of: the sense that one is doing what one should be doing; the satisfaction, perhaps even happiness, that this engenders; the sense that one belongs to a complete and self-contained community; and the support of the individual by this community.

Women bear the brunt of this process. The annoyance many men feel at having to take into account the corporate presence of women is—however noisy the men's complaints—insignificant compared to the conflicting demands on women of the public sphere and the home. Moreover, the socialization of women to value behaviors that are more strongly inherent in maleness, and to devalue behaviors that are more strongly inherent in femaleness, has had a terrible—and terribly ironic—effect: it has only minimally increased women's tendency to effectively behave in male ways while it has severely decreased women's ability to effectively behave in female ways.

Through most of our history one could assume of women an understanding of men. This understanding meant every woman had, in her armamentarium, a host of weapons with which to defend herself against male stupidity by deflating the male. Few women felt the need of the protection of dubious laws against the wolf whistle; women knew how to handle men. Today many young women, not having learned the self-defense that gives confidence, tremble at the sight of a male aggression they cannot handle.

The aspects of modernization mentioned above render unavoidable women's being socialized and educated to see the roles associated with males as the worthwhile roles. It is hardly surprising, therefore, that many contemporary women derogate the feminine. (There are feminist attempts to "redefine femininity," but the "redefinitions" are simply an acceptance of the non-feminine, supported by claims about how well women can do the things men do.)

In any case, the public arena, the marketplace, is becoming for great numbers of women the primary status arena. It is an arena in which femininity is far less powerful than it is when status is determined by marriage and family. The conflicts encountered by women represent not just the clash of physiological impulse with social reward (i.e., maternal possibility vs. the status now given women in the public arena), but also incongruous social demands (expectations of feminine and maternal behavior away from the job vs. the behavior expected in the battle for public status). When the physiological nature of those concerned conflicts with social expectation and when the natures of the required social abilities conflict with each other, a woman is being asked to possess a universality that very few human beings possess.

All this might be less of a problem if men were wired to respond to the infant as readily as women do. But the experience of China, the Soviet Union, Scandinavia, and a number of other countries—combined with the evidence of physiology—shows that equal child-rearing is an impossibility. American women are painfully and rapidly realizing that there are some things a man just won't do, and taking equal responsibility for child care is one of them.

A Masculinization of the World

Even if modernization did not offer women any rewards and even if the costs were higher, our bond to modernization has long since been rendered indissoluble.

We are, in short, experiencing a masculinization of the world: the modern economic system tends to socialize and reward women for behaviors required in the public arena more highly than for the once-primary feminine, maternal, and familial behavior. This masculinization dwarfs in importance the more obvious, but superficial, feminization seemingly implied by cosmetic alterations of customs of male dominance and by denial of temperamental, cognitive, and behavioral sex differences that are obvious to all. And it forces women to neglect a game that they cannot lose in order to enter a game that nature has stacked against them. . . .

The socialization is, of course, far from totally successful; women are, after all, women, and, when the bullet hits the bone, they know only they can fill the only role that ultimately matters. They know men are expendable: if 90 per cent of the males were lost, the lucky 10 per cent would assure that there was no population loss to the next generation; each woman lost reduces the size of the next generation.

The psychophysiological reality guarantees that many women will always harbor doubts—whether acknowledged or not— about the value of roles in the public arena when compared to those in the home. Thus, even today over half of American women *acknowledge* that they would prefer to devote themselves to home and children, were that a financial possibility.

Real Life

And real life does still have some influence. Young wives see that their daughters would rather have a doll with dresses than a G.I. Joe figure, and that their sons would rather have their heads catch fire than be caught playing with a doll that lacks even a rudimentary weapon for wasting the bastards.

They also quickly see that their husbands don't seem to be getting with the program. Even when national policy (as in the Chinese, Soviet, and Scandinavian examples mentioned above) charges men with sharing the work at home when women join the labor force, men simply ignore the charge, and women, or at least those not able to afford "nannies" and "mother's helpers," are forced into two full-time roles. These roles, each potentially life-satisfying in itself, can become back- and spirit-breaking when combined without compromise.

To some extent, of course, women will cope with the impossible demands by devoting less time to former roles. This may be for the best when it represents, say, a decrease in the obsession with cleaning the home that was fashionable in the Fifties. However, it is difficult to be sanguine about the effects on children of the analogous reduction of maternal accessibility. That many women worry about this is clear from the endless discussions of "quality time" and its ability or inability to substitute for the constant background proximity of mother to infant.

Feminism and Marriage

Feminist "theories" deny the physiological roots of maleness and femaleness. In doing this they persuade the contemporary woman not merely that she can have it all (an eventuality impossible for those with male physiologies to believe about themselves), but that marriage can ignore crucial differences between males and females, differences that (if acknowledged at all) are incorrectly alleged to be "merely cultural" and, therefore, amenable to elimination.

Dad Is No Substitute for Mom

Most fathers have become reluctant warriors in a social revolution. Now that even the most traditional women are going off to work, the pressure is on dad to help more—if not share equally—on the home front. He is supposed to be the new sensitive man, caring and warm. Yet most men were raised to succeed at work, not at home. When his role as breadwinner is undermined, often his ego is too. . . .

Some fathers are downright angry about having to get involved. Studies show that marriages are more volatile when the father is forced to help around the house because the mother has taken a job. A Penn State study that followed blue-collar newlyweds for three years found that fathers in dual-earner marriages quarreled with their wives more than fathers in single-earner families. Mothers, meanwhile, sometimes feel threatened by a challenge to their traditional role and reinforce the husband's role as odd man out by treating him like an employee. "Mothers tend to be the experts. There is a natural tendency for the mothers to take over," says Glen Palm. "It's hard for the father to build confidence in himself as a parent." In a *Parenting* magazine survey, 64 percent of the fathers said mother knows best about daily child care. Only 1 percent said father knows best.

Evan Thomas et al., *Newsweek*, December 19, 1988.

Most wives of fifty years ago understood that men were just men, and that men cannot be expected or socialized to be anything else. This made the marriage agreement a realistic one that was not inherently enraging to the woman (in the way it is when there is a pretense that men are simply less lumpy women who could just as easily accept an "egalitarian" role).

The woman of the contemporary ideology—unlike all the

women of all other societies that have ever existed—no longer recognizes this. When wives have expectations of an "equality" that demands not merely equal reward for different behavior, but equal reward for the same behavior, marriage as an institution is in trouble, and would be even were there not numerous other forces tending toward this end. (There is, to be sure, a range of possibilities in practical terms; the treatment of women in the United States is different from that in Saudi Arabia. But the core statistical male-female differences of cognition, temperament, and behavior are the same everywhere: no society—and only a feminist sub-culture in ours—claims to believe that women could be as aggressive as men or men as nurturant as women; no society fails to associate dominance and crime with males or familial stability and child care with females.)

Similarly, the conflicting demands of feminine attractiveness and the maternal disposition, on the one hand, and success in the public arena, on the other, have generated a feminist psychosocial view of the world as protective armor. For example, it is received wisdom among the more feminist-oriented career women that men are threatened by female success, and there is no doubt a great deal of truth to this. Unexpected competition from former allies always causes anxiety, even if the new competitors do not add to the competition one faces.

The Bases of Attraction

But the deep cause of the feminist emphasis on this male anxiety is the realization that even those men who are not threatened by female success are not especially drawn to it. While the perimeters of conceptions of femininity vary from time to time and culture to culture, the core behavior that defines the feminine and attracts males everywhere and at all times does not much vary. And dominant behavior is not a vital component of this femininity. Women through the ages knew that males are drawn to the feminine and that characteristics not disproportionately associated with the female elicit, at best, a male lack of interest.

But women through the ages were not told that they had to exhibit these male characteristics. Contemporary women are told that their status will, to a great extent, be determined by their ability to mimic qualities associated with the male, and women know that these are, at best, qualities that do nothing to attract males. Males have never faced an analogous conflict because women everywhere have—for reasons rooted in female physiology—been drawn to men who exhibit dominance. Despite contemporary values claiming the desirability of males with a female portion of sensitivity and nurturance, the actual behavior of even those women who give lip-service encouragement to

281

men who claim to agree casts serious doubt on the attractiveness to women of such men.

The change in the attitude of each sex toward the other is at the heart of the matter. As women have come to have less use for men, and have refused to grant their husbands the special position both sexes once took for granted, men have come to have less use for women. Both look for satisfaction on an occupational playing field on which, statistically speaking, men as a sex cannot lose and women as a sex cannot win.

At the Head of the Table

The women of every society save our own have understood that the male's nature is such that he must be given a special position in the family if he is to peacefully take his place in it. These women have understood the male's greater readiness to choose competition over compromise, his greater resistance to socialization, his inevitably lesser role in his children's lives, his lower threshold for sexual arousal, and, perhaps most powerfully, the attraction to the new that constantly threatens to overwhelm his mere social and moral agreements. Women have realized that men will not even attempt to suppress these tendencies if they are offered no distinctive and respected position in the family, a position that can act as counterpoise to both the limits marriage sets on male behavior and the centrality that the woman's unique physiological and psychological bond to the infant automatically gives her. If being "the man of the family" means nothing special, many men will find it not worth the cost.

Men have always expected the family to be a respite from the war outside, a peaceful harbor that they protect from attack. It is a fact—a fact so obvious that only a sociologist or a feminist could deny it—that male physiology is such that males react to competitive situations by fight or flight, usually fight or, in the context of marriage, a stonewalling that reduces the marriage to a formal understanding and replaces intimacy with civility (at best). In response to the refusal to grant them their traditional role men will tend to either a) disrupt the family as they attain through aggression that which they were once granted, or b) channel their energies into sexual conquest outside the family. Women will find that they are raising their children either on a battlefield or alone, wondering why loudmouthed Rambos have replaced strong, silent defenders of justice and protectors of women.

Contemporary values, for example, see as indefensible the idea that the husband be seen to deserve the favored seat at the table and be deferred to in other, analogous, ways. Often ignored—for obvious psychological reasons—is the cost inherent in the elimination of *any* former benefit of marriage to the man: an increase in the number of men who stay single or who find the marriage they are in less worthy of effort.

In 1970 only a sixth of Americans older than 17 had never married. In 1980 it was a fifth. In 1993 it is nearly a quarter. Between 1980 and 1991, the percentage of 35-to-39-year-old women who had never married doubled to 12 per cent. Various factors undoubtedly played causal roles here: demographic changes, the invention of "the pill," women putting off marriage for career and then facing the reality that it becomes more difficult with each year after the mid-twenties to find someone to marry, a recession that made the choice of marriage and children a heroic act, a greater acceptance of homosexuality, and the like. But the view I have given makes this prediction: when these factors have reversed or been accounted for, the future will a) still exhibit an increasing percentage of never-married people and b) provide clear evidence that the increase in single males represents a male refusal to marry, while the increase in single females represents primarily the loss of the males from the pool. And this increase in never-married people will complement a marital discord that is already mirrored in an unprecedented rate of divorce. . . .

Marriage Is Not a Democracy

Just as the women's movement has found that, for all the energy it has expended, it has had no serious effect on male attainment of positions of power, so does the wife find that marriage is not a democracy for the same reasons that bed is not a democracy. She finds that the basic male impulses she so enjoys in bed preclude marital equality of the sort she has envisioned (however she may attempt to explain this fact).

And there will be many women—perhaps the large, if less vocal, majority—who will find that they prefer a man to be a man. In some cases men will repay this with loyalty and love, in others with the astonishing selfishness that this arrangement permits. These are the women who are grateful that they belong to the sex that has the option of deciding to do that which is most important—even those among them who choose not to take the option. But there will be other women who have been so completely socialized that they consider the female's unique ability to act as agent for the continuation of the species and culture as insufficient recompense for the male retention of positions of dominance. Such is the power—and limit—of socialization.

There's a sense, of course, in which none of this matters. Whatever their beliefs, men and women are still men and women, and beliefs that require the impossible are not taken seriously by reality. But the attitudes and values held by men and women *do* determine whether they live their lives on a dance floor or a battlefield, and this is not such a little thing.

"For many, mixing work and sex is inherently inappropriate, and [coworker] reactions from righteous outrage to serious discomfort are not uncommon."

Sexual Attraction in the Workplace Is Often Counterproductive

Lisa A. Mainiero

With the ongoing entrance of large numbers of women into paid employment, intimate relationships between men and women in the workplace are inevitable. Sometimes these relationships are even productive, concedes Lisa A. Mainiero in the following viewpoint. But, Mainiero warns, the dangers of sexual attraction in the office are numerous, not only for the work couple involved, but also for their company and their coworkers. Mainiero, assistant professor of management at Fairfield University's School of Business in Connecticut, is the author of *Office Romance: Love, Power, and Sex in the Workplace.*

As you read, consider the following questions:

1. What are some of the pressures favoring office romance, according to Mainiero?
2. How extensive does the author report office romances to be in American businesses?
3. What dangers involved in workplace sexual relations does Mainiero list as relevant to the man and woman involved, to the couple's coworkers, and to the company employing them?

Lisa Mainiero, "Office Romance," *Ethics: Easier Said Than Done*, nos. 7 & 8 (1990), © 1990, The Joseph and Edna Josephson Institute of Ethics. Reprinted with permission.

Love in the office is a powerful aphrodisiac. Indeed, the office of today has become a very sexy place in which men and women are meeting, dating, falling in love, and mating.

And why not? Meeting Mr. or Ms. Right has become a difficult and time-consuming venture fraught with disappointment. Expecting to meet our mate at the local bar on a Saturday night is out of the question these days. Blind dates can turn into evenings in which one's entire goal becomes "the great escape." Many singles have simply resigned themselves to stopping off at their local video store for a safe, if bland, evening's entertainment.

But more and more, the idea of dating a coworker—someone we already know, someone we feel safe and secure with—appears to offer a solution. The long hard hours put in together on an important project can create both an intellectually and emotionally stimulating climate. Cocktail parties, business lunches, and business trips all add up to the right ambiance for romance.

A Prevalent Practice

The fact is we tend to become involved with people who are in close proximity to us. Indeed, in some respects, today's office has taken the place of church, neighborhood, and even family in bringing people closer together. We develop friendships and romances these days more often with our coworkers than with anyone else. More than half of America's workforce have become workaholics and that investment of time means intimate and potentially romantic opportunities.

A survey in the February 1986 issue of *Personnel* magazine indicated that more than 86% of those interviewed had known about, or had actually been involved in, an office romance. Another survey in a 1987 issue of *Men's Health* magazine showed that over half of the survey's 444 respondents had been sexually propositioned by a fellow employee. The survey also said that 25% actually had had sex in their workplace, and 18% had sex with a coworker during office hours.

Contrary to popular myth, not all office romances turn out badly. Many seem to transcend their questionable roots and bloom into lasting meaningful unions. Others burn out but end in ways that injure no one. And while the affair is going on and love is in the air the spirit of harmony may actually help office conditions.

Still, engaging in such liaisons involves a complex array of moral, emotional, and practical problems.

An Ethical Quagmire

Even in the simplest case, where both parties are unattached, the relationship is open and above board, and neither party has conflicting responsibilities to the workplace, there are many other stakeholders who are affected by office romance. Superiors, subordinates, coworkers—all are likely to be caught up in the ebb and flow of evolving love. Depending on the duties of the lovers and the obviousness of their attraction, the relationship may be so powerful and pervasive that it affects radically the chemistry of the workplace. For many, mixing work and sex is inherently inappropriate, and reactions from righteous outrage to serious discomfort are not uncommon. And this is just in the simple cases.

Office romances present a veritable ethical quagmire if one or both parties are married or "involved"—a situation in which the relationship has to be kept a secret from some or all work colleagues. If one mate has decision-making authority over the work of the other, this can create a conflict of interest. In these situations, deceit and concealment are almost inevitable and they exact a high toll on all involved.

In my research on this subject, coworkers told me a number of their own fears, such as the couple's declining productivity, lack of concentration on their work, and conflict of interest issues.

Romantic Risks

There are numerous risks to carrying on an office romance. Based on the research I did for my book *Office Romance: Love, Power, and Sex in the Workplace*, I found seven areas that represent risks to those who find themselves at work and shot by Cupid's arrow.

1. An office romance can threaten your career. In a survey I did of executive women, some 63% said their careers could be compromised by an office romance.

2. Professional relationships can be destroyed. Not all office romances have happy endings. The termination of a romantic relationship can be a messy matter, especially when you will still have to see and perhaps work with your ex-mate. In my research with 100 executive women, I found that one of the most common concerns that women had about an office romance was fear of the breakup. They recognized that being forced to see your ex-lover at work on a daily basis—as if nothing has happened—can be excruciatingly painful.

3. Office romance can cause coworkers to feel contempt. Colleagues can be confused about whether to deal with the couple as individuals or a team. Sometimes a department does not treat the news of an office romance with affection but with scorn. They might even go so far as to ostracize the couple, especially if they act unprofessionally at work by fighting or displaying their affection in public.

4. Just as office romances can cause one's performance to increase, so they can also cause one's performance to decline.

Romance can distract from the concentration necessary to get a job done. A change in productivity can cause suspicion and distrust. In my survey I found that less than 25% of those involved showed a productivity decline, yet more than half of the women I polled expected work performance to decrease as a result of romance.

5. An office romance can lead to self-doubt and loss of objectivity. The jealousy-induced gossip that can accompany a romantic office liaison can undermine the couple's professionalism. Sometimes the gossip makes it appear as if the couple's professional decisions were affected by their personal relationship. Keeping personal feelings from affecting professional decisions takes a concerted effort.

Work and Sex

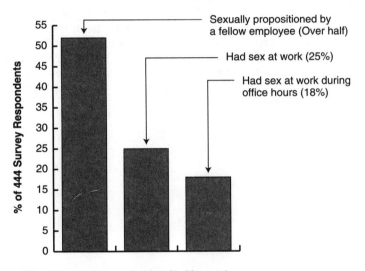

Source: Adapted from 1987 survey in *Men's Health* magazine.

6. Sometimes competition and conflict are the outcomes of an office romance. Perhaps your lover has just blown up in a meeting you attended, or maybe you find yourself at odds with your mate because your department is in competition with his on a project. Either can cause conflict. Sometimes there can be intense career competition between the two lovers which can cause serious friction.

7. Office romances can cause conflicts of interest. As professionals, employees must exercise independent professional

judgment—the basis upon which they were hired and continue to be employed. Yet when their judgments can affect their mates, either directly or indirectly, a conflict of interest arises. The trust their employer has in them can be compromised. For instance, when couples work together it is only natural that they discuss their jobs over dinner at home. But some work information can cause a conflict of interest. Sometimes in situations such as accounting audits it can even become necessary to transfer one member of the couple to prevent even the appearance of impropriety.

Diverting Cupid's Arrows

It is no surprise then that office romances are disfavored and in some cases forbidden by company policies (as if rules could divert Cupid's arrows). More liberal companies may simply caution employees not to allow their personal involvement to interfere with their work or the workplace. Employees involved in a romantic relationship may also be required to report to their superiors potential conflicts of interest arising from their relationships. Though written policies will not solve all potential problems associated with bringing love to the job, they can clarify expectations ahead of time in a way that might deter involvement at an early stage. This way, prospective employees can know what is expected of them.

"The problem is not that sexual attraction inhabits the workplace, but that the options we traditionally give ourselves for recognizing that passion are far too limited."

A New Sexual Dynamic in the Workplace Can Be Beneficial

David R. Eyler and Andrea Baridon

In the following viewpoint, David R. Eyler and Andrea Baridon explain that sexual attraction between men and women at work, though a somewhat new and potentially disruptive phenomenon, does not have to be either awkward or dangerous. The energy from these romantic liaisons can, in fact, be channeled into increased productivity and creativity, say the authors. They propose a new sexual etiquette that allows for intense feelings within mutually agreed upon and well-maintained boundaries. Everyone will benefit from the new rules governing sexual attraction in the office, Eyler and Baridon contend, especially the work "couples" themselves. Eyler and Baridon are professional management consultants.

As you read, consider the following questions:

1. What incentives do Eyler and Baridon mention for developing a new sexual etiquette for the workplace?
2. What are the five steps the authors outline for developing the new sexual etiquette? What do they say are the benefits?

Our ways of living and loving have changed radically since the 1970s and 1980s. Today men and women are thrust together on the job, sharing the workplace in equal numbers and, increasingly often, as professional peers. Work is becoming a major source of intimate interaction between them as they daily share the physical proximity of working side by side, the stimulation of professional challenge, and the powerful passions of accomplishment and failure.

Like every other kind of intimacy, the workplace variety brings with it the likelihood of sexual attraction. It is natural. It is inevitable, hard-wired as we are to respond to certain kinds of stimuli, although it sometimes comes as a surprise to those it strikes. But sexual attraction in the office is virtually inevitable for other reasons as well: The workplace is an ideal pre-screener, likely to throw us together with others our own age having similar socioeconomic and educational backgrounds, similar sets of values, and similar aspirations.

It also offers countless opportunities for working friendships to develop. As teams come to dominate the structure of the business world, the other half of a business team is increasingly likely to be not only a colleague with complementary skills and interests, but an attractive member of the opposite sex. As close as the collaboration between men and women workers can get at the office, it may be even more so outside it, as workers today function in an extended workplace of irregular hours and non-office settings. We are now more likely than ever, for example, to share the intimate isolation of business travel.

The New Workplace

Such opportunity for interaction between the sexes is, in the grand scheme of things, really rather new. Only since the early 1970s, and particularly since 1980, have women worked in equal numbers with men, and as equals rather than subordinates. Traditionally, society limits the opportunities for relationships between the sexes—how it does so is typically one of the distinguishing features of a culture. Until recently, unmarried men and women who were attracted to each other could date, court, or marry without raising eyebrows. For attracted couples who were already committed to others, the only option was to avoid each other or give in to an affair that consumed great energy just to be kept secret. So new is our sharing of the workplace that we have not yet created rules or social structures for dealing with today's unfamiliar intermixture of men and women working together.

The problem is not that sexual attraction inhabits the workplace, but that the options we traditionally give ourselves for recognizing that passion are far too limited. Conventional thinking tells us there is only one place to take our sexual feelings—to bed together. The modern American mind equates sexual attraction with sexual intercourse—the word "sex" serves as a synonym for physical contact. But intercourse is only one possible outcome among many.

Sexual attraction can be managed. It is not only possible to acknowledge sexual attraction, but also to enjoy the energy generated by it—and without acting on it sexually. The positive energy of sexual attraction is instead focused on work as it pulls men and women into a process of discovery, creativity and productivity. This thinking is part of a broader ethic emerging in this country: It's possible to have a lot without having it all.

We propose a new, psychologically unique relationship for which no models currently exist in American culture. It is a positive way for men and women to share intimate feelings outside of marriage or an illicit affair. It rejects altogether the saint-or-sinner model of colleague relations as too simplistic for modern life. In our own work as management consultants, we see the new relationship slowly unfolding in the American workplace. Confused coworkers, lacking guidance of any kind but responding to today's workplace realities, are stumbling toward new ways of relating to each other as they find the old alternatives too confining or otherwise unacceptable. The relationship they are inventing is not quite romantic—but it's not Platonic, either. It adds a dimension of increased intimacy to friendship and removes the sexual aspect from love. We call this relationship More than Friends, Less than Lovers.

Incentives for Change

The new sexually energized but strictly working relationship has already been officially documented. In a study conducted by researchers at the University of Michigan, 22 percent of managers reported involvement in such a relationship. Moreover, the relationship, unleashing as it does a great deal of creative energy, was shown to benefit both "couple" and company. And a study at the University of North Dakota found that work teams composed of men and women were more productive than those of same-sex colleagues. . . .

There is another incentive for welcoming this new, intimate relationship. Traditional thinking assumes there is only one appropriate place for sexual attraction—between lovers or spouses. But that leads to an untenable burden on our primary relationships—the spouses or lovers with whom we share it all romantically and sexually. As seasoned observers, we believe that it is naive to assume that a single intimate relationship will fulfill us in every way. As busy people leading complex lives outside the home, we cannot expect our primary relationships to also bear the burden of providing total personal and professional satisfaction. We need to grow comfortable loving one person romantically and deeply valuing another intellectually, artistically, or in any of a variety of ways that do not diminish our commitment to a primary partner. . . .

The New Etiquette

On the basis of our experience, we have developed a practical, two-person model of sexual etiquette for those who wish to exploit the energy of workplace attraction without physical sex or falling in love, or avoiding each other altogether and pretending that the workplace is genderless. At its heart is a consciously managed relationship founded on mutual trust, respect, and acceptable boundaries that are openly agreed on, communicated, and monitored by both parties. Unlike friends, these partners share moments of great personal revelation. But unlike lovers, they do not expect to share bodies and souls. They divulge only what they choose to.

Natural human desire is something any two people should be able to feel without guilt or awkwardness. Where we set our boundaries is what distinguishes committed, romantic relationships from the near-loving feeling of those who come to know each other intimately through work. These are the five keys to pulling off the new relationship:

• *Setting boundaries.* Our personal boundaries are the psychological barriers that define us as individuals. You need a strong sense of your own values and purpose to risk sharing them intimately with someone else—even more so when you rely on your boundaries to permit tremendous personal intimacy yet prevent its becoming physical. You and your partner openly discuss and decide what is and is not off-limits.

You establish boundaries and expectations for the relationship right at the outset, as a means for defining and consciously managing it. You agree that you will not develop a personal life together and that your relationship will not be allowed to become a love affair. Some boundaries, notably the sexual one, are lines you agree never to cross; they remain forever out of bounds. Similarly, neither physical contact nor the language of lovers has a place in the relationship—they will only send misunderstood signals.

Other boundaries may be set and changed as you grow safe and comfortable in this new, unfamiliar relationship: defining the kinds of situations in which you allow yourselves to be alone, discussing certain facets of your personal lives, the giving and accepting of compliments, allowing your partner to see you when you are not at your best, and admitting the high value you place on the relationship without fear of being misunderstood.

You will also have internal boundaries to contend with—very personal ones you set and maintain without the knowledge of your partner. These are the lines you draw for monitoring your own thoughts and behavior; coping with near-love feelings is a personal matter each partner handles in his/her own way. . . .

Myths of Attraction

• *If work partners are sexually attracted, they can't possibly do the job effectively—their minds will be on sex rather than work.* Sexual energy can stimulate creativity and actually drive them into a better working relationship instead of into bed or a sexual harassment confrontation.

• *Managers have an obligation to break up a work team they suspect of being sexually attracted because embarrassing and disruptive consequences are inevitable.* Managers should deal with actual outcomes, not fears of what might happen. If productivity suffers, someone complains or the company is embarrassed, managers should intervene. Otherwise, they should leave workers alone to be productive *and* enjoy their work together.

Psychology Today, May/June 1992.

• *Conscious management.* There are no sure paths to ideal relationships between mutually attracted men and women under any circumstances. But without conscious management of this relationship, personal attraction can lead to destructive consequences—from ruined marriages to tainted professional reputations. Consciously managed, the relationship becomes a series of purposeful, directed events, rather than random ones that could drift into unplanned physical intimacy. You expect to have differences that you will resolve openly, instead of dancing around issues and leaving them open to ambiguity.

Through discussion, you create a voluntary contract in which you both agree that you will divert your sexual energy from personal attraction between you to the working relationship supporting it. You agree that your attraction is a positive thing that makes your working relationship exciting. You define ways to behave that will help you maintain your mutual boundaries. You communicate honestly with each other about your feelings and expectation. You make no attempt to hide the relationship from your spouse or lover on the one hand, or your company managers on the other, although you maintain discretion.

At first, you will probably find it difficult and awkward to discuss the emotional issues involved in creating and managing this relationship. It's new and unfamiliar turf and you're not sure what constitutes the right measure of trust. Your best guide is to sense when tension builds—that's when something needs to be brought into the open for honest discussion.

Staying Open

• *Monitoring each other.* Two people seldom approach a relationship—any relationship—with perfectly matched expectations. You and your partner both know that adjustments in your behavior will sometimes be necessary to keep things on an even keel. You share the responsibility for keeping your own behavior, feelings and expectations in line with the boundaries you establish. Monitoring each other ensures that open communication takes place when you sense your partner may infringe on a boundary or yield to temptation.

Monitoring each other also sets the expectation of open communication. You come to your relationship with respect for each other's intellect, tastes, and competencies. You look to each other to supplement what you individually bring to your work— to stimulate your thinking and enhance your creativity.

• *Open discussion.* You are making deliberate use of sexual chemistry to become both more personally satisfied and more successful and productive. The overarching technique you use to keep behavior within the boundaries you set is open discussion. It short-circuits problems that tend to build with time. Instead of maintaining the relationship by one-sided internal coping, you raise concerns to the level of two-person reasoning.

You clarify areas of misunderstanding where individual interpretations of events or intentions may be wrong. In time, you'll probably be laughing at simple misunderstandings. You vent frustrations to each other as well as understanding and being understood—eliminating the need to reject and the pain of rejection. The secret is not some perfect progression through an ideal set of relationship-building steps, but rather in the openness that says, "Ask me. Let's talk about it. We can work this out."

• *Cooling-off periods.* Unlike husbands and wives, you have the advantage of regular time-outs from each other, away from a nonphysical but demanding association. In permanent relationships, a large tolerance quotient is both desirable and required. In this relationship, by contrast, you are not obligated to keep each other happy or to take care of each other or to tolerate differences in food or music or television preferences on a daily and nightly basis. You deny yourselves some of the privileges of a fully committed couple while you avoid some of their frictions.

On the rare occasions when work isn't going well, or your conscious management techniques are flagging, you can acknowledge this is not going to be the right day to accomplish much together and step back to a comfortable distance.

On the good days, this relationship fosters inspired work that is intense, demanding and fulfilling. When it ends, parting involves ambivalence. You enjoy what you do so you are reluctant to stop, but you feel a sense of relief in getting away for a time to relax and be nourished in different ways with your family and friends. Down time spent apart allows you to keep a view of your work partner as someone special. . . .

Company Benefits

What partners get out of non-loving intimacy [should now be] clear. Their relationship is amazingly satisfying psychologically, and very workable. They pursue their work with an abandon they never could afford if they were lovers who had to get along both at work and at home. They do genuinely inspired work together and honestly love it, their creative energy flowing from a sexual attraction they've chosen not to indulge physically or force into love. They have friends and family at home, where they recharge themselves.

Companies also benefit. They get highly motivated workers who are enthusiastic and happy. The relationship enhances creativity. And partners are not deceiving anyone or stealing work time. They waste no energy on feeling guilty.

Men and women bring differing and complementary orientations to shared work. A tremendous amount of energy can flow from their sex-based differences when they are allowed to keep their sexual identities, rather than suppress them in conformance with the corporate ideal of a safe, genderless workplace. Nonsexual intimates willingly spend time together to achieve great results—and avoid behavior that would threaten the relationship.

And so love is much as it's always been. Sexual, romantic love has been and will be the many splendored thing, driven by a desire for fusion and physical intimacy and achieving that blurring of boundaries that takes place only in sex. But our model promises legitimacy for what many men and women have felt but dared not admit or act on—the reality that sexual chemistry can be safely shared with an associate and play a constructive role in their lives.

It works because what has changed the workplace has crept onto the domestic scene as well. The days of insecure spouses who waited at home has passed, part of the revolution that has swept women into jobs in large numbers. Simply put, peers understand peers. Newly equal husbands, wives and lovers accept what they know from common experience—colleagues may be sorely tempted to become lovers, but they will settle for being more than friends. The trust that makes it all possible is, after all, the only valid measure of romantic fidelity.

Periodical Bibliography

The following articles have been selected to supplement the diverse views presented in this chapter.

David Brock "The Real Anita Hill," *American Spectator*, March 1992.

Maureen Dowd "Everything but Sex: The New Office Affair," *Mademoiselle*, February 1991.

Austen A. Ettinger "Mum's the Word," *The New York Times Magazine*, February 3, 1991.

Suzanne Fields "Battle of the Sexes Drifts into Dangerous Territory," *Insight*, July 5, 1993. Available from 3600 New York Ave. NE, Washington, DC 20002.

Patricia Mainardi "The Politics of Housework," *Ms.*, May/June 1992.

Ian Miles "Consequences of the Changing Sexual Division of Labor," *The Annals of the American Academy of Political and Social Science*, July 1992.

Moody "Men & Women: Seeing the Value in Our Differences," (entire issue), July/August 1992.

Thomas Moore "Soul Mates," *New Age Journal*, January/February 1994.

Lance Morrow "Are Men Really That Bad?" *Time*, February 14, 1994.

Lillian B. Rubin "People Don't Know Right from Wrong Anymore," *Tikkun*, January/February 1994.

Alisa Solomon "One Year After Anita Hill . . . ," *Glamour*, November 1992.

Michelle Stacey "Work and Love and the Whole Damn Thing," *Mademoiselle*, December 1992.

Carol Tavris "The Man/Woman Thing," *Mademoiselle*, February 1992.

Jon Tevlin "Why Women Are Mad As Hell," *Glamour*, March 1992.

Utne Reader "Men & Women: Can We Get Along? Should We Even Try?" (entire issue), January/February 1993.

Iris Marion Young "Making Single Motherhood Normal," *Dissent*, Winter 1994.

For Further Discussion

Chapter 1

1. Both Anthony Layng and Carol Tavris open their viewpoints by attacking their opponents' arguments. What does Layng say about "social liberalism's" impact on sociobiology? What does Tavris imply about sociobiology in her description of one of its proponents, Sam Kash Kachigan? Do these attacks address the opposition's arguments or their motives? Explain.

2. James C. Dobson is president of Focus on the Family, an advocacy group for Christian and conservative family values. Ruth Hubbard is a professor of biology and a feminist writer on scientific and social issues. Are the authors' backgrounds and affiliations reflected in their views on why the sexes develop differently from each other? Support your answer with examples.

3. Le Anne Schreiber and Yves Christen cite much of the same brain research to reach opposite conclusions on whether the sexes have the same or different aptitudes and abilities. Do you think their preconceptions may have influenced their interpretations of the evidence? Cite the sexes' work-related skills in your answer.

Chapter 2

1. The Business and Professional Women's Foundation marshals statistics to show that women and minorities are clustered on the middle and lower rungs of the job ladder. What evidence does the foundation offer to support its belief that this phenomenon is a result of discrimination? What abilities does George Gilder cite to show that men "naturally" outperform women?

2. Phyllis Schlafly divides the debate over women's roles in the military into two camps. Who are the players in each camp? What values do they represent, according to Schlafly? Whose opinions does Schlafly want the reader to agree with?

3. In her viewpoint, Nancy Pearcey says that birth statistics show that "motherhood is becoming popular again." But her viewpoint is about a special kind of mother: the type who stays at home. What evidence does Pearcey cite to show that *this* kind of motherhood is becoming more popular?

Chapter 3

1. What aspects of men's lives are important to Warren Farrell in his viewpoint? Compare this with what Sam Julty indi-

cates is important to men about their lives. Do you think these differences account for the authors' divergent views on whether men's lives are changing for the better? Explain.

2. In his viewpoint criticizing the men's movement, whom is Fred Pelka attacking? Do you think that the author's criticism of an important person in the men's movement helps or harms his case against the movement itself? Explain, using examples from the viewpoint.

3. What kind of information do Wade C. Mackey and Ursula White use to show that fathers have no incentive to be with their families? What is the source and the type of information that Kathleen Gerson employs to show that fathers are becoming more family oriented? Which argument seems more compelling and why?

Chapter 4

1. In her viewpoint, Sylvia Ann Hewlett describes a "burgeoning parenting deficit increasingly threatening the well-being of children." What emotion do you think the author wants to inspire in the reader by using such words as "burgeoning" and "threatening"?

2. Faye J. Crosby, Susan Faludi, and Rosalind C. Barnett all argue in their viewpoints that day care is beneficial to children's development. In their arguments, do the authors seem on the offensive or the defensive? What perceived bias in American society or in the media do these authors confront to make their case for day care?

3. Sheila B. Kamerman is a professor of social policy and planning (a subject dealing with how government should help people). Allan Carlson is president of the Rockford Institute, an advocacy group promoting traditional family values. Citing examples, explain how the authors' affiliations are reflected in their arguments for and against government-subsidized day care.

Chapter 5

1. In their viewpoint, Arlie Hochschild and Anne Machung point out that women work two shifts a day: one at work and one at home. What evidence do the authors use to show that men must help women at home? What part of their argument do you think Steven Goldberg most disagrees with in his viewpoint?

Organizations to Contact

The editors have compiled the following list of organizations concerned with the issues debated in this book. The descriptions are derived from materials provided by the organizations. All have publications or information available for interested readers. The list was compiled on the date of publication of the present volume; names, addresses, and phone numbers may change. Be aware that many organizations take several weeks or longer to respond to inquiries, so allow as much time as possible.

Catalyst
250 Park Ave. S.
New York, NY 10003-1459
(212) 777-8900

Catalyst is a national research and advisory organization that helps corporations foster the careers and leadership capabilities of women. The organization studies and reports on a variety of human resource issues such as flexible work arrangements, child care options, and women's leadership and management styles. Its publications include research and survey reports, such as *Women in Engineering: An Untapped Resource*; "infobrief" summaries of occupational issues; and the monthly newsletter *Perspective*.

Catholics United for the Faith (CUFF)
50 Washington Ave.
New Rochelle, NY 10801
(914) 235-9404

CUFF supports, defends, and advances the teachings of the Roman Catholic Church. Its members do not object to women in the workforce but believe every effort should be made to allow women who wish to stay home to do so. CUFF explores women's religious issues in its publications. These include books, such as *St. Theresa: Doctor of the Church* and *Blessed by the Cross: Five Portraits of Edith Stein*; a monthly newsletter, *Lay Witness*; and the organization's quarterly update, *Bulletin*.

Center for the American Woman and Politics (CAWP)
Eagleton Institute of Politics
Rutgers University
New Brunswick, NJ 08901
(908) 828-2210

The center is a think tank and resource center dedicated to the advancement of women in public leadership. The center's program offers public leadership programs for women; research on the importance of electing women to all levels of government; and current information on the women's political movement. Many of these published materials, including the organizations newsletter, *CAWP News & Notes*, are available through the *Subscriber Information Services* packet, published three times a year.

Child Care Action Campaign (CCAC)
330 Seventh Ave., 17th Fl.
New York, NY 10001-5010
(212) 239-0138

CCAC is an advocacy group that works to help bring about child care legislation, employer-provided child care, and other quality, affordable child care benefits and options for parents. It also conducts a variety of programs to help businesses and parents implement these benefits. CCAC's publications include series and guides, such as *Employer Tax Credits for Child Care: Asset or Liability?*; policy papers, including *Child Care: The Bottom Line*; fact sheets, including *Who's Caring for Your Kids?—What Every Parent Should Know About Child Care*; and the newsletter *Child Care ActioNews*.

Eagle Forum
Box 618
Alton, IL 62002
(618) 462-5415

The Eagle Forum is an educational and political organization that advocates traditional family values. To expose what it believes is radical feminism's goal to break up the family, the forum examines and disseminates its position on issues such as women in combat, family leave, child care, tax credits for families with children, and "outcome based" education. The organization offers several books by its president, Phyllis Schlafly, including *Child Abuse in the Classroom, Who Will Rock the Cradle?*, *Meddlesome Mandate: Rethinking Family Leave*, and *Equal Pay for Unequal Work*. It also publishes a monthly newsletter, *The Phyllis Schlafly Report*.

Men's Rights Association
17854 Lyons St.
Forest Lake, MN 55025-8854
(612) 464-7663

The association works to restore to men the dignity that it believes feminism has diminished. Toward that end it seeks to obtain equal rights for all people under the law, offering an attorney referral service to men who believe they have been discriminated against. The association conducts extensive research, compiles statistics, and publishes several legal-assistance guides, such as *Divorce: What Everyone Should Know to Beat the Racket. The Liberator* is its monthly newsmagazine on men's rights and divorce reform.

National Coalition of Free Men
PO Box 129
Manhasset, NY 11030
(516) 482-6378

The coalition is a nonprofit educational organization whose mission is to examine men's lives, with particular emphasis on how sex discrimina-

300

tion affects men. Antimale discrimination occurs on several fronts, the coalition believes: in male/female relationships, where men are denied equality in matters of child custody and divorce; in the courts, where men are put on the defensive by sometimes false accusations of rape and sexual harassment; in employment, where men are expected to fill the dangerous occupations, such as military combat positions; and in matters of general health, where men are observed to live measurably shorter lives and to commit suicide more often than women. The coalition conducts research, sponsors educational programs, and maintains a computerized library on Compuserve. Its newsletter, *Transitions*, offers statistics, book reviews, movie reviews, and events affecting men.

National Federation of Business and Professional Women's Clubs, Inc.
2012 Massachusetts Ave. NW
Washington, DC 20036
(202) 293-1100

The federation works to promote women's civil rights, including the elimination of sexual harassment and violence against women; women's health, including reproductive choice and the funding of women's special health care needs; and women's economic equality, including pay equity, equal educational opportunities, and affordable quality child care. The organization publishes papers, such as *Crime of Power: Sexual Harassment in the Workplace*; technical resource manuals, including *Vote Women Power: A Woman's Guide to Voter Registration, Voter Education and Get-out-the-Vote Activities*; and fact sheets on the status of working women and legislation affecting women.

National Organization for Men Against Sexism (NOMAS)
54 Mint St., Suite 300
San Francisco, CA 94103
(415) 546-6627

NOMAS is an activist organization of men and women working to challenge traditional ideas of masculinity and to help men become more caring and nonabusive. Previously known as the National Organization of Changing Men, the group is pro-feminist, gay-affirmative, and antidiscrimination. NOMAS's projects include The Campaign to End Homophobia and BrotherPeace: An International Day of Men Taking Action to End Men's Violence. *Masculinities*, a quarterly academic journal, and *Brother*, the organization's newsletter, are NOMAS's publications.

The Rockford Institute
934 N. Main St.
Rockford, IL 61103-7061
(815) 964-5819

The institute seeks—by educating the public on religious and social issues—to return America to Judeo-Christian and traditional family values. It believes that day care is harmful to children and that every effort should be made to allow mothers to raise their children at home.

Home-based business is one opportunity the organization has researched as a means of allowing mothers to stay home. The institute publishes a monthly monograph, *The Family in America*, and its supplement, *New Research*; a monthly magazine, *Chronicles*, which explores a variety of cultural issues; and a newsletter, *Mainstreet Memorandum*.

Tradeswomen, Inc.
PO Box 40664
Berkeley, CA 94140
(510) 649-6260

Tradeswomen, Inc., is a nonprofit membership organization developed for the purpose of peer support, networking, and advocacy for women in blue-collar jobs. The organization publishes *Tradeswomen*, a quarterly magazine that explores a variety of issues affecting women in the trades—cases and evaluations of affirmative action legislation and sexual harassment laws, racism on the job, and the operation of workers' compensation laws, to name a few—in addition to offering lists of local tradeswomen groups and other networking opportunities. Tradeswomen also publishes a monthly newsletter, *Trade Trax*.

Women for Racial and Economic Equality (WREE)
198 Broadway, 6th Fl.
New York, NY 10038
(212) 385-1103

WREE is a political activist organization representing women of all races. It works with grassroots groups and activists through a variety of public forums, including demonstrations, to reduce military spending and increase the funding of various social services, such as the construction and maintenance of child care centers. WREE lobbies federal, state, and local governments to legislate the demands in its Women's Bill of Rights, including the right to equality, economic justice, housing, education, health care, reproductive choice, and several others. The organization publishes the quarterly *WREE-View for Women*.

Women's Legal Defense Fund
1875 Connecticut Ave. NW, Suite 710
Washington, DC 20009
(202) 986-2600

The fund is a national advocacy organization that works at the federal and state levels to develop and promote policies that help women achieve equal opportunity, quality health care, and economic security for themselves and their families. The fund offers a range of publications, including a guide on how to utilize the 1993 Family and Medical Leave Act, fact sheets on sexual harassment and what to do about it, and books on women's legal issues, such as the primer *What's at Stake: A Preview of Supreme Court Cases Vital to Women*.

Bibliography of Books

Patricia Aburdene and John Naisbitt — *Megatrends for Women.* New York: Villard Books, 1992.

Margaret L. Andersen and Patricia Hill Collins, eds. — *Race, Class, and Gender: An Anthology.* Belmont, CA: Wadsworth Publishing, 1992.

Sandra L. Bem — *The Lenses of Gender: Transforming the Debate on Sexual Inequality.* New Haven: Yale University Press, 1993.

Cynthia Berryman-Fink, Deborah Ballard-Reisch, and Lisa H. Newman, eds. — *Communication and Sex-Role Socialization.* New York: Garland Publishing, 1993.

Barbara Boxer and Nicole Boxer — *Strangers in the Senate: Politics and the New Revolution of Women in America.* Washington, DC: National Press Books, 1994.

Timothy H. Brubaker — *Family Relations: Challenges for the Future.* Newbury Park, CA: Sage, 1993.

Judith Frankel, ed. — *The Employed Mother and the Family Context.* New York: Springer Publishing Co., 1993.

Marilyn French — *The War Against Women.* New York: Summit Books, 1992.

Kathleen Gerson — *No Man's Land: Men's Changing Commitments to Family and Work.* New York: Basic Books, 1993.

Diane F. Halpern — *Sex Differences in Cognitive Abilities.* 2nd ed. Hillsdale, NJ: L. Erlbaum Associates, 1992.

Pat Kirkham and Janet Thumin — *You Tarzan: Masculinity, Movies, and Men.* New York: St. Martin's Press, 1993.

Terry Allen Kupers — *Revisioning Men's Lives: Gender, Intimacy, and Power.* New York: Guilford Press, 1993.

Sherri Matteo — *American Women in the Nineties: Today's Critical Issues.* Boston: Northeastern University Press, 1993.

Nancy Dodd McCann and Thomas A. McGinn — *Harassed: One Hundred Women Define Inappropriate Behavior in the Workplace.* Homewood, IL: Business One Irwin, 1992.

Michael Meade — *Men and the Water of Life: Initiation and the Tempering of Men.* San Francisco: Harper, 1993.

Michael A. Messner — *Power at Play: Sports and the Problem of Masculinity.* Boston: Beacon Press, 1992.

| John Money | *The Adam Principle: Genes, Genitals, Hormones, and Gender: Selected Readings in Sexology.* Buffalo: Prometheus Books, 1993. |

Robert L. Moore and Douglas Gillette — *The Magician Within: Accessing the Shaman in the Male Psyche.* New York: William Morrow, 1993.

Peter M. Nardi, ed. — *Men's Friendships.* Newbury Park, CA: Sage, 1992.

Mariah Burton Nelson — *Are We Winning Yet?: How Women Are Changing Sports and Sports Are Changing Women.* New York: Random House, 1991.

Frank S. Pittman — *Man Enough: Fathers, Sons, and the Search for Masculinity.* New York: G.P. Putnam's Sons, 1993.

Barbara F. Reskin and Patricia A. Roos — *Job Queues, Gender Queues: Explaining Women's Inroads into Male Occupations.* Philadelphia: Temple University Press, 1992.

Anthony E. Rotundo — *American Manhood: Transformations in Masculinity from the Revolution to the Modern Era.* New York: Basic Books, 1993.

Felice N. Schwartz and Jean Zimmerman — *Breaking with Tradition: Women and Work, the New Facts of Life.* New York: Warner Books, 1992.

Beth Anne Shelton — *Women, Men, and Time: Gender Differences in Paid Work, Housework, and Leisure.* Westport, CT: Greenwood Press, 1992.

Linda Jean Shepherd — *Lifting the Veil: The Feminine Face of Science.* Boston: Shambhala, 1993.

John Stoltenberg — *The End of Manhood: A Book for Men of Conscience.* New York: Dutton, 1993.

Tine Thevenin — *Mothering and Fathering: The Gender Differences in Child Rearing.* Garden City Park, NY: Avery Publishing Group, 1993.

Barrie Thorne — *Gender Play: Girls and Boys in School.* New Brunswick, NJ: Rutgers University Press, 1993.

Christine L. Williams, ed. — *Doing "Women's Work": Men in Non-Traditional Occupations.* Newbury Park, CA: Sage, 1993.

Naomi Wolf — *Fire with Fire: The New Female Power and How It Will Change the Twenty-First Century.* New York: Random House, 1993.

Index

abortion
  rates of, 247
  and women in politics, 101-103,
    106, 110, 114
Act for Better Child Care (ABC), 221,
  240, 244-45
Aid to Families with Dependent
  Children (AFDC), 154-55, 200, 240,
  242
AIDS, 148, 150
Ainsworth Strange Situation Test,
  233-34
American Association of University
  Professors, 88
amygdala
  and gender differences, 49
androgens, 58
androgyny, 79, 81, 126
animal research
  and gender roles, 21-22, 25-30, 49
anorexia, 218
Arnold, Arthur, 51
Aspin, Les, 119-21, 126, 128
Auden, W.H., 257

baby boomers
  and marriage, 255-60
Bakke, Eileen, 137, 138, 140
Bardwick, Judith, 258
Baridon, Andrea, 289
Barnett, Rosalind C., 129, 229
Barrett, Jackie, 102
Barrow, Robert H., 118
Bateman, Angus John, 25-26
Becker, Gary S., 95
Beckwith, Jonathan, 61, 62, 64
Belsky, Jay, 227, 231-32
Bem Sex Role Inventory, 81
Benbow, Camilla, 54, 63-64
Berne, Rosalyn Wiggins, 131
Bible
  on sexual differences, 34, 39
biology
  determines gender roles, 32-39,
    95-97, 279-81
  con, 40-47
birth rates
  factors affecting, 198-99
  increases in, 137, 256
  statistics on, 197
blacks
  in academia, 88

  in labor force, 86, 87, 89
  as slaves, 69, 70, 71
Blakeslee, Sandra, 259
Blau, Francine D., 66
Bleier, Ruth, 62
Bly, Robert, 158, 168-73, 178, 181
Bottigheimer, Ruth, 171
Boxer, Barbara, 104, 105, 112, 114,
  115
boys
  need initiation rites, 162-63, 164
  sexual abuse of, 171-72
Bradley, Bill, 216
brain
  gender differences in, 33, 37, 41
  and sexual activity, 50-51, 59
  structure of
    development of, 58-59
    explains male/female differences,
      48-56
    con, 57-65
  hemispheric functions of, 51, 59
  research on
    is sexist, 58, 65
Brock, William, 215
Buckley, William F., Jr., 127
Buczynski, Alan, 180
bulimia, 218
Bush, George
  as against working mothers, 232
  and parental leave bill, 239
  political appointments of, 102, 106,
    109, 117
  right-wing agenda endorsed by,
    110-11
Business and Professional Women's
  Foundation, 85

Canada
  and women in the military, 123,
    125
Carlson, Allan, 243
Carter, Pamela, 101
child abuse
  of boys, 171-72
  in day care, 226-27, 230, 237
child care
  benefits of, 206-207
  costs of, 237
  and family arrangements, 191-92
  and fathers, 133, 147, 278
  federal legislation for, 221

funding for, 240
government-subsidized
  families need, 236-42
    con, 243-49
  historical, 232
  increases in, 237
  is harmful, 220-28
    con, 229-35
  by relatives, 237, 245
  shortages in, 244-45
Child Care and Development Block
  Grant, 221, 240, 241
Child Care Law Center, 230
children
  and absent fathers, 156, 213, 218
  adult responsibilities of, 208
  are not valued, 246-47
  bonding with mothers
    child care harms, 223-25
      con, 231-32, 233-34
  child care for
    benefits of, 206-207
    health risks of, 225-26
    is harmful, 220-28
      con, 221-22, 229-35
  and eating disorders, 217-18
  emotional problems of, 216-17
  family roles of, 69, 71
  health insurance for, 242
  in home schools, 249
  and illiteracy, 215
  latchkey, 213, 225
  poor academic achievement of,
    214-16
  and poverty, 237, 244, 247, 248
  responsibility for, 247-48
  schools perpetuate stereotypes of,
    81
  stereotyped roles of, 75
  television's effect on, 79-80
  toys and gender roles of, 76-77,
    79-80, 279
  working mothers and
    benefits for, 133-34, 206-10
  working parents and
    benefits to, 205-11
    are harmed by, 212-19
    time spent with, 133, 271, 274-75,
      280
Christen, Yves, 48
Christian men's groups, 183-85
Civil Rights Act of 1991, 91, 99
Clarke-Stewart, K.A., 222-23, 230,
  234
Clinton, Bill
  political agenda of and women,
    106, 111
  position on women in military, 120,

126, 128
Cohen, Abby, 230
Collins, Mary, 123
Cornum, Rhonda, 117, 120, 121
corpus callosum
  and gender differences, 50, 51,
    59-61, 65
Crosby, Faye J., 205
culture
  can overcome genetics, 23, 41-46
    con, 33-34, 38, 95
  determines gender roles, 74-81

Danowitz, Jane, 103
Darwin, Charles
  theory of evolution, 21, 25
day-care. See child care
de Beauvoir, Simone, 41
Defense Advisory Committee on
  Women in the Services
  (DACOWITS), 124
Democratic Party, 110-11, 154
divorce
  and custody of children, 193
  effects of, 277
    on children, 213, 217, 259, 265,
      277
  as good, 262
  rates of, 197, 218, 256, 262, 264,
    277
  reasons for, 198, 262, 264, 267
  and working parents, 213, 217
Dixon, Carlie, 138, 141
Dobson, James C., 32
domestic responsibilities
  men and women should share,
    268-75
    con, 276-83
  traditional division of, 274
domestic violence, 172
Donnelly, Elaine, 120, 122
double standards, 20
Driesenga, Morrie, 183, 185
Dwiggins, Cathy, 139, 140

Eccles, Jacquelynne, 64
economics
  determines gender roles, 66-73
Emerson, Thomas I., 126
EMILY's List (Early Money Is Like
  Yeast), 104, 110
empty-nest syndrome, 141
England, B., 224
Entitlement Funding for Child Care
  Services, 240
Equal Employment Opportunities
  Commission (EEOC), 91
Equal Remedies Act, 91

306

Equal Rights Amendment (ERA), 20
Etzioni, Amitai, 263
evolution
    explains traditional gender roles,
        17-23
        con, 24-31
Eyer, Diane, 231
Eyler, David R., 289

fairy tales
    used by men's movement, 161-62,
        170-71, 172
Faller, Kathleen, 227
Faludi, Susan, 130, 134, 229
families
    and child care, 191-92, 224, 230,
        231
    childlessness is increasing in, 210
    determine gender roles, 75
    dysfunctional, 216-18
    economic roles in, 67-73
    effect of government subsidies on,
        152-57, 198-201, 247-48
    health care costs for, 226
    low-income, 224, 230, 231
    nuclear, 198
    as political issue, 110-11, 115
    should be responsible for children,
        247-49
    traditional, 71-73
    two-income, 209
    of working mothers
        benefits for, 133-34, 206-10
Family and Medical Leave Bill, 239
Farber, E.A., 224
Farrell, Warren, 151
fathers
    absence of harms children, 156
    are getting better, 187-94
        con, 195-201
    and child care, 133, 147, 278
    and flexible work schedules,
        192-93, 275
    government discriminates against,
        154-56
    lack of connection to sons, 161,
        163-66, 169
    must teach sons, 165-66, 170
    reasons for becoming, 199
    studies on, 196-97
Fausto-Sterling, Anne, 58, 62
Federal Pregnancy Discrimination
    Act, 152
Fein, G., 222-23
Feinstein, Diane, 104, 105, 112, 115
feminism
    effect of on men
        as negative, 152-57

    as positive, 147-49
    as unnatural, 98
Feminist Majority Foundation, 88
feminists
    and androgyny, 126
    and child care, 221
    history of movement, 148-49
    and myth of glass ceiling, 93
    on women in military, 123, 126
Ferber, Marianne A., 66
Focus on the Family, 180, 184, 249
Framingham Heart Study, 131-32
French, Marilyn, 28
Fuchs, Victor, 218

gender issues
    help women win in politics,
        100-107
        con, 108-15
gender-norming, 124, 125, 127
gender roles
    animal research on, 21-22, 25-30,
        49
    biology determines, 32-39, 95-97,
        279-81
        con, 40-47
    and children with working
        mothers, 207-208, 230
    culture determines, 74-81
    economics determines, 66-73
    history of, 67-73
    and language, 77-78
    as reflected in titles, 78-79
    research on is flawed, 46-47
    social policy can affect, 23
    traditional
        evolution explains, 17-23
        con, 24-31
        universality of, 18-20
General Social Survey, 263-64
Gerson, Kathleen, 186
Geschwind, Norman, 61-62, 64
Gilder, George, 92
glass ceiling
    limits women at work, 85-91
        con, 92-99
Glenn, Norval D., 261
Goldberg, Steven, 94, 276
Goldberg, Whoopi, 79
Gordon, Suzanne, 168, 169
Gore, Al, 111
government
    competes with fathers, 152-57, 198,
        199-201
    discriminates against men, 152-57
    should subsidize child care, 236-42
        con, 243-49
    subsidizes women, 152-57, 198-201

Grimm, Brothers, 170-71, 172
Gulf War
  women's participation in, 117, 118,
    120, 123

Harris, Karla, 140, 142
Head Start, 200, 240
Heffner, Elaine, 137
height, body
  social effects on, 42-44
Hetherington, E. Mavis, 217
Hewlett, Sylvia Ann, 212
Hill, Anita, 103-105, 109-10, 113, 155
Hilton, Margaret, 141
Hochschild, Arlie, 190, 268
Hollywood Women's Political
  Caucus, 105
hormones
  and aggression, 95
  and brain differences, 58-59, 61-62,
    65
  brain regulation of, 37, 50-51
  and gender roles, 34-36, 41
  and growth rates, 43-44
Howes, Carolee, 221, 222, 224
Hrdy, Sarah Blaffer
  on primates' sexuality, 27, 29, 30
  on sexual stereotypes, 25-26, 31
Hubbard, Ruth, 26, 40, 62, 65
Hunter, Brenda, 139, 141, 223
hypothalamus
  gender differences and, 37, 49, 50

illiteracy, 215
Industrial Revolution
  and changes in family roles, 70-71,
    147, 165, 249
infants, in day care, 237, 238
  day care harms, 223-25
    con, 231, 233-34
intelligence tests, 53, 54
Iron John, 162, 168, 170

Jackson, Peb, 180
Julty, Sam, 146

Kamerman, Sheila B., 236
Kessler, Ronald, 132, 134-35
Kimbrell, Andrew, 177
Kreisher, Otto, 119
Kreyche, Gerald F., 155
Kupers, Terry A., 148, 174

Lacoste-Utamsing, Christine de, 50,
  51, 60
language
  shapes gender roles, 77-78
Layng, Anthony, 17

leisure gap, 271-72
Letich, Larry, 174
Lindsey, Linda L., 74

Machung, Anne, 268, 272
Mackey, Wade C., 195
Mainiero, Lisa A., 284
marriage
  benefits of, 256-58, 265, 267
  and children, 259
  after divorce, 262
  economic roles in, 67-73
  effect of children on, 199
  effect of working women on, 133,
    134, 272, 280-81
  expectations for, 266
  and glass ceiling, 97
  is not a democracy, 28
  and language, 78
  popularity of is increasing, 253-60
    con, 261-67, 277, 283
  premarital contracts, 263
  quality of, 263-65
  and romance, 256-57
  soft men in, 160-61
  as a tradition, 255
  as a value, 262-63, 266-67
  and women's dowries, 67, 69, 70
matriarchies, 94
McMartin Pre-School case, 226, 230
media
  distort facts on working women,
    130
  singles lifestyle portrayal in, 255,
    285
Medved, Diane, 253
men
  aggressiveness of, 33, 38, 95-98, 157
  and AIDS, 148, 150
  are accepting women's changing
    roles, 106
  are biologically different from
    women, 32-39, 95-97
    con, 41-47
  attracted to feminine women, 281
  and children
    are becoming better fathers,
      186-94
      con, 195-201
    equal parenting, 190-92, 196
    guidance of boys, 162-63, 164-65
    as single fathers, 193
    time spent with children, 274, 278
    won't handle child care, 278, 280
  and competition, 177-78
  culture affects physical traits of,
    42-43
  domestic participation by, 20, 196,

272-75
housework gap, 187-88, 190-91,
   206
should share domestic
   responsibilities, 268-75
   con, 276-83
   time spent on, 271, 274
earnings capacity, 97-98
feminine side, 148, 160, 162
friendships among, 148
   are already forming, 180-85
   are not close, 176
   barriers to, 175-78, 185
   and homophobia, 175, 176
   how to form, 179
   and marriage, 177
   need to form, 174-79
   rules for, 175
gender roles of
   are changing, 187, 196-97, 255-56
   biology determines, 32-39, 280-83
   as breadwinner, 71-73, 96-98, 134,
      189, 196, 263
   is decreasing, 187, 189, 263, 280
   culture determines, 41-47, 74-81
   historical, 67-71
glass ceiling limits, 93
homeless, 150
as househusbands, 97
and Industrial Revolution, 165
initiation rites for, 162-63
intelligence quotients (IQs) of, 53
as intolerant of infidelity, 20, 22,
   26, 30
and linguistic aptitude, 55, 56
lives of are changing
   for better, 146-50
   for worse, 151-57
and male bonding, 168, 177
and marriage, 19-20, 22
mathematical aptitude is superior,
   54-55, 56, 96
   con, 59, 60, 63-64
must be head of household, 282-83
need to become more manly, 158-66
   con, 167-73
office romance can be detrimental,
   286-88
as physically stronger than women,
   96, 124, 127
prefer younger women, 18, 19, 22
promiscuity of, 19-22, 25, 26
reproductive strategies of, 21-23
self-esteem of, 38
sex discrimination in hiring, 152
sexual behavior of
   traditional views, 19-20, 22-23
should protect women, 126, 127

spatial aptitude of, 53
study habits of, 55
support groups for, 148, 149-50, 184
types of, 172
   Fifties male, 159-60
   historical, 159
      are romanticized, 170, 173
   soft male, 159-62, 168
   myth of, 169-70
and work
   are biologically suited to be
      executives, 94
   and difficulty of parenting, 189-94
men's movement
   blames older men, 162-63, 164-65
   Christian, 184
   fallacy of, 147-48
   is antiwoman, 168-73
   is based on mythology, 161-62,
      170-71, 172
   is growing, 168
   and misogyny, 171-73
   problems of, 168
menstrual cycle, 34-37
Mikulski, Barbara, 93, 114
military
   women in
      opportunities are dangerous,
         122-28
      opportunities are improving,
         116-21
minorities
   in academia, 88
   in labor force, 86, 87, 89
mommy track, 130, 135
Monkerud, Don, 79
monkeys
   sexual behavior of, 21-22, 27-29, 30
Morin, Richard, 113
Moseley Braun, Carol, 104, 105, 113,
   114
motherhood
   difficulty of, 138, 140
   emotional fulfillment of, 138-40,
      142
   as growth experience, 140-41
mothers
   bonding with child
      child care harms, 223-25
      at home, 244-45, 248
   and men's movement
      as evil, 171
      must break from sons, 163-64
   and military service, 117, 123, 126

National Organization for Women
   (NOW), 126, 155
National Women's Political Caucus,

104, 110
Nelan, Bruce W., 116

Paget, Karen M., 110
Pagnozzi, Amy, 116
Palley, Marian Lief, 108
parental leave
  is necessary, 242, 275
  legislation on, 239
parents
  benefits of, 198-99
  impact of on children's grades, 64
  men are becoming more involved
    as, 187-94
    con, 195-201
  stereotyping of children by, 75-77,
    80
  working
    benefit their children, 205-11
      con, 212-19
    guilt of, 234-35, 239
    at home, 249
    time spent with children, 133,
      271, 274-75
    is not enough, 213, 218-19, 247
patriarchy
  is romanticized, 170, 173
  and men's movement, 168, 170
Pearcey, Nancy, 136
Peery, J. Craig, 220
Pelka, Fred, 167
Perry Pre-School Project, 231
Persian Gulf War. *See* Gulf War
Phillips, Deborah, 132, 221, 222, 224,
  233, 234
physical strength
  social effects on, 44-45
politics
  women in
    gender issues and, 100-107,
      108-15
pregnancy
  effect of on women's emotions, 37
  and women in the military, 123
premarital contracts, 263
premenstrual tension, 36
Presidential Commission on the
  Assignment of Women in the
  Armed Forces, 117, 126, 128
primates
  sexual behavior of, 21-22, 27-30
Public Awareness About Child Care,
  227

Reagan, Ronald
  as against working mothers, 232
  as Fifties male, 159
  judicial appointments of, 102, 109

Republican Party
  and women, 110-11
Restak, Richard, 33, 38
Richards, Ann, 104, 106
Rivers, Caryl, 129
Robertson, Brian, 223
Robinson, John, 219
Rogers, Mary Beth, 100
romance and marriage, 256-57

Schlafly, Phyllis, 93, 111, 122, 248
Scholastic Aptitude Test (SAT), 54, 56,
  63, 96, 215-16
schools
  gender role stereotyping and, 80-81
Schor, Juliet B., 94-95
Schreiber, Le Anne, 57
Schroeder, Pat, 107, 239
Selective Service
  women and, 121
sex-change operations, 33-34
sexual abuse
  in day care, 226-27, 230
  at home, 230
  McMartin Pre-School case, 226, 230
  "psychic incest," 171
  victims of, 172
sexual attraction
  forming a new kind of relationship,
    291-95
  at work
    can be beneficial, 285, 289-95
    is counterproductive, 284-88
    risks of, 286-88
sexual harassment
  effect on women and politics, 103
  Hill-Thomas charges, 103-105,
    109-10, 155
  in the military, 105, 117, 123, 128
  suits harm business, 97
Shapiro, Jerrold Lee, 182
Shreve, Anita, 207
singles lifestyle, 255, 256, 285
society
  changes in
    cost to women of, 277-78
    and rise of feminism, 149
  gender roles in earlier types of
    agricultural, 68-69, 277
    Colonial America, 69
    horticultural, 67-68
    hunting and gathering, 67
    pastoral, 68
  is unkind to children, 213-14
  "stalled revolution" in, 275
  will benefit from women in politics,
    107
sociobiology

310

on gender roles, 21-23, 25
 is incorrect, 25, 27-31
Specter, Arlen, 103, 113, 114
suicide, 216-17
Szalai, Alexander, 271, 272

Tailhook scandal, 105, 117-20, 128
Tavris, Carol, 24
taxes
 credits for child care, 240, 242, 248
teenagers
 and eating disorders, 218
 and substance abuse, 213, 217
 and suicide, 216-17
television
 effect on women's roles, 106
 as sexist, 79-80
Thomas, Clarence, 103, 105, 109,
 110, 112-15, 155
Thomas, Evan, 280
Title VII, 86, 91
Title XX, 240
titles, social
 effect on gender roles, 78-79

United States
 Armed Services Committee
  hearings on women in military,
  118, 124, 125
 Department of Labor
  employment statistics, 86
  Glass Ceiling Initiative, 86, 89, 91
  Workforce 2000 report, 130
 failure of educational system in,
  215-16
 funding for child care in, 236-42
 Supreme Court
  Roe v. Wade decision, 102, 103

Wagner, Kathleen, 139
weight, body
 social effects on, 44
welfare state, 247-48
White, Ursula, 195
Whitehead, Barbara Dafoe, 256
Wild Man, 170, 172
women
 are biologically different from men,
  32-39, 95-97
  con, 41-47
 are not aggressive, 96-99
 are physically weaker than men,
  96, 124, 127
 biological instincts for children, 97,
  280
 black, in labor force, 86
 can have it all, 129-35
  con, 136-42, 280

changing roles of, 147, 255-56
and childbearing, 67, 69-70
 biological clock, 142, 154
 birth rates increasing, 137, 197
  con, 210, 246
 emotional fulfillment of, 138-39
 postponement of, 141-42, 210, 254
culture affects physical traits of,
 42-43
and domesticity, 20, 22, 37-38
and domestic responsibilities, 271,
 273-74
earnings capacity of, 97-98
educational history of, 41-42, 131
emotions of
 and brain activity, 51-52
 menstrual cycle's effect on, 34-36
 and pregnancy, 37
and empty-nest syndrome, 141
and equal parenting, 190-92
gender roles of
 biology determines, 32-39
  con, 24-31
 brain structure explains, 48-56
  con, 57-65
 culture determines, 28, 40-47,
  74-81
 and defeminization, 277-78, 281
 economics determines, 66-73
 historical, 67-71
 traditional role develops, 71-73
glass ceiling limits, 85-91
 con, 92-99
government subsidies for, 152-57,
 198-201
health of
 heart attacks, 130, 131
 housewives' problems, 132, 135
 working is healthier for, 130-33
  con, 272
and housework gap, 187-88, 190-91
and Industrial Revolution, 70-72
intelligence quotients (IQs) of, 53
and linguistic aptitude, 55
and marriage, 19-20, 22
 dowries paid for, 67, 69, 70
 effect of working on, 133, 134,
  272, 280-81
masculinization of, 277-79, 281
maternal instinct of, 37, 38
mathematical aptitude of is inferior,
 54-55, 56, 96
 con, 59, 60, 63-64
men's movement blames, 160, 163,
 168-69
in the military
 are not as qualified as men,
  124-25, 127-28

311

con, 118-21
cannot meet physical standards,
117-18, 124-25
combat restrictions on, 118, 119,
121, 125-26
deaths of, 118
drafting of, 121
flying combat planes, 117, 119,
120
and gender-norming, 124, 125,
127
have better records than men, 118
and killing, 118, 120
opportunities are dangerous,
122-28
opportunities are improving,
116-21
and sexual incidents, 117, 123,
126
will harm male morale, 127
con, 118
in politics, 106
are increasing, 101-102, 111-12
changes in society due to, 107
and fund raising, 104-105, 110
gender issues affect, 100-107
reasons for victories, 109-15
statistics on, 101-102, 106, 111-15
and poverty, 198
prefer older men, 18, 19, 20, 22
reproductive strategies of, 21-23
"right to choose" of, 156
self-esteem of, 38, 132
sexual behavior of
are monogamous, 19-23, 25, 26
modern views about, 27-28, 30
promiscuity, 27-28
tolerance for infidelity, 19, 20
traditional views about, 18, 19,
21-23
single lifestyle is difficult for,
254-55
as single parents, 213, 217, 237,
242, 259
birth rates of, 197, 262
economic concerns of, 209
and fathers, 199
raising sons, 69, 163-64
as slaves, 69, 70
violence against
military training and, 126-27
voting for women, 110-12
working
are healthier, 130-33

con, 272
costs of, 137-38
economic contribution of, 209
effect on family, 191-94, 272-74
effect on marriages, 133, 134, 272,
280-81
glass ceiling limits, 85-91
con, 92-99
guilt of, 234-35, 239
harm their children, 212-19, 247,
279-80
con, 133, 206-10, 231-35
history of, 67-73
increases in, 213, 218, 219, 237,
244, 262, 269-70
and mommy track, 130, 135
necessity of, 238-39, 240, 245-46
con, 223, 225, 246
office romance can be detrimental
to, 286-88
and part-time employment, 135,
270
positions for are improving, 95,
105
salaries of compared with men's,
209-10
social pressures on, 137, 138, 140
traditional jobs for, 87-90
Women, Infants, and Children
Program (WIC), 152, 154, 155, 156,
200
work
cultural roles in are arbitrary, 45-46,
70-73
force is changing, 86-87
gender aptitudes and, 53-54
as place to meet people, 285, 290
sexual attraction at
can be beneficial, 285, 289-95
is counterproductive, 284-88
new etiquette for, 292
risks of, 286-88
women and
glass ceiling limits, 85-91
con, 92-99
positions for are improving, 95,
105
traditional jobs for, 87-90

Yeakel, Lynn, 103, 113, 114
Year of the Woman, 101, 105, 107,
109, 113, 155
Yorkey, Mike, 180